The Violent Woman

SUNY series in Feminist Criticism and Theory

Michelle A. Masse, Editor

The Violent Woman

Femininity, Narrative, and Violence in Contemporary American Cinema

Hilary Neroni

State University of New York Press

Published by
State University of New York Press, Albany

For information, address State University of New York Press,
194 Washington Avenue, Suite 305, Albany, NY 12210-2365

Production by Kelli Williams
Marketing by Susan M. Petrie

Library of Congress Cataloging-in-Publication Data

Neroni, Hilary, 1969–
    The violent woman : femininity, narrative, and violence in contemporary American
cinema / Hilary Neroni.
        p. cm. — (SUNY series in feminist criticism and theory)
    Includes bibliographical references and index.
    ISBN 0-7914-6383-4 — ISBN 0-7914-6384-2 (pbk.)
    1. Women in motion pictures.   2. Violence in motion pictures.   3. Motion pictures—
United States.   I. Title.   II. Series.
PN1995.9.W6N47 2005
791.43'6522—dc22
                                                                                        2004007575

10   9   8   7   6   5   4   3   2   1

to Diana Cataldi,
for her extraordinary strength and generosity

Contents

Preface

"Of course, I'm not *pro*-homicide," a friend once said to me after she had expounded on her fascination with the latest appearance of violent women on-screen. To me, her statement represents the attitude of most film viewers today, who are both undeniably drawn to the violent woman but unsure what this might say about their character. No one is "pro-homicide," but if a writer discusses violence in cinema today without at one point expressing some degree of disapproval toward violence itself, it appears as though she advocates violence. Both George W. Bush and Al Gore made the condemnation of filmic violence a central issue in the 2000 presidential campaign. And while multiple articles and political speeches seem to suggest that the simple answer to a peaceful society would begin with eliminating all violence from film, they ignore the complex way in which violence exists in society at every level, but especially the way in which violence is an integral part of changing gender expectations.

Until recently, on-screen violence has primarily been a masculine activity. There have been periods in cinema in which violent women have appeared (usually within a particular genre, such as the femme fatale in film noir), but since the late 1980s, they have been ubiquitous. Violent women today can be found across all genres. In the midst of the debate on violence in film, it is imperative to look at these new violent women and understand both why we are so fascinated—even excited—by them and what they reveal about violence in our society and its cinema. Rather than embodying some mythical "pro-homicide" movement, violent women actually disrupt the

ix

structure of filmic narratives, call into question our conceptions of masculinity and femininity, and reveal the limits of, or failures of, ideology. Our simultaneous condemnation of and fascination with the violent woman stems from this disruptive position that she occupies. On the one hand, we want to preserve our society against the threat of the violent woman, but, on the other hand, her threat excites us because it involves overturning the ideological structures (most especially those involving gender) that regulate our experiences.

This book investigates the history of violent women on film, the history of the female murderer and the public's reaction to her, the aesthetics of the representation of the filmic violent woman in contemporary cinema, and the theoretical relationship of masculinity and femininity to violence. The first three chapters make up part one, "The Development and Background of the Filmic Violent Woman." They concentrate on the history of the violent woman (both on- and offscreen) and discuss the relationship of masculinity and violence on-screen. Chapter 1, "Complementarity and Its Discontents: An Overview of Violent Women in American Film," considers the history of the violent woman on film from silent films to today's action heroines. In chapter 2, "Expressions of Masculinity: The Traditions of Violence in American Film," I focus on the theoretical importance of violence through an exploration of the association of violence with masculinity. Chapter 3, "Female Murderers: America's Recurring Nightmare," investigates how society reacts to female violence by examining the public reaction to three well-known female murderers: Lizzie Borden (1892), Ruth Snyder (1927), and Susan Smith (1992).

In part two, "The Violent Woman on the Contemporary Screen," I concentrate in four chapters on the phenomenon of violent women in contemporary cinema. By providing wide-ranging cultural analysis as well as analyzing individual films, I hope to bring about a clearer understanding of the theoretical and aesthetic issues surrounding the violent woman on-screen. In chapter 4, "Romancing Trauma: The Violent Woman in Contemporary American Film," I suggest that one commonality among many of the films featuring violent women is that, unlike in the traditional Hollywood film, violent women do not end up in a romance at the film's end. Through films such as John Dahl's *The Last Seduction* (1993), Steven Soderberg's *Out of Sight* (1998), Ridley Scott's *Thelma and Louise*

(1992), and F. Gary Gray's *Set It Off* (1997), I investigate what this lack of romance suggests both about filmic narrative and society's concepts of masculinity and femininity. In chapter 5, "Violent Women in Love," however, I look at a handful of films—Oliver Stone's *Natural Born Killers* (1994), Kathryn Bigelow's *Strange Days* (1995), the Coen Brothers' *Fargo* (1996), and Roger Spottiswoode's *Tomorrow Never Dies* (1997)—that do end with the violent woman in a romantic union. In my analysis of these exceptions, I uncover the multilayered cultural and filmic responses that a violent woman provokes, for example, often the traditional Hollywood film form is disrupted, or traditional gender roles are completely reversed, or the film attempts to split a woman's violence from her femininity. In chapter 6, "Feminity on the Front Line: Portrayals of Violent Women in Recent Military Films," I delve further into this attempt to split violence from femininity through an analysis of the two films in which this is especially prevalent: Edward Zwick's *Courage Under Fire* (1996) and Ridley Scott's *G.I. Jane* (1997). I also consider here the role of the military's relationship to female violence. In the conclusion, I investigate Renny Harlin's *The Long Kiss Goodnight* (1996) as a film which most dramatically depicts the contradictions involved in representations of the violent woman and her influence on the filmic form. Thus, this film provides a way of more completely understanding the complex relationship between Hollywood narrative, filmic violence, and the ideology of gender.

Acknowledgments

The publication of this book could not have happened without the support of numerous individuals and institutions. Portions of chapter 2 originally appeared as "Expressions of Masculinity: The Traditions of Violence in American Film" in the *Journal for the Psychoanalysis of Culture and Society* 5, no. 2 (Fall 2000).

I would like to thank my colleagues and students at the University of Vermont for being especially supportive of this work. They encouraged and challenged me at every step.

This project would be unimaginable without the support of James Peltz, editor in chief and acting director at State University of New York Press.

For their emotional and intellectual support, I am also indebted to: Diana Cataldi, Chadwyk McGowan, Beth Cowett, Walter "Mac" Davis, Marvin D'Lugo, John Gennari, Cindy Karlson, Lillian Kessler, Henry Kessler, Sheila Kunkle, Amor Kholi, Tony Magistrale, Sandra McGowan, Jane Neroni, Delmont Neroni, Christine Pierce, Claire Scanlon, Nicodemus Taranovsky, Meredith Willoughby, and Jean Wyatt.

Thanks also to Todd Boyd, Marsha Kinder, and Douglas Thomas, whose mentoring and intellectual tutelage helped give birth to this project.

In a way that is hard to put into words, I am especially grateful to those who read part or all of this manuscript, generously giving their time, energy, and invaluable comments: Emily Bernard, Paul

Eisenstein, Phil Foster, Jonathan Mulrooney, Sarah Nilsen, Sharon Preves, Renata Selecl, and Slavoj Žižek.

Finally, this work would be quite impossible without Todd McGowan.

Introduction

Filmic violence has recently received a great deal of critical attention. Four edited collections of essays dealing with the topic have appeared between 1999 and 2001. The salient feature—and lasting contribution—of these collections is their determination to investigate violence as a filmic element with its own logic and with its own particular effect on spectators. Prior to 1999, filmic violence tended to be the province of quantitative researchers in the social sciences rather than film scholars. Because they are fully aware of this, the editor of each collection points out the historical importance of their contributions. J. David Slocum's claim that "while 'quantitative' studies by social science researchers have accompanied such popular attention and concern, humanities and film scholars have undertaken the 'serious' study of film violence haltingly"[1] is echoed either explicitly or implicitly by each editor. Despite this link between them, however, each collection has a relatively distinct approach to theorizing filmic violence.

Stephen Prince (*Screening Violence* 1999) sees worth in the work of the social researcher and brings together such work with personal memoirs, film critics' original reactions to violent films such as *Bonnie and Clyde*, as well as discussions on the causes and prevention of violence. In combining these myriad approaches, Prince hopes to inaugurate an interdisciplinary discussion on film violence. Christopher Sharrett (*Mythologies of Violence* 1999), on the other hand, takes a more theoretical (and, at times, psychoanalytic) approach to filmic violence, as he investigates the meaning of this violence in a political and social framework. In general, the essays

1

in Sharrett's collection concentrate on narrative content and cultural contextualization of various kinds of violence (i.e., that of the serial killer, fears of alien takeovers, and so on) rather than specific investigations into film form and the filmic aspects of violence on the screen.[2] J. David Slocum (*Violence and American Cinema* 2001) begins with a thorough history of the way that film criticism has understood film violence.[3] Slocum's collection resembles my own approach when he calls for more in-depth analyses of filmic violence through investigations of filmic "narrative strategies, production practices, and formal operations of Hollywood cinema."[4] The essays in this collection provide some of the more comprehensive interpretations of filmic violence written today. Notably, however, none of these three collections has a single essay specifically devoted to investigating violent women in film. Martha McCaughey and Neal King's *Reel Knockouts* (2001) begins to fill this gap.[5] Their collection is an encomium. Rather than involve themselves in a debate concerning the violent woman—either condemning the violent woman as merely a masculine trope or questioning her political status (i.e., whether she is sexist or feminist)—the editors explain that they want to celebrate the violent woman. The essays in this collection restrict their focus to analyses of individual films or film trends (female cop films, rape revenge films, violent women in the Hong Kong Kung Fu films, and so on) while eschewing broader theoretical inquiry into what these films reveal about the social order.[6] Building on all these studies, *The Violent Woman* both argues for a psychoanalytically influenced investigation into the larger issues surrounding violence in film and, at the same time, offers a broader exploration of the recent trend of the violent woman as she exists across multiple genres.

Before beginning this investigation, we must first consider the relationship between filmic violence and narrative (a question that Slocum's collection begins to take up). This relationship is fundamental for any inquiry into filmic violence because of the way we experience this violence. Violence, especially on film, has a seemingly nonverbal, nonnarrative quality to it. Narrative is a mediating structure that creates meaning through its interrelating elements, but violence seems foreign to any type of mediation. It typically seems more like an immediate experience rather than an element within—and relating to—a larger narrative structure. American film accentuates this aspect of violence at almost every turn. Most often films do this through rhythmic editing that depicts acts of violence in a rapid montage sequence. Such violent sequences tend to utilize many different filmic techniques—such as cutting on action, slow motion, shot-reverse shot—in a short period of time. The violent scenes in Andy and Larry Wachowski's *The Matrix* (1999) provide an extreme example of this style. At one point Neo (Keanu Reeves) and Trinity (Carrie-Anne Moss) arrive at the top of a building where a fierce opposition of enemy agents awaits. The outcome of this battle bears on the plot, yet it still places the plot on pause as it revels in this display of violence. Just as in a musical when the narrative pauses for the musical number, the plot of this action/science fiction film stops for a prolonged display of violence. Within the scene, Andy and Larry Wachowski cut between moments with the characters fighting at top speeds in long or medium shots (interspersed with a quick close-up of moments of contact and accompanied by foley sounds that emphasize each contact through loud crunching), and slow-motion shots emphasizing especially fantastic moments (such as a slow-motion shot in which Neo bends backwards to avoid a bullet whose progress we can track in this slower speed). *The Matrix* may be an extreme example, but the pattern is the same for most American action films. Violence seems to arrest the narrative as the viewer waits with tension and excitement for the outcome while immersed in the spectacle.

This description of the violence of *The Matrix* owes a clear debt to contemporary film theory, which has developed a distinct approach to film violence emphasizing the discontinuity between violence and narrative. Historically, film theory approached violence as just another plot element, one indistinct from other elements in the larger narrative structure.[8] For film theorists looking at narrative in the 1970s and 1980s, violence did not confound narrative altogether; instead, violence is just another aspect of narrative. For instance, in *Narration and the Fiction Film*, David Bordwell does not see violence as unique but as simply part of the narrative structure of a film, cueing the audience expectations concerning conflict and plot twists. In fact, Bordwell never mentions filmic violence as such but rather describes violent scenes in terms of their place within the larger narrative structure. Other film theorists also subsume violence within the rubric of filmic narration. In his *Film Language: A Semiotics of the*

Cinema (1967), for example, Christian Metz says, "*it was precisely to the extent that the cinema confronted the problems of narration* that, in the course of successive groupings, it came to produce a body of specific signifying procedures."[9] For Metz, narrative alone structures film form, and this position erases any possibility of other structuring forces, such as violence.

It was a contribution from an unexpected source—film theorist Tom Gunning's work on silent cinema (his conception of silent cinema as predominately a cinema of attractions)—that fundamentally transformed the scholarly debate surrounding filmic violence. Gunning's work allowed film theorists to begin to think about violence as distinct from—rather than as just an element within—narrative. But before having an impact on the discussion of filmic violence, Gunning's primary contribution was to the study of silent cinema. Until the appearance of his "cinema of attractions" argument, the dominant view of silent cinema was that its popularity with audiences—and its role in the history of film—was the result of its incipient narrative strategies. In other words, the major filmic techniques that developed in the silent era (cutting on action, crosscutting, shot-reverse shot, the 180-degree rule) resulted from efforts to tell stories in better and more efficient ways. According to this once predominant view, cinema began with little to no filmic vocabulary in 1895, and yet, by the coming of sound in the late 1920s, it developed into a sophisticated narrative machine. But Gunning convincingly argues that the key features of early silent cinema were its images of physical violence, action, and humor—its "attractions"—not its developing narrative. In this argument, he emphasizes that these attractions were a sophisticated filmic endeavor, not an indication of the banality of silent cinema; he suggests that theorists are ignoring a significant part of a filmic text by concentrating solely on narrative (whether on narrative form or content).[10] He suggests: "Rather than early approximations of the later practices of the style of classical film narration, aspects of early cinema are best understood if a purpose other than storytelling is factored in. Cinema as an attraction is that other purpose."[11] Gunning's contribution both provoked further research into silent cinema and encouraged theorists of contemporary cinema to be aware of violent spectacle as a separate element of a film, an element as important as narrative and with its own logic, structure, and relationship to the viewer.

Gunning concentrates on cinematic spectacle in response to the overwhelming emphasis on narrative at the time he was writing, but recent theorists realize that the spectacle alone cannot explain everything. Most viewers experience violence on the screen as exciting not only because of the highly stylized techniques, but also because violence often marks moments of tension, and moments of life and death for the main characters. In other words, while violence on screen may arrest the movement of the narrative and may rely on nonverbal expressions, it cannot exist on its own. It must be situated within a narrative framework. Even films today, receiving the most criticism for relying on pure violent spectacle, such as Jan de Bont's *Speed* (1994), John McTiernan's *Die Hard* (1988), David Fincher *Fight Club* (1999), Andy and Larry Wachowski *The Matrix* (1999), and Oliver Stone's *Natural Born Killers* (1994), have a plot. This is why J. David Slocum points out:

> Indeed, the threat of violence caused by a narrative can often be more powerful than any graphic single image in provoking viewer responses. Further, even images of blatant violence on-screen, physical or otherwise, beg for multiple and complexly determined responses from viewers: slapstick pratfalls and battlefield kills and acts of noir sadism and boxing matches and serial killings necessarily elicit different kinds of responses and call for different kinds of critical approaches.[12]

That is to say, even those most stylized violent films need narrative in order to exist, because narrative provides the background through which the violence acquires its significance and meaning.

While Gunning led film theory to recognize the unique structure of the violent spectacle, Slocum, Marsha Kinder, and Leo Charney—film theorists who have brought Gunning's insights about the cinema of attractions into the theorization of filmic violence—realize the importance of the narrative and theorize extensively about its relationship to spectacle in their articles in *Violence in American Cinema*. While Kinder points to the ever-increasing spectacle of violence,[13] Leo Charney investigates theoretically this phenomenon of increasing violent spectacle and decreasing narrative.[14] For Charney, theorizing the spectacle of violence and its relation to the narrative in contemporary cinema is pivotal to understanding contemporary subjectivity. Thus, he moves from an analysis of the relationship between violence and narrative to a larger philosophical conclusion about viewer subjectivity.

Thinking through the importance of the relationship between violence and narrative is essential to understanding violence in film, but film theory, in my view, has not yet gone far enough in this direction. It has yet to explain the ideological function of, and political possibilities inherent in, this relationship. This may at first be counterintuitive because though they never considered the role of violence in narrative, earlier film theorists—especially the first psychoanalytic film theorists—stress the ideological dimension of filmic narrative. Film theorist Christian Metz, for example, suggests that when looking at film narrative it is essential to break the narrative down into two categories, *histoire* (the story itself) and *discours* (the way that the film tells the story). From another direction, David Bordwell relies on the Russian Formalist distinction that refers to the narrative as *fabula* (what really happened) and the order of events presented in the narrative as *szuyhet* (how the story presents the events).[15] While they may not say so explicitly, both approaches hint at the way narrative can have an ideological function.[16] Metz's distinction between story and discourse is not only an attempt to map out the structure of narrative, but also implicitly an attempt to grasp how the viewer understands the film text. Clearly, a viewer can understand a film only if it uses a filmic and cultural vocabulary with which the viewer is conversant. This is, for example, the theory behind continuity editing. Over time, Hollywood developed a number of visual codes with its audiences that indicate spatial or temporal coherence (such as the crosscut or cutting-on-action). Learned and accepted as a visual vocabulary, these codes are essential for the viewer's overall understanding of the narrative. In other words, narrative theorists suggest that narrative is not only a linear plot, but also the form in which that plot is presented, and that this form equally informs the viewer about the overall meaning(s) in the text.[17] Because these meanings come out of the viewer's culture, and thus have ideological resonance, narrative becomes an expression of ideology, and one might even say that it is ideology itself. Even popular critiques of Hollywood films—that they objectify women, for example—rely on the notion that narrative enforces ideology.

Ideology often has a clear narrative quality to it, as it works to represent social relations. This is apparent throughout Louis Althusser's analysis of ideology in his famous essay on "Ideology and Ideological State Apparatuses." According to Althusser, *"Ideology is a 'Representation' of the Imaginary Relationship of Individuals to their Real Conditions of Existence."*[18] To express this imaginary relationship, individuals and the social order as a whole need to narrativize their identity and society's expectations of them. These narratives provide meaning and identity. For example, the ubiquitous ideological narrative of two people falling in love and finding happiness is a powerful force in shaping individual identity, and thus in shaping the larger social order. Obviously, Hollywood film often uses a romantic narrative in order to begin and end even action films—whose linear plot has little to do with romance—and this in turn reinforces the ideological myth of love (the foundation for the formation of the family). Similarly, America's reliance on the ideological narrative of "manifest destiny"—the settler's "divine right" to conquer the continent—justified western expansion and became part of American national identity. Ideology, then, is constantly being narrativized, just as narrative reinforces ideology. But cultural texts are often as much about the failure of ideological narratives as about their success. For example, though Westerns capitalized on and worked to reinforce the larger myths of western expansion in America, these films eventually began to explore the inadequacy of this myth, particularly its basis in racist violence and white supremacy. This turn is possible because ideology never completely explains everything about identity; instead, it seems to be incomplete, a narrative with gaps.

Similarly, film violence both produces and resists ideology. For example, violence often appears to erupt when ideology fails: when the symbolic or narrative structure breaks down, we turn to violence. On the one hand in this scenario, violence can serve as a stopgap for that failure, an action that hides the limits of language and narrative. In other words, violence aids ideology—or acts as the supplement to it—whether that be, for example, the ideology, of the state or the ideology of masculinity. On the other hand, however, violence can be a challenge to ideology, because it exists at the very limits of language and narrative. That is to say, violence can also represent a threat to the functioning of ideology. It erupts when

ideology becomes vulnerable—at moments of ideological failure—
and thus can exacerbate these failures.

In one way or another, all cultural texts must struggle with ideological failure. The Marxist and psychoanalytic attempt to shed
light on the nature of these failures is especially important to my
project and to my analyses of filmic violence. Much of Marxist and
psychoanalytic theory exists to explain the way these ideological
failures affect everything from the individual psyche to the entire
social order. In fact, it is the failure of ideology that created the theoretical space in which Marxist and psychoanalytic thought could
emerge. For Marxists, ideological failures—ideology's inability to
explain everything and its incessant propensity for contradiction—
indicate the existence of a fundamental antagonism underlying society: the antagonism of class conflict. Ernesto Laclau and Chantal
Mouffe focus on the way in which antagonism results from the inevitable failure of any social order to become complete, to take
everything into account without contradiction. As they assert in
Hegemony and Socialist Strategy, "antagonism, as a witness of the impossibility of a final suture, is the experience of the limit of the social. Strictly speaking, antagonisms are not *internal* but *external* to
society; or rather, they constitute the limits of society, the latter's impossibility of fully constituting itself."[19] Since this antagonism constitutes the limits of the social, it fundamentally structures society.
But ideological narratives work to make us blind to the way that antagonism structures our existence. The American Dream, for example, suggests that all it takes is hard work to move up in social class.
It encourages us to believe that we are only isolated monads who
can become wealthy through sheer determination. In this dream,
there is no "class conflict," only monetary rewards for those who
work the hardest. This narrative hinders even those in the poorest of
conditions from understanding that the very structures of society
depend on class antagonism and that this prohibits all but a token
few from rising in class status. As Marx explains,

> Only as an exception does the worker succeed through will
> power, physical strength and endurance, greed etc., in trans-
> forming his coin into money, as an exception from his class and
> from the general conditions of his existence. If all or the major-
> ity are too industrious [. . .], then they increase not the value of

their commodity, but only its quantity; that is, the demands which would be placed on it as use value.[20]

Moreover, the American Dream reinforces an understanding of human relations as based on exchange value and hierarchies rather than on social equality. Ideology, however (like the ideology of the American Dream), eliminates the appearance of class struggle to present the illusion of a society without antagonism—an image of society as already fairly and equally structured. Ideology works to erase signs of its own failure, of antagonism, and instead creates a sense of wholeness.

Like Marxism, psychoanalysis also focuses on the gaps or failures in ideology. For instance, in *Seminar XX* (entitled *On Feminine Sexuality: The Limits of Love and Knowledge*), Jacques Lacan insists repeatedly that ideology (i.e., meaning) always and necessarily comes up short. He claims that "meaning (*sens*) indicates the direction toward which it fails (*échoue*)."[21] Psychoanalytic cultural theorists who follow Lacan take as their point of departure his claim that these failures or gaps in ideology are the Real, an unsymbolizable void that marks a hole in the symbolic order. Slavoj Žižek, for example, explains that "the Real [. . .] in itself is nothing at all, just a void, an emptiness in a symbolic structure marking some central impossibility."[22] For psychoanalysis, antagonism lies in the impossibility to explain our emergence as speaking beings and the emergence of our symbolic social structure. This central impossibility is the origin of the symbolic order. The symbolic, in other words, can make sense of everything except itself. Lacan attempts to capture the spirit of this central psychoanalytic idea when he says: "I always speak the truth. Not the whole truth, because there's no way, to say it all. Saying it all is literally impossible: words fail. Yet it's through this very impossibility that the truth holds onto the real."[23] Just as words cannot "say it all," the symbolic order cannot explain it all. Most importantly, it can never explain its own coming into being.

Lacan's theory of subjectivity is tied to his understanding of this crisis of origin, which is why he describes the subject as barred. The subject is barred, because it can never know itself: as a being of language, it cannot have full knowledge of itself. For Lacan, the Real is the central emptiness that the subject cannot traverse in order to communicate successfully with itself. Ultimately, this lacuna of the Real manifests itself in myriad ways in the psyche and throughout culture/ideology. [24] For example, Lacan lectures extensively on the way that this Real affects desire. He suggests that subjects can never know their own desire, that their desire is always the desire of the Other. He also explains that the object-cause of desire—the *objet petit a*—partakes of this same lacuna of the Real. Desire is structured so that there is no real object that could actually satisfy desire. In other words, if the subject is barred from knowledge of itself, then the satisfaction of desire is also barred. Ideology, however, encourages the subject to believe that desire can be realized.[25] Ideology pushes the consumer to believe, for example, that various objects (such as the new car, house, or digital camera) are imbued with the potential to make him or her whole. These objects, however, never have the effect that ideology promises, and the subject must continue his/her search.[26]

Early psychoanalytic film theorists attempted to show how Hollywood film form and content elided antagonism. Laura Mulvey analyzes film form in terms of its link to ideological standards of patriarchy. In explaining this, she says: "Woman then stands in patriarchal culture as a signifier for the male other, bound by a symbolic order in which man can live out his fantasies and obsessions through linguistic command by imposing them on the silent image of woman still tied to her place as bearer, not maker, of meaning."[27] For Mulvey, film form serves ideology when it turns women into the objectified spectacle for the male gaze. While she does not explicitly use the word "antagonism," Mulvey's article strives to have a political impact by tearing away the ideological purpose of film form. This will make it impossible for the film viewer to experience pleasure after hearing her analysis. As Mulvey says: "It is said that analyzing pleasure or beauty, destroys it. That is the intention of this article."[28] Once this pleasure is destroyed and the social antagonism becomes visible, Mulvey contends, political/feminist action is possible.

Unlike Mulvey, contemporary film theory's discussion of film violence has not been concerned with whether violence elides or reveals antagonism. This is ultimately an underlying aim of *The Violent Woman*: a new line of inquiry into the study of film violence, one which imbues film theory with a Marxist and psychoanalytic understanding of antagonism.[29] My argument emphasizes the way that film's deployment of the violent woman can both elide and express antagonism. I argue that the representation of violence—and specifically the representation of the violent woman—is either ideological or revolutionary on the basis of the relation it takes up to antagonism. Its relation to antagonism is the key to understanding the political valence of violence. For example, a film can use the violent woman to conceal antagonism by offering narrative explanations for this violence (associating it with her job as a police officer or providing the rationale of self-defense). But at the same time, the extraordinary lengths to which the narrative must go to explain or situate the violent woman reveals the trauma caused by her violence. In fact, the very existence of the violent woman as such testifies to ideology's propensity for failure. As viewers, we have a double relation to the violent woman: the violent woman and her effect on the traditional Hollywood romance plot reveals that narrative can expose antagonism as much as it can elide it. After recognizing this, what matters in the end is the attitude that we take up toward her. Do we embrace the antagonism that her violence exposes, or do we take shelter within the attempts to narrativize that antagonism?

PART ONE

The Development and Background of the Filmic Violent Woman

CHAPTER 1

Complementarity and Its Discontents

An Overview of Violent Women in American Film

Since the late 1980s, the violent woman has become a staple in contemporary American cinema. In looking at films from *Thelma and Louise* (1991) to *Strange Days* (1995) to *Tomorrow Never Dies* (1997) to *Girlfight* (2000), we quickly see that action and violence are no longer the exclusive province of men. Rather than waiting for men to protect them, female characters have begun to protect themselves. When we first look at the emergence of the violent woman in the films of the late 1980s and early 1990s, we cannot but be startled by the dramatic change that her emergence seems to indicate in cinematic representations. She seems, in short, to have sprung into existence as if shot out of a cannon, taking the cinema-going public completely by surprise (as the very public debate about *Thelma and Louise* seemed to suggest). Even though the current phenomenon is unprecedented in the number of films that contain a violent woman, this figure itself is not unique to contemporary cinema. The violent woman has antecedents throughout the history of film and an investigation into the significance of the violent woman's emergence in the films of today must therefore begin with a brief look at the history of the violent woman in American cinema. I aim in this chapter not to provide a comprehensive history of the violent woman but instead a survey of her various historical manifestations in the cinema in order to highlight better the theoretical, cultural, and aesthetic foundations of her origins.

An overview of the violent woman in cinema allows us to see more clearly the various ways in which the violent woman has been not only present throughout the history of cinema, but also connected to the historical situations of women from all backgrounds within American society. The earliest filmic manifestations of violent women are the heroines of the Serial Queen Melodramas, films that Hollywood produced in large numbers (nearly eight hundred series) between 1912 and 1925, as Ben Singer has detailed in his pathbreaking article "Female Power in the Serial-Queen Melodrama." Each series consisted of anywhere from six to twelve episodes that were shown each week as viewers anticipated the twists of their extended plots. In these series—the soap operas of their day—the action inevitably revolved around a heroine in danger who went to unusual lengths to save herself or someone she loved. The films were filled with action—adventure, car chases, melodramatic villains, and close calls—and were aimed primarily at women (who made the serials a viable cinematic product for seventeen years). Moreover, the heroines in these films participated in many activities usually reserved for male characters. They used guns, took part in car chases, and held jobs (such as a detective or a novelist, occupations that few women of that time had an opportunity to pursue).

In films starring violent women, the mise-en-scène that surrounds the violent woman is almost as important as the actual violence itself in shaping our ideas about the woman and subsequently about her violence. In the Serial Queen Melodramas, the woman interacts with the mise-en-scène by setting out in each episode to investigate and conquer her surroundings. More often than not this means that the films depict her at first in the domestic sphere and then depict her adventure in various rural or urban environments, as she follows her free spirit and investigates mysteries. The typical serial heroine is able to master both domestic spaces and rural or urban spaces, for she fears very little of what she encounters. In this way, the Serial Queen Melodramas are more like the Western, in which the adventure lays somewhere "out there," and any perils are expected and even eagerly anticipated. In the end, the mise-en-scène of the serial queen melodrama serves as a kind of playground for the heroine, which is an unusual scenario for a female character in Hollywood. Traditionally in Hollywood, women characters are more

often trapped by their mise-en-scène, either emotionally or physically.

One of the best known and most popular early serials, *The Perils
of Pauline* (1914) depicts a young woman who wants to pursue her
own adventures before she settles down and marries.[1] Though
Pauline (Pearl White) herself is not actually violent, she is certainly
a precursor for the violent woman. Even though she is a single
young woman with a guardian, she is also extremely rebellious. For
example, in "Deadly Turning," Pauline signs up for a car race
against the will of her male guardian. In the end, her guardian
agrees to her demands, on the condition that he drive the car during
the race, and she sit in the passenger seat. Although this seems to indicate a taming of her original desire, her rebellion nonetheless continues to exist and have an effect on others: by desiring nonfeminine
adventures she calls into question feminine norms. In the years before and after World War I, women faithfully attended serials depicting such freedom and adventure. In "Female Power in the
Serial-Queen Melodrama," Ben Singer argues, "The clearest and
most interesting indication of the genre's address to a female audience lies in its sustained fantasy of female power. Every serial-queen
melodrama, without exception, places an overt polemic about female independence and mastery at the center of its thematic design."[2] In this way, early films did at times cater to female fantasies
of empowerment.[3]

What is even more significant for the history of violent women
on film, however, is that eventually such independent behavior did
lead to violence. A good example is the serial *The Woman in Grey*
(1921). A mystery surrounds the serial's main character Ruth Hope
(Arlene Pretty), who happens herself to write mystery novels. The
mystery involves a fortune buried in an old house, numerous relatives, love interests, and hidden identities, all of which have Ruth
constantly probing and investigating. Haviland Hunter (Fred
Jones), the main villain, tries to thwart Ruth's investigation and
even attacks her throughout the series. And although a friend (who
becomes Ruth's lover at the end of the film), Tom Thurston (Henry
G. Sell), is always there to save her at the last minute, Ruth does
quite a bit of violent fighting with Hunter. She also jumps from a
fast moving car, is thrown from a bridge, and is almost killed with a
dagger (in "The Deadly Dagger" episode, of course). Firing a gun,

and defending herself during fights with Hunter, Ruth appears far more daring and independent than Pauline was just eight years earlier. This heightened quality of independence is indicated in some ways by her ability to be violent. Although not discussing violence per se, Ben Singer echoes this thought when he points out that "the depiction of female power self-consciously dissolves, sometimes even completely reverses, traditional gender positions as the heroine appropriates a variety of 'masculine' qualities, competencies, and privileges."[4] One of those qualities is obviously the ability to handle oneself in a fight, to be violent. Nevertheless, all these serials had men who saved the heroines in the end, ostensibly because they couldn't save themselves. Likewise, even though these women were capable of being violent, rebellious, independent, and adventuresome, the serials invariably depicted their heroines as completely virtuous and entirely bereft of any tendency toward promiscuity. Clearly, having chastity and a male protector were two commodities that allowed these women some latitude in the direction of adventure and freedom—and even violence. These commodities blunt the disruptive power of her adventurousness and violence.

Since the period of the Serial Queen Melodramas, the violent woman has continued to crop up in isolated instances in the history of American cinema. She is never entirely absent from the American cinematic landscape, but it is when depictions of the violent woman appear in large numbers and in similar roles that they tell us about the functioning of ideology. That is to say, insofar as she appears in a historically related group of films, the violent woman is most clearly related to social problems and contradictions—and to the ideological response to these contradictions. The violent woman appears at moments of ideological crisis, when the antagonisms present within the social order—antagonisms that ideology attempts to elide—become manifest. Though antagonisms always exist within the social order, they emerge most forcefully at moments of ideological crisis.

Such an ideological crisis occurs when strictly defined gender roles—roles that give a logic and a sense to sexual difference—break down. Ideology works to produce clear gender distinctions in order to provide stable symbolic identities for both male and female subjects. Without this kind of coherence, identity loses its guarantees:

male and female subjects begin to question, rather than invest themselves in, symbolic identities. This process destabilizes the social order, and popular culture often responds by producing cultural images that work through, contain, or expose, this destablization. One powerful example—one that almost always acts as a nexus for concerns about gender identity—is the violent woman in film. If there is one characteristic that defines masculinity in the cultural imagination, it is violence. The depiction of a violent woman upsets this association of violence with masculinity. Yet, at each moment when the violent woman emerges on a wide scale in film history, the films in which she appears go to great lengths to frame her violence within the very symbolic system that her violence threatens to undo. In this way, these films are an effort to ameliorate the social antagonism at the same time as they are explorations of it.

After their appearance in the Serial Queen Melodramas, the next filmic trend in which the violent woman emerged *en masse* was in film noir (from the late 1930s through the 1940s); she reappeared in horror and blaxploitation films in the 1970s and early 1980s; and she has most recently appeared in full flower in a wide range of films from the late 1980s through to the present. In these current films, the violent woman has undergone a fundamental transformation from her earlier incarnations: when she appeared in Serial Queen Melodramas, film noir, blaxploitation films, or horror films, the violent woman was strictly a generic figure, limited to a particular kind of film. Beginning in the late 1980s, however, depictions of the violent woman began to cross generic boundaries. She has appeared in action films, neo-noirs, comedies, and dramas. This widening of the violent woman's berth suggests that the antagonism—the ideological disruption that the appearance of the violent woman marks—has become more dramatically exposed than in the earlier eras. Because the violent woman in contemporary films has escaped the confines of isolated (and often marginalized) types of film, her violence indicates that the antagonism of the sexual relationship has become imagined to be increasingly precarious. But each of these contemporary manifestations of the violent woman owes a debt to the femme fatale and film noir.[5]

Masculinity and violence were intimately linked in Hollywood during the time of the classic film noir. Westerns, gangster films, and war films concentrated on masculinity, and they all connected violence with masculinity.[6] Westerns depicted men using violence to bring law and civilization to the lawless while conquering untamed parts of the country. Gangster films showed how honor and masculinity stem from proving oneself violently. Similarly—although not as prolific or widespread as the other genres—war films during this time clearly connected honor and respectability with professionally administering the kind of violence that would crush the enemy and save American lives. With all these images of masculinity and violence covering the American screens, what provoked the image of the femme fatale?

Outbreaks of violent women in film—such as the femme fatale in film noir—occur at moments in history when a clear difference between genders ceases to be operative. There are, of course, many different characteristics that we associate with maleness and many that we associate with femaleness, but, as I have said, one of the most significant is the identification of violence with masculinity. The very idea of masculinity implies, to some extent at least, the propensity to be violent, to protect oneself and one's family. In *Violence: Reflections on a National Epidemic,* James Gilligan, a psychoanalyst who spent much of his career working within the Massachusetts prison system, points out that "Violence is primarily men's work; it is carried out more frequently by men; and it is about the maintenance of 'manhood.'"[7] Violence—or at least the ability to be violent—is one of the main ways that men differentiate themselves from women. If gender difference becomes elided, then there is seemingly nothing to stop a woman from taking up violence as well, from being as violent as a man. In a sense, the appearance of the filmic violent woman, then, is a cautionary tale about the elision of difference. It is as if films with violent women are saying: "If we continue to disregard the proper difference between the genders, look at what kind of chaos will erupt." These films are also dealing with the problem of their own existence—that is, they offer violence as a cautionary tale on the level of narrative, but also as an attraction on the level of spectacle. This contradiction, between narrative and spectacle, underscores the conflict between the violent women as cautionary tale and the violent woman as role model. In the last instance, films with violent women remain ambiguous insofar as they struggle with the ultimate possibilities of the elision of gender difference and the ideological crisis that it signals.

The years of classical film noir—the late 1930s through to the end of the 1940s—were years of rapidly changing gender roles. These revolutions/transformations were, of course, not new: women had been making active moves to change their lives and to enter the public world for decades. During World War II large numbers of women, however, were called upon to work for the factories left vacant by men who had gone off to war but were subsequently fired once the soldiers returned.[8] At the conclusion of the war, the United States government called upon women to willingly take up the feminine position once again. But the demand did not immediately create the reality. Women could not take up their previous position so easily, and men and women both were left with a growing understanding that the female "role" in life was no longer well defined.[9] Women had now—simply because of the exigencies of the war—shown that they could work and support themselves without men, and the job of provider no longer seemed uniquely male.

The new violent woman of the 1940s cinema, the femme fatale in film noir, became a site for the exploration of the angst and fantasies that surrounded this elision of gender difference. The influence of the femme fatale on the history of violent women in film is far reaching. From Paul Verhoeven's *Basic Instinct* (1992) to Renny Harlin's *The Long Kiss Goodnight* (1996), there are many films today whose leading female characters either are influenced by, are in direct conversation with, or are recapitulations of the femme fatales of film noir. Film noir has become a much disputed category among film scholars because unlike genres (such as the Western or the gangster film), noir does not have as fixed a set of patterns or criteria. In fact, noir's styles and themes often run across genres. Certainly the long scholarly debate on whether or not noir deserves its own generic category indicates the uncertainty of its status. Indeed, film noir was not even a category (unlike Westerns, gangster films, etc.) that the studios themselves used.[10] It was, of course, French theorists who coined the term and created the category.[11] In "American Film Noir: The History of an Idea," James Naremore suggests the amorphous quality of this category. He claims:

> If we want to understand it or to make sense of genres or art-historical categories in general we need to recognize that film noir

belongs to the history of ideas as much as to the history of cinema; it has less to do with a group of artifacts than with a discourse—a loose, evolving system of arguments and readings, helping to shape commercial strategies and aesthetic ideologies.[12]

One of the main elements found in noir—whether it is a genre or just a style—is the femme fatale. Just like the category of film noir itself, the category of the "femme fatale" does not involve rigid definitions. She is an ambiguous character who varies dramatically from film to film. She has also been the nexus for much theoretical work concerning sexual difference. For instance, Elizabeth Cowie claims that "femme 'fatale' is simply a catchphrase for the danger of sexual difference and the demands and risks desire poses for the man."[13] What continues to feed this theoretical work on the femme fatale is her ambiguous status: she seems to be both society's fantasy screen and, on the other hand, she seems to be a hard rock of the real that threatens the stability of patriarchy. She is both a manifestation of society's fantasy of the underside of femininity (and thus in the service of ideology) and also something more elusive (and thus undeniably threatening to society). But there are characteristics that remain constant: a self-centered nature, an overt sexuality, and an ability to seduce and control almost any man who crosses her path mark the femme fatale of the late 1930s and 1940s. She is almost always glamorously beautiful and wears highly stylized clothes (from long trailing gowns to cocked hats and trench coats). Trapped in the famous mise-en-scène (influenced by German Expressionism) of highly contrasting shadows in an urban setting, the femme fatale seems to spring to life from the depths of these city shadows that eventually swallow her up. The extreme mise-en-scène that provides the backdrop for the femme fatale works to emphasize that she is the embodiment of a "bad girl."[14] In Billy Wilder's *Double Indemnity* (1944), Phyllis Dietrichson (Barbara Stanwyck) perfectly captures this image when she tells Walter Neff (Fred MacMurray): "I never loved you or anyone else. I'm rotten, rotten to the core." One of the main characteristics of the femme fatale is her inability to maintain a romantic relationship. And this is the reason—along with her proclivity toward violence—why she is unacceptable to society. In "Women's Place: The Absent Family of Film Noir," Sylvia Harvey points out the position love occupies in society as depicted in film noir: "And if successful romantic love leads inevitably in the direction of the stable institution of marriage, the point about film noir, by contrast, is that it is structured around the destruction or absence of romantic love and the family."[15] As a result, if the femme fatale does fall in love—usually with the detective character—this relationship ends up ruining both herself and the male character (although, on rare occasions, love can also have the reverse effect and end up making an honest woman of the femme fatale).[16]

The fate of the femme fatale usually involves violence: either she meets a violent death or resorts to using violence on someone else. Of course, not all femme fatales turn to violence, but a large majority of them evince a capacity and a willingness to be violent. The femme fatale's violence often appears to be a last resort for her, but she nonetheless performs violence proficiently and without compunction. Within the context of the films, her violent act marks the femme fatale as truly bad and dangerous. Often the narrative trajectory of the film noir gradually reveals an explanation of how and why she resorts to violence. But I would not claim that the femme fatale's violence is the one thing that defines her character and makes her dangerous. If anything, violence is just a by-product of the overall persona of the femme fatale. For example, in *Double Indemnity*, Phyllis Dietrichson seduces Walter Neff into helping her in an insurance scam in which he kills her husband, and they split his insurance money. Essentially, she lies, cheats, flaunts her body in front of Walter, and generally acts promiscuously, all in order to get the money that she wants. Billy Wilder famously introduces Phyllis dressed only in a towel at the top of the staircase. When she returns after dressing, the camera follows her legs only as she walks down the stairs and then displays her again as she finishes buttoning her shirt and putting on her lipstick while looking in a mirror. The dialogue here also calls attention to her looks as she asks Walter if her "face is on straight," forcing Walter and the viewer to stare one more time at her face and lips before the plot continues on.

All these moves are cleverly executed by a woman who is well aware of society's ideas about femininity and women. Phyllis plays upon social ideas of femininity to entice Walter, and every other man, to help her. In the first half of the film, Wilder depicts Phyllis as clever and manipulative (even Walter is aware of this, and yet he doesn't care), but she still pretends to play second fiddle to Walter, who directs the murder plans. Because he is the man, the film suggests, he understands how to deal with violence and how to set up plans that involve violence. Hence, the initial machinations of the femme fatale leave the traditional relationship between the sexes in place and do not make any antagonism between the sexes evident. The relationship between the femme fatale and her man usually begins with an image of sexual complementarity, as it does in *Double Indemnity*.

In the second half of the film, as Walter begins to lose his nerve, Phyllis reveals that she is actually calmer and more prepared for this murder—and its aftereffects—than Walter. When the plan has gone somewhat awry and Phyllis realizes that she is in trouble, she calmly and quickly turns to violence—placing a gun under her seat cushion in order to kill Walter and continue with her scam to get her dead husband's insurance money. It is at this point, when the femme fatale becomes violent, that the antagonism between the sexes manifests itself. The film presents a glimpse of the insurmountable stumbling block that exists in the sexual relationship, allowing us to see that this relationship involves incompatible desire and cannot work out. Any implicit complementarity that existed between Phyllis and Walter is shown to be pure fantasy. In other words, the film uses the viewer's assumptions about an innate complementarity between masculinity and femininity to explain the characters and their attraction to each other. It also provides the tension in the plot as the viewer realizes that this complementarity was manufactured by the femme fatale. Phyllis has coldly calculated all the options and, by hiding the gun, is taking the next step she deems necessary in her plan. Because Phyllis is entirely selfish and coldhearted, the film emphasizes, she is able to behave violently in her relationships with others. Ultimately, then, the film depicts her, as a femme fatale, as so far from the "average" American woman that she inevitably ends up turning to violence. This distancing of the femme fatale from the average woman blurs the antagonism that the femme fatale's violence engenders. In other words, if we can dissociate her from all other women, then we can protect ourselves from the trauma that she represents.

In Joseph H. Lewis' *Gun Crazy* (1949), Annie (Peggy Cummins) is also far from an average woman. She is a sharpshooter in a circus. When Bart (John Dall), a man obsessed with guns, sees her, he feels he has found his perfect mate and joins her act. After running away and getting married, Annie tells Bart: "I've never been much good at least not up till now. You're not getting a very good bargain." The film does not go into detail as to why she is "no good." That she is in a circus, that she likes and is good with guns, and that she sleeps with her boss seems self-evident enough, according to the film, to explain her "badness." Soon after they are married, Annie tells Bart that she wants more than they have, and she coldly demands that they commit crimes to get more money. She doesn't care whom she hurts in the process, in this manner, her "badness" has been firmly established before she is violent.

Importantly, female violence at this period in film history is always the exclusive province of the licentious femme fatale. These women, of course, represent quite a shift from the virtuous heroines in the Serial Queen Melodramas. In film noir, no other woman—only the wayward woman who has already transgressed social mores in her dress, behavior, and life style—is considered capable of violence. Yet, even for this woman, violence is considered her last action, a last resort (whether or not this action comes at the end of the film). In this group of films, any woman depicted as violent must first be securely identified as a femme fatale.

By limiting female violence to the femme fatale character, film noir makes a gesture toward dulling the trauma involved with female violence. If we know that only bad women become violent and if we connect the violent woman to the social antagonism (the failure of complementarity), then we can deduce that the emergence of antagonism in the social order—manifested by the loss of clear gender definitions—is not the result of the inherent functioning of the social order itself, but of a few bad women. In short, we can reduce an ontological problem to an empirical one. What's more, even in the case of these women, violence is not something intrinsic to their femininity; it is a last resort—the result, not the cause, of the failure of their femininity. But this is not the only way that the film noir attempts to situate and symbolize the femme fatale's violence. It also puts clear restrictions on the violence itself in order for the idea of the feminine to be preserved.

The femme fatale hardly ever commits actual physical violence, such as engaging in hand-to-hand combat, stabbing someone with a knife, or choking someone with a wire. Instead, she almost always uses a gun. One of the famous images from classic film noir is that of the femme fatale with a smoking gun. This sleek, cold, phallic weapon is the perfect accessory to the femme fatale; it both matches her highly stylized representation and her insensitive demeanor. The prevalence of the gun, however, also reveals that these films could not conceive of women—even the coldhearted femme fatale— as strong enough to do anything more than pull a trigger. This weapon also allows the femme fatale to continue looking beautiful when committing violence. She doesn't need to sweat, grunt, move into awkward positions, or even mess up her hair while killing someone. Hence, her violence doesn't completely disrupt the traditional gender categories; on the contrary, it leaves much of femininity intact. To continue with the example of *Double Indemnity*, we can see how Phyllis retains her femininity even in her moment of lethal violence. In the crucial scene, she does not hesitate to use her gun as soon as possible when she realizes that Walter intends to kill her. Again Wilder uses the dark shadows to highlight the deranged depths of the femme fatale. Phyllis has drawn all the shades and turned out the lights. When Phyllis shoots Walter, the camera remains on Walter, who is giving a speech revealing that he knows about her sordid past. As he talks, shrouded in the darkness of the room, we see him being shot rather than Phyllis shooting him. The next reverse shot is a long shot of Phyllis, backlit, standing in the middle of the living room with the recently fired gun pointed at Walter. She still looks elegant. Her long white dress flows down to the floor, and her striking hair remains in perfect condition. She just stands there—glamorous and silent—waiting to see what Walter will do next. Oddly enough—after all her "badness"—Phyllis is suddenly overcome with a love for Walter (a love she says she has never felt for anyone before), and during this moment of "weakness," Walter shoots her twice and kills her. This ending to their relationship, and to the femme fatale, is a dramatic example of the horribly destructive nature of the relationship between the femme fatale and the "detective" figure (an insurance agent in this film). By not allowing the femme fatale and the detective to stay together (and often even to live) film noir highlights social antagonism by making clear that there is an insurmountable divide between men and women. For in the end, what each does best is destroy the other's life.[17]

After the femme fatale in film noir, the violent woman appears *en masse* again in the 1970s, concurrent with another widespread elision of sexual difference. It was during this decade that the feminist movement reached its apogee, with the push for the Equal Rights Amendment and the proliferation of consciousness-raising groups. Second-wave feminism dramatically transformed the American social landscape. At the same time, women pushed further into the public realm by joining the workforce. In *The Employment Revolution*, Frank Mott states: "In 1960 only 15 percent of married women with children under the age of 3 were in the workforce, but by 1970 this percentage had grown to about 16 percent and by 1980 fully 41 percent of women with preschool children were either on the job or looking for one."[18] For all the importance of consciousness-raising and challenges to masculine modes of discourse, it was perhaps this movement of women into the workplace that had the greatest ideological impact. By going to work, women deprived men (and other women) of one of the crucial markers of sexual difference. The 1970s also saw women experimenting with appearance and sexuality. Feminists made clear that femininity was a construct that they no longer believed in and intended to destroy.

In response to this new crisis of the elision of gender difference, a different kind of violent woman made her appearance in film. Even though the feminist movement was very public in the 1970s, violent women on film during this time can be found more toward the margins of cinema, in horror and Blaxploitation films.[19] Though some were very successful and popular, these films were not entirely mainstream. This marginalization allowed for a certain amount of experimenting that wasn't possible in mainstream cinema, which depended so much more on appealing to a wide audience. Oftentimes, films at the margins of cinema are able to experiment with fears and desires that would be too controversial for mainstream cinema. And this is certainly the case with both Blaxploitation and horror films in their depictions of the violent woman.

Typically, Blaxploitation films are characterized by black-centered low-budget action films that featured ultramasculine men who inspired cult-like followings, in films such as Gordon Parks' *Shaft* (1971), Gordon Parks, Jr.'s *Superfly* (1972), and Melvin Van Peebles *Sweet Sweetback's Baad Asssss Song* (1971).[20] But there was also another side to Blaxploitation. In films such as Jack Starrett's *Cleopatra Jones* (1973), Jack Hill's *Coffy* (1973), and *Foxy Brown* (1974), and Arthur Marks' *Friday Foster* (1975), it is a woman who violently saves the day, cleans up the streets, or pursues her own adventures. As Ed Guerrero, who has written extensively on Blaxploitation films, says in *Framing Blackness*, "Between 1973 and 1975, Tamara Dobson and Pam bolted into Blaxploitation stardom as they cranked out a series of cheap ghetto action adventures that on almost every count replicated the values, visual style, and exaggerated sex and violence of their male-focused counterparts."[21] Starting on the margins, Blaxploitation films quickly became box office hits, and many film historians credit them with saving some Hollywood studios from going bankrupt.[22] The movement, however, lasted only from 1969 to 1974. While relying financially on the box office returns from Blaxploitation films, Hollywood did not see these films as targeting mainstream America. Instead, they considered Blaxploitation as tapping into an as yet underutilized African-American consumer base. Hoping to make fast, easy money off these cheaply made films, Hollywood did not pay a great deal of attention to the content of these films, which allowed for a degree of experimentation. It is no coincidence, I would contend, that the first "contemporary" violent women in cinema—after the explosion of new violence marked by the appearance of *Bonnie and Clyde* and *The Wild Bunch*—occurs in Blaxploitation films. Within this particular genre directors could explore with impunity the subject of the violent heroine. In other words, the generic exigencies themselves elide any apparent threat.[23]

Ed Guerrero argues that the films, and especially their representations of violence, were clearly tied to the political struggles of that time period. He explains: "No matter how imperfectly rendered its narratives, violence in much of Blaxploitation either depicted or implied the shaking off of the oppression of 'the Man,' and, significantly, the movement toward the dream of a liberated future."[24] I would add that the very presence of a violent heroine marks a political statement of feminist implications as well. Combining the political purposes of the Civil Rights movement and radical black movements with feminist politics, the Blaxploitation heroine's violence often serves her community. Blaxploitation films with a violent woman are a complex combination of over-the-top stereotypes, gritty realism, standard action plot lines, and political messages.

The heroines of these films are characterized by their independence, toughness, violence, and intelligence. Like the femme fatales of the 1930s and 1940s, they are also glamorously beautiful, and the films emphasize their beauty throughout, even during the acts of violence. Similar to the femme fatale, the Blaxploitation heroine uses her beauty to get what she wants or to get closer to what she is looking for. But unlike the virtuous and sometimes violent heroine of the female melodramas, and unlike the cold and vicious femme fatale, the Blaxploitation heroine is neither virtuous nor vicious. She is a complex combination of the desiring woman and the upstanding detective or community protector, which does not mean that she is immune, any more than the heroine of the melodrama or the femme fatale, to the female stereotypes of the time, stereotypes that allow for the films to symbolize the antagonism that she represents.

Blaxploitation films often seem to be predominantly "camp" precisely because of their overly sexualized depictions of women, and this applies even to violent women in these films. The heroine's bared breasts often appear, and exploitative scenes appear throughout the blaxploitation world, such as a scene with a bar full of rowdy lesbians presented as spectacle in *Foxy Brown* (1974).[25] But the films all also involve story lines about a woman fighting against the dominant structures of society to clean up her streets and save her family and friends. She is often propelled into these adventures because someone in her own family—or someone she loves—is killed by drug pushers or other criminals.[26] Thus, whereas the most popular male leads in Blaxploitation films are frequently heroic outlaws who purposely take up the position of the criminal (even if it is to further "good" causes), female heroines in Blaxploitation are more on the side of the law. They may not be working *for* the law, but somehow the police are not against them; in the end, they usually deliver the criminals to the authorities. In *Foxy Brown*, for example, Foxy Brown's (Pam Grier) boyfriend, a police detective, testifies against a criminal group, and they subsequently murder him in front of Foxy. Foxy then proceeds to go after this group for revenge, but along the way she becomes concerned about the women whom this group has enslaved as call girls—and thus Foxy's quest takes on a feminist as well as a personal meaning. While the police do not help her (she doesn't call on the police but instead asks for aid from the "neighborhood committee," a group of neighborhood men who create their own justice), they do not try to stop her, and in the end the film suggests that the criminal mastermind will get her comeuppance in court, as well as in life, once Foxy has finished with her. In Jack Starrett's *Cleopatra Jones* (1973), Cleopatra Jones (Tamara Dobson) is more literally on the side of the law. She is a special agent working for the United States government and has the police on her side (although she still looks more toward neighborhood friends to help her get things done than to the police, who were known and depicted as the primary violent servant of white patriarchal power).

In many ways, these heroines are *forced* into situations where they must use violence. They are violent—and have learned how to be violent—because of the extreme circumstances in which they live. In other words, the criminals and racists that surround her provoke the Blaxploitation heroine to learn violence and to use it. Her violence is much more physical and bloody than that of the femme fatale. She does use a gun on occasion, but the gun is by no means her only available weapon. She often fights in hand-to-hand combat and gives out more punishment than she receives. Cleopatra Jones, for example, is a martial arts expert, and she deftly uses any available object in her battles. Foxy Brown, to choose another example, at one point makes use of a bunch of hangers, which she fashions into a weapon. And unlike any of the femme fatales, the Blaxploitation heroine always survives and *almost* always triumphs in her quest for justice.

Importantly, male heroes from Blaxploitation films never appear simultaneously with these violent heroines. Each has their own film, and it seems impossible to imagine them being able to share the screen. Indeed, most of the men with whom the Blaxploitation heroine is linked romantically die violently, disappear early in the film, or play a very small role. This clearly allows the heroine not only to be sexual with more men throughout the story, but it also eliminates the problems or conflicts that would arise if the male partner were around. The insinuation in each of these films is that if her male partner were still alive or still present, the violent heroine wouldn't have to do all that she does. For example, Foxy Brown, while she is clearly a tough woman, learns to shoot a gun only because her boyfriend gave it to her and implored her to learn to use it in case she needed to protect herself while he was gone. In the 1970s, then, strong, violent women could appear in films, but only if they lacked male protection and their violence arose from absolute need. In fact, Foxy's most gruesome violence arises only after she has been horribly raped and abused by two white redneck racists. In retaliation, Foxy brutally wounds one of the men with the hangers, and then she incinerates them along with their house. The extreme circumstances that surround this eruption of female violence instantly make it more comprehensible within the structure of contemporary ideology, thereby limiting its disruptive power.[27]

The violent woman in the 1970s was not confined solely to Blaxploitation. Many of the same themes and violent acts appear in horror films, though it is usually white adolescent girls who are violent in these films, not black women. In horror films, as in Blaxploitation films, the woman's violence most often arises only after much abuse. But unlike the Blaxploitation heroine, the violent woman in horror films seldom transcends the position of victim and only becomes more violent with the slow progression of the genre throughout the decade of the 1970s. By consigning the violent woman to the position of victim, horror films leave her in a traditional female role. But horror films also produced many different types of violent women. In her *Men, Women, and Chainsaws*, Carol Clover points out that women in horror films of the 1970s and early 1980s exist in three categories: "not only figures like Carrie, whose power somehow derives from their female insides, [but also] the boyish knife-wielding victim-heroes of slasher films and the grim avengers of their own rapes in films like *Ms. 45* and *I Spit on Your Grave*."[28] Slasher films, such as Tobe Hooper's *The Texas Chain Saw Massacre* (1974), John Carpenter's *Halloween* (1978), Tom DeSemone's *Hell Night* (1981), Amy Jones' *Slumber Party Massacre* (1982), and Wes Craven's *A Nightmare on Elm Street* (1984), represent their violent women as more boyish. In her extensive study of horror films, Carol Clover calls the women in slasher films "victim/heroes" and "final girls." This "final girl" is usually the only person to escape a murderous criminal who has killed all her friends. The killer hunts her down, but in the end she defends herself enough to escape or even kill the attacker. She is a combination of the investigator, the rescuer, and the female victim—clever and determined to live, but also young and innocent. As Clover explains: "She alone looks death in the face, but she alone also finds the strength either to stay the killer long enough to be rescued (ending A) or to kill him herself (ending B). But in either case, from

1974 on, the survivor figure has been female."[29] This young woman is almost always beautiful and usually of middle or lower class.[30] Her youth, beauty, and innocence tend to deflect the trauma of her violence by highlighting her victim status and in this way, justifying any means she uses to save herself.

Like the Blaxploitation heroines, all of the disparate horror film heroines deal with violence in a way significantly different than the femme fatale. In general, their violence is far more gruesome, physical, and bloody than that of the femme fatale, and it is usually based on physical strength (rather than the act of firing a gun). These women tend to rely on weapons besides guns (knives, chainsaws, and knitting needles—really anything handy, including their own hands). In fact, women's violence in horror takes on a physical dimension that would have been unthinkable in the 1930s and 1940s. But these films can only imagine a woman as capable of violence if she is entirely enraged, and this anger can only occur when she is tortured, violated, and pushed into a state of total fright. It is the mise-en-scène itself that provides much of the terror in horror films. The final girl in slasher films is most often trapped and terrorized by her surroundings. And it is the mise-en-scène that illustrates her violence and the violence done to her through bright red blood and gruesome attackers. It is these half-psychotic, half-monster men who push the women to such extremes. Any normal men in these films either die early or prove feckless in protecting the female victim. The men who do try to protect the woman in danger often end up dead before the end of the film; if they survive, they do not have much of an overall presence, appearing only in the last two minutes to save the final girl. This marginalization of the "normal" man allows us to see the violent woman without immediately thinking about her implications for gender roles.

In many of the earlier horror films, the young woman—although at points violent—does not kill the male monster in the end. In *Halloween*, she survives, but the monster's psychiatrist arrives in the end and shoots him. In *Texas Chain Saw Massacre*, she makes it through a night of torture, escapes to the highway, and gets away in a pickup truck that happened to be driving down the road. But the late 1970s slasher films and rape revenge films depict the woman triumphantly killing her torturer in the end. The violence that these women commit (a final response after enduring torture from men) is a direct result of the feminist movement of the time.[31] Feminist consciousness-raising in the 1970s served to make women aware of their oppression and, at the same time, aware of their strengths. Thus, rather than emanating from the worst attributes of a wayward woman (as in film noir), violence now emerges out of women's burgeoning consciousness and desire to protect themselves. Instead of depicting the woman's violence as just another malicious and manipulative act, as is the case with the femme fatale, the 1970s horror films depict the woman's violence as something she must resort to as the victim of horrible things that men do to women. Nonetheless, female violence remains, in the 1970s, a response to victimization, and in this sense, it continues to fit with a traditional image of femininity.

A more ubiquitous violent woman burst into mainstream cinema in the late 1980s.[32] Resembling a combination of the femme fatale, the blaxploitation heroine, the final girl, and the monster, these new violent women both shocked and fascinated the public as they became the center of a debate about feminism and filmic representation. In fact, the 1980s was the first time in the history of violent women in film that the public reacted so loudly to the violent woman. The fervor also made for box office success. Violent women in contemporary cinema make up a large trend in mainstream American film (at least three to ten major films each year feature violent women). When Adrian Lyne's *Fatal Attraction* opened in 1987—and even more so four years later when Ridley Scott's *Thelma and Louise* opened in 1991—people began to have conversations about violent women that were qualitatively different than any that came before.

The violent woman in *Fatal Attraction*, Alex Forrest (Glenn Close), is as malicious as the femme fatale and, at the same time, her violence is as gruesome as that depicted in horror and Blaxploitation films. Here the violent woman is definitely one to fear, and yet audiences who flocked to see the film seemed to enjoy hating her more than they feared her. The film stages a typical opposition—especially for the 1980s—between the good housewife, Beth (Anne Archer), and the bad career woman, Alex. The film depicts Alex as essentially a psychotic. But rather than suggesting that this is a part of Alex's individual makeup, the film suggests that it is her lifestyle that makes her psychotic. In other words, a woman who has chosen to pursue her career instead of a family life will eventually be so depressed and unhappy that she can become psychotic and violent.

Director Adrian Lyne uses the mise-en-scène to define Alex through her home décor (as well as her business-oriented attire). Alex lives in a cold barren loft and this—it is hinted—will be the state of her reproductive organs if she does not hurry up and find a mate fast. Even Alex emphasizes that point when she says, "I'm thirty-six years old. It may be my last chance to have a child."

Her violence stems entirely from her desire to coerce Dan Gallagher (Michael Douglas) into a relationship. She directs her first violent act toward herself—slitting her wrists—in order to elicit Dan's sympathy and encourage him to stay with her. Later, she kills the pet rabbit that Dan bought for his daughter, and, finally, she tries to kill Dan's wife, Beth. In many of the scenes, common household items become weapons, and the film confines the violence to a domestic space. In one of the final scenes of the film, Beth prepares to take a bath, but as she wipes the steam off the bathroom mirror, she sees Alex standing behind her. Alex immediately attacks her and tries to kill her. Alex's other violent acts occur in reaction to Dan's violence. On one occasion, he attacks her in her apartment, and she brandishes a huge kitchen knife, which he easily takes away from her. And in the very last scene of the film, Dan saves Beth and fights with Alex. He almost drowns her, but she retaliates, and in the end, it is Beth who shoots Alex. The violence Alex initiates, then, is only directed toward women (herself and Beth), children, or animals (the daughter's pet rabbit); in other words, she aims directly at the heart of the family. And although she fights back when Dan attacks her, she is never able to triumph in these fights. In the end, however, it is the housewife, Beth, who breaks from her femininity to fire a gun at Alex and save her family.

Fatal Attraction shows us an out-of-control, violent, and promiscuous woman—a woman who is hell-bent on destroying the family—as the logical outcome of a woman choosing career over family.[33] It is easy to see why this film emerged when it did. After the feminist movement of the 1970s, the 1980s put feminist ideas into practice. Women entered the workforce in droves and either chose not to have a family or tried to juggle family and a fast-paced career. These changes, of course, affected the whole family, and by the end of the 1980s, much of America began to grumble and complain. *Fatal Attraction*'s director Adrian Lyne was only echoing many others when he said,

You hear feminists talk, and the last ten, twenty years you hear women talking about fucking men rather than being fucked, to be crass about it. It's kind of unattractive, however liberated and emancipated it is. It kind of fights the whole wife role, the whole childbearing role. Sure you got your career and your success, but you are not fulfilled as a woman.[34]

Obviously Lyne's definition of a woman is particularly limited to traditional ideals.[35] But these feelings are also representative of a larger backlash against the feminist movement that *Fatal Attraction* embodied and fueled. As Gabriele Griffin points out in her *Feminist Activism in the 1990s*, many women felt that the women's movement was dead by the end of the 1980s. She contends, however, that "feminist activism [in the 1990s] is still very much in evidence and perhaps more diverse, far-reaching and impact-achieving than ever before."[36] This activism has taken place not on the spectacularly large scale that 1970s and 1980s feminism (such as mass mobilization and general political spectacles in the public domain) relished but instead has taken on a multiplicity of forms. In other words, if the 1980s saw public attempts to define and assert the women's movement—marches on Washington and so on—it also saw public backlash in the form of films, magazines, and newspapers constantly recounting the problem with the working woman and her relationship to femininity and domesticity.[37] This seemed to have led not only to the death of the activist-oriented women's movement in the 1990s, but it also gave birth to the more complete infiltration of institutions: women's studies became more fully ensconced in academia during the 1990s, and women became much more of a mainstay in the workforce. In this way, the appearance of the violent woman *en masse* and across genres during this time could be seen as partly triggered by the more permanent change in gender relations.

Thus, for a third time in the history of film, violent women appeared *en masse* in reaction to an elision of gender differences, which—as in the 1940s—occurred in the workforce and then had ramifications in the family. But this time the image of the violent woman did not remain in the realm of the psychotic female killer where the initial film, *Fatal Attraction*, attempted to confine her. Instead, she began to show up in many different genres of films and television shows—that is, from action, to drama, to comedy and even to video games—becoming an established presence in the universe of contemporary media.[38] The continuation and proliferation of films starring violent women was also a reaction to the continuation of and proliferation of ways in which gender differences were elided. Whereas in earlier decades the elision of gender difference was either temporary or confined to a particular group of politically active women, in the late 1980s and the 1990s this elision of difference touched upon all aspects of society and all aspects of the relations between men and women. During the Gulf War, for example, the public realized for the first time that large numbers of women were a mainstay of the military. And women also gained attention in the world of sports. The 1990s also saw the inauguration of the first large-scale female professional basketball league. In addition, we no longer singled out the career woman in the 1990s, and, instead, it became more common for women to have careers than for women to stay home. During the 1990s, therefore, women's roles continually changed, and each change seemed to have further emphasized the elision of gender differences. Hence, it is not surprising to find the violent woman—the filmic response to the elision of gender differences—across all genres and in all types of film.

Before this proliferation really settled in, however, one film appeared that both provoked the most reaction and solidified the trend: *Thelma and Louise* (1991). Films like *Fatal Attraction* (1987) and *Basic Instinct* (1992) did occasion some public discussion, but neither elicited the kind of response produced by *Thelma and Louise*. In fact, the reaction to *Thelma and Louise*—a film about two friends who begin a vacation together but end up running from the law after killing a man who tries to rape one of them—more closely resembles society's past reactions to actual female murderers than to other films. The public tried hysterically to define real life femininity, feminism, and violence in reaction to this film. It is easy to understand why these issues would be important to work through in the public realm, but why would this particular film provoke such a response at this time?

Some viewers asserted that they were reacting strongly to *Thelma and Louise*, because they thought that the violence committed by the women throughout the film, as they raced across the country eluding the police, was purposeless and worked to glorify violence. And while it is true that the violence Thelma and Louise committed in the film was both aggressive and extreme—from killing a man, to robbing a convenience store, to blowing up a tanker truck, and so forth—compared with other standard action films in which the body count often ranges between fifty and two hundred, *Thelma and Louise* is practically nonviolent, with its body count of only one. Others said that Thelma and Louise were antifeminist representations of women, and still others said that they were too radically feminist. It's possible that the public was taken aback by the "averageness" of the characters: Thelma and Louise are working-class women who, besides being very feminine, live very normal lives. After considering the important role that mise-en-scène plays in defining the violent woman throughout her history, it is no surprise that much of the film's impact is a result of the mise-en-scène. Thelma and Louise seem trapped by their domestic and working-class environments at the beginning of the film, as director Ridley Scott cuts back and forth between Thelma's suburban home and the busy, crowded diner where Louise works. Later, however, Thelma and Louise drive through the wide-open spaces of the west as they shed the trappings of femininity and enter a new realm of freedom and open spaces.

The public outcry over *Thelma and Louise* was fueled in part by the film's attempt to explore how the *average woman* could be involved with violence (rather than the wealthy psychotic woman), a topic that perhaps hit too close to home. The outcry was also provoked by the way the film connected violence so directly with femininity and feminism. To begin a more in-depth analysis of this public reaction, one must locate both these interpretations within film history and within the political and cultural climate at the time it was released. *Thelma and Louise* came out during a time of transition from films depicting psychotic and maniacal violent women to an era in which a violent woman could appear in any profession, situation, or environment. Audiences experienced violent women in films before *Thelma and Louise*, I think, as particular occurrences tied only to certain current issues, not as simply "violent women." For example, the media discussed *Fatal Attraction* (1987) as a response to the emergence of the career woman.[39] Film scholars analyzed James Cameron's *Terminator 2: Judgment Day* (1991) as tied to a fear of loss of humanity in the face of burgeoning technology. And films like Kathryn Bigelow's *Blue Steel* (1990) and Stephen Frears' *The Grifters* (1990) originally seemed more tied to past violent women in horror and noir than to an incipient filmic trend. By the end of the early 1990s, however, the theme of the monstrous career woman had run its course (after also spawning films such as *Basic Instinct* and *The Hand That Rocks the Cradle*), as had the rape revenge film, and violent women characters began to appear in many forms. From quirky leading ladies (*To Die For*, *Fargo*), to straightforward action heroines (*Strange Days*, *The Long Kiss Goodnight*, *Broken Arrow*, *Charlie's Angels*), to dramatic heroines (*Set It Off*, *G.I. Jane*, *Girlfight*), today it is rarer to see a woman who can't fight for herself or help out in a fight than one who can. *Thelma and Louise* signaled the beginning of this transition, and allowed us to recognize a trend that had been building. That is to say, by the time we recognized this cultural transformation, it had already occurred. In other words, even though we were noticing it for the first time, the underlying transformation had already fully flowered, making it impossible to stop. Reviewers, critics, and the public at large recognized *Thelma and Louise* as representative of a new trend (including the films, like *Fatal Attraction* and *Blue Steel*, which had previously only been thought of singularly). In reaction to this burgeoning trend—and trauma—of violent women in cinema, *Thelma and Louise* provoked a frenzy of symbolization. Whether the media represented this female violence as antifeminist, unladylike, feminist, or liberating, all these descriptions dealt directly with the representation of the violent woman as such. This frenzy of symbolization should then be recognized as not only a marker that points to the importance of the violent woman, but also as a way to contain her. The symbolization anchored her image into a more specified universe of meaning so that films with violent women that came after *Thelma and Louise* would make sense.

To put it in another way, *Thelma and Louise* tapped into unconscious anxiety—both because of the time in which it was produced and the content of the film—and this eruption of the unconscious manifested itself in an onslaught of film analyses, proclamations about womanhood, and heated arguments about gender roles—all of which ended up solidifying some meaning for what seemed traumatic about *Thelma and Louise*. This intense public response indicates the importance of *Thelma and Louise*, revealing a break from the way that the public had previously interacted with films featuring violent women.[40] After *Thelma and Louise*, the violent woman herself became a figure in the landscape of contemporary film. And because of *Thelma and Louise*, and public reaction to it, society had an opportunity to symbolize the violent woman as such. Once symbolized, the appearance of the violent woman in film ceased to be traumatic. Now she existed within a symbolic universe of meaning, one which worked to obviate the underlying antagonisms that the violent woman had the potential to reveal. I say this to explain why *Thelma and Louise* was the only film with violent women to provoke the kind of reaction that it did, but this does not mean that after *Thelma and Louise* the violent woman's radicality completely disappears and that she no longer represents an attempt to grapple with the trauma of the elision of sexual difference. In fact, as I will argue in detail in the following chapters, I believe that the trauma exists instead—in the rest of the films in the 1990s and 2000s featuring violent women—in the cinematic manner in which the violent female is represented and the disruptive effect that the violent woman has on the narrative. In other words, the trauma of the violent woman manifests itself in the defense mechanisms that films must utilize in order to depict this figure.[41]

In this chapter, I have illustrated the most important episodes in filmic history for the emergence of the violent woman as a filmic element, and described the historical circumstances (including especially the conflicts and antagonisms of these moments) behind these emergences. Here, however, we must again consult Ernesto Laclau and Chantal Mouffe's understanding of such cultural eruptions, as they articulate it in *Hegemony and Socialist Strategy*. They suggest, "The usual descriptions of antagonisms in the sociological and historical literature [. . .] explain the *conditions* which made antagonisms possible, but not the antagonism as such."[42] Laclau and Mouffe go on to say that theorists often describe these conditions by saying that this or that "*provoked* a reaction." In other words, we can see what provoked the reaction and we can see what the reaction is, but this does not necessarily explain or describe the antagonism itself. For example, I have explained how large numbers of women had jobs during World War II, which unsettled and provoked fear among society at large. This was accompanied by a huge push on the part of the United States government to reconstitute the traditional roles of masculinity and femininity. These feelings of anxiety, at this particular time, also manifested themselves in a spate of films featuring violent women. The violent woman is, then, a way to displace this anxiety into an aesthetic realm, but she also provokes more anxiety and very complex defense mechanisms within the film in which she appears. Regardless of this outcome, her place in history seems particularly tied to moments of crisis in male and female gender roles. But all this still does not get to the "antagonism itself." I have given an overview of the historical context and the cultural product but not yet theoretically elaborated on antagonism itself. The violent woman in American cinema reveals that there is an antagonism between masculinity and femininity that is both essential to the working of society and also its potential undoing. In order to approach this antagonism and to grasp its relationship to female violence, we must look at masculinity and the central role that violence plays in its construction.

CHAPTER 2

Expressions of Masculinity

The Traditions of Violence in American Film

Graeme Newman begins his discussion of violence in *Understanding Violence* with this caveat: "Violence is anything but a unitary phenomenon. Rather it is a catchall word that is used to refer to a wide range of often very different events and behaviors."[1] Many accounts of violence begin similarly, with warnings that there can be no universal theory about violence because even the word "violence" seems inadequate for all the different acts that it describes. Violence is so rooted in the particular that theorists such as Newman claim it is almost impossible to universalize about it. Such an attitude also mirrors the common feeling that violence often erupts spontaneously, as a highly irrational response to a conflict or problem. While it may be true that violence is a concept that is strongly rooted in the particularity of specific violent acts—precisely what makes them seem to erupt spontaneously—this chapter begins with the basic idea that it is essential to look at how those particulars work in relation to society as a whole. In this way, I hope to illustrate theoretically that violence does not necessarily erupt spontaneously or as an irrational response to a situation, but rather that violence plays a very specific role in creating individual and social identities. To understand this, one must consider the individual, and the individual acts of violence, but also the larger social totality that might provoke, demand, or provide an environment for the said violence.

41

Serving as a fundamental signifier of masculinity, we not only consider violence more the province of men than women, but it is also an activity that inevitably enhances a man's masculinity as much as it would conversely detract from a woman's femininity.

Since its inception, American film has relied on this connection between masculinity and violence. Indeed, entire genres—such as the gangster film, the Western, the war film, and the contemporary action film—have been built around various permutations of this connection. As Lee Clark Mitchell points out about one such genre, "The Western's obsession with violence grows out of a larger fascination with what is now termed the construction of masculinity."[2] The task of this chapter is to understand some of the basic ways in which American film expresses masculinity through violence, as well as the role that masculine violence has in obscuring social antagonism. My investigation is thus solely concerned with how violence and masculinity are represented culturally. Clearly, this topic alone warrants its own book-length study. My purpose here, however, is to understand how masculinity enhances our understanding representations of femininity and violence. In lieu of surveying a large number of films, however, I will analyze several in detail in order to investigate this connection and provide a context for discussing femininity and violence.

The myriad ways that American film has narrativized and depicted masculinity illustrate that ideals of masculinity often change with each historical period. The historic trajectory of filmic masculinity has always been complex: from the funny man (Charlie Chaplin, Buster Keaton, Mack Sennett's keystone cops) and the romantic hero (Rudolf Valentino) in silent cinema, to the song and dance man (Gene Kelly, Fred Astaire) and the hardened "tough" guy (John Wayne, Humphrey Bogart, and Paul Robeson) in classical Hollywood cinema, to the muscled action hero of the 1980s (Arnold Schwarzenegger and Sylvester Stallone), to the more sensitive thinking man of the 1990s and 2000s (Tom Hanks, Denzel Washington, and George Clooney). One way to begin generalizing about filmic masculinity is to consider how an individual's masculinity is often defined by his link to a larger group or institution. Genres are built on these very links when they pit one type of masculinity against another, such as in the gangster genre (gagsters vs. the police), the Western (the law man vs. the criminal), and so on. Revolving around seemingly binary masculine standoffs, these genres rely on violence as a marker of symbolic status: to be the most violent is to attain the group's highest symbolic status, a status that connotes ultramasculinity.[3]

Providing both a critique and an illustration of this association, Carl Franklin's *One False Move* (1992) uses this hierarchy of violence—and thus of masculinity—to play a central role in the very unfolding of the film's plot. This film is a perfect example because the plot revolves around masculinity in crisis. The plot itself would not make sense without the violence. In the film, tough urban police officers investigate a crime in a rural area, where they cannot help but view the local sheriff as less competent because he rarely sees action or violence. Carl Franklin makes this distinction clear on the level of mise-en-scène from the very beginning by introducing Dale Dixon (Bill Paxton), the rural sheriff, in a shot in which he is comforting his child, while introducing Dud Cole and McFeely (Jim Metzler and Earl Billings), the Los Angeles officers, in a shot that depicts them looking calmly over dead bodies. Cole and McFeely are familiar with violence and death, because they interact with it everyday (as the first shots of them inspecting a gruesome murder scene make obvious), and this signifies their toughness and their masculinity. The majority of Dixon's experience, however, involves dealing with arguing couples, shoplifters, and troubled kids. All these experiences happen within a domestic, more feminized, realm that is free of real violence. Dixon even admits this when he tells Cole and McFeely, "Hell, I've been police chief going on six years. I never even had to draw my gun."

Through comments like this, through his enthusiastic eagerness, and through the more domestic mise-en-scène that Franklin places him in, Dixon appears naïve or boyish while Cole and McFeely appear fully masculine and adult. What seems to go along with their masculine violence is a calm and cool attitude. This is emphasized in their business-like demeanor (especially when contrasted with Dixon) and their patronizing—however kindly—attitude toward Dixon. But what is most obvious is that Dixon himself feels less masculine because he sees little or no "action." He tells Cole and McFeely that he is thinking of joining the Los Angeles police department. He explains, "I've been on the force down here since I was grown. Hell, after ten years of busting peeping Toms and stop sign runners, I'd like to take a crack at the big time." In other words, he wants to acquire extreme violence as a signifier of his masculinity. In one of the film's key scenes, all his fears about his own masculinity receive explicit confirmation when he overhears Cole and McFeely laughing about him as if he is a child—or a woman—trying to fit into a man's clothing. In order to prove himself after this moment of emasculation, Dixon attempts to battle the city criminals on his own while Cole and McFeely are scrambling to find their way among the country roads. In the end, Dixon kills the criminals and through this violence claims the masculine signifier. Even the city officers reveal their new respect when one remarks, "That son of a bitch nailed 'em." Here, we see the way in which violence acts as a signifier of masculinity within state-sponsored organizations whose purpose—ironically, but not coincidentally—is to protect its citizens from violence. And the film replicates this through character trajectory, narrative, and form. *One False Move*, in fact, becomes increasingly noirish in style as it progresses. While Dixon begins as an innocent rural "keeper of the peace," depicted in the sunny countryside, by the end of the film, he is creeping through the shadows, wrestling with the femme fatale, and actually killing criminals, all of which further aligns him with the troubled but certainly masculine hero of film noir.[4]

Though the preceding example illustrates the representation of violence in legal organizations, this sense of hierarchy accorded to violence and masculinity exists in a parallel fashion in criminal organizations, such as the Mafia and other street gangs. Like state-sponsored organizations, these insurgent groups engage with violence for initiation into the group and continued respect within the group. To enter the group the would-be member must kill an outsider and/or be beaten by other members, and to continue receiving respect, he must continue being violent. As in legal organizations, the most violent person earns the most respect and embodies the greatest degree of masculinity. Still, in both kinds of organizations the violence must be in the service of the organization; violence that only serves personal revenge or jealousy can be dangerous to the entire organization. The ideological narrative linking gang violence and its masculine quality with the underside of American ideology is classically presented in Francis Ford Coppola's *The Godfather* (1972), which pivots on a scene in which Michael Corleone (Al Pacino) becomes a man, and a member of the Mafia, by murdering a police chief. Previous to this murder, Michael has been a family member but not a member of the family business. His brothers—and the other members of the "business"—do not take him seriously when he says he wants to be involved. At the beginning of the film, Michael comes home from the army a decorated soldier. In this legal organization, he has proved his masculinity. But the men in his family do not consider the military a true rite of passage toward masculinity. They see the violence they interact with as much more gruesome, much more intense, and thus they see themselves as more masculine than those in the military. Murdering the police captain, however, is the rite of passage that establishes not only Michael's manhood, but also secures his position as head of the family. As filmic representations continually make clear, in the Mafia, as in the local police department, violence goes hand-in-hand with respect and masculinity.

They both are structured around the link between masculinity and violence. Investigating this link, the later *Godfather* films depict Michael working to make his Mafia family a legitimate business, and the narrative in Francis Ford Coppola's *Godfather Part II* (1974) and *Godfather Part III* (1990) explores just how intricately legal and illegal organizations are linked. In effect, they both need each other for survival. The underlying suggestion is that violence supports both and that for both organizations violence is a man's realm, as well as a defining characteristic of masculinity.

Of course, violence is just one signifier among many that point to maleness. Violence itself doesn't entirely make up masculinity, but it is also not possible to entirely erase violence from masculinity. One cannot separate ideas of masculinity from violence in our society—which is why, for example, a woman committing violence is inevitably at some point referred to as masculine. Even if a man purposefully avoids engaging in violence and disdains it, his identity is still formed in opposition to violence. In this sense, his nonviolent actions accentuate the importance of violence all the more. In all arenas of violence—war, domesticity, criminality, law enforcement—it is masculinity that gives violence its meaning. The intertwined nature of violence and masculinity is one of the reasons the violent woman is so threatening: she breaks up this symbolic relationship between violence and masculinity. Every book on violence is—at least unconsciously—also aware of this relationship. Film theorists writing on violent genres, or on masculinity in general, may not make this link explicit, but it inevitably structures their assumptions. For example, in his discussion of "Masculinity as Spectacle," Steven Neal begins by commenting that "current ideologies of masculinity involve [. . .] notions and attitudes to do with aggression, power, and control."[5] Theoretical discussions on masculinity within film rely on the implicit assumption that violence is a masculine activity.

Jan de Bont's *Speed* (1994) serves as an ideal example of how this association between masculinity and violence resonates filmically. *Speed* is a standard Hollywood action film, a summer blockbuster, and it provides a near-perfect illustration of how the signifiers of violence (guns, bombs, handcuffs, and so on) are also signifiers of masculinity. This film also adheres to Marsha Kinder's theory regarding the "narrative orchestration of violence in American film."[6] The violence is spectacular, stops the narrative flow, and is often peppered with pithy jokes. It is, in short, an exemplary case of American filmic violence. When the male hero first appears in *Speed*, he is laden down with masculine signifiers. During his entrance, his car bounds onto the screen and screeches to a halt. His driving seems reckless, suggesting a potential for violence. When he gets out of the car, he puts on a gun and other accessories, which indicate that he is a Los Angeles police officer and mark his masculinity.[7] Jack's (Keanu Reeves) bravery is similarly displayed for the viewer as another moniker of his masculinity. Jack is a member of the L.A.P.D. who takes on one of the most dangerous jobs—dismantling bombs—and has, by association with this job, a reputation for being among the bravest on the force. When he and the rest of the bomb squad are listening to their leader describe a bomb threat—a bomber has placed a bomb under an elevator in an office building and has demanded a large amount of money or he will blow the bomb and kill the people—Jack volunteers himself and his partner, Harry (Jeff Daniels), for the dangerous task of investigating the bomb. His cavalier and casual attitude about the mission indicates his bravery and his love of danger. Through these clues at the beginning of the film, the audience already understands that Jack is our hero at the same time that we are also given some indication of his masculine prowess.

In *Speed*, Jack's sexual prowess, his ability to be violent, and his lack of fear in the face of violence all act as symbols of a supposed "authentic" masculinity. It is often humor that makes the connections between these signifiers of masculinity obvious. For example, when Jack has again demonstrated his driving prowess by catching up with a bus that has a bomb on it, a man on the bus says that Jack "really has a hard on for this bus." Most of the comments that characters in the film make about Jack, like this one, affirm his masculinity and sexual prowess. After Jack convinces the bus driver that there is a bomb aboard, he climbs into the bus and explains the situation to the bus patrons. From this moment, he encounters a series of difficult obstacles, including a panicked rider shooting the bus driver and Annie (Sandra Bullock), a young woman on the bus, taking the place of the driver. Eventually Jack tries to defuse the bomb by lowering himself under the moving bus. He is unsuccessful, but it is such a daring attempt that one of the riders remarks admiringly, "You're not too bright, but you've got some big hairy *cohones*." Again, it is Jack's masculinity—"his big hairy *cohones*"—that others point to when complementing him. Filmically, the spectacle of the daring rescue has also allowed the viewer to stop and revel in Jack's masculinity. Everyone admires Jack's gut reactions and bravery, and they inevitably link these to his sexuality.

The comedic moments of the film add to this notion that violence proves Jack's masculinity as well. For example, at the beginning of the film the bomb in the elevator explodes, and Jack, with the aid of Harry, daringly and successfully saves all the people before the elevator crashes to the ground floor. After the elevator crashes, Jack and Harry sit down and take a breath, and they say to each other, "Was it good for you?" "It was great for me." Joking about their heroic actions as if they were sexual intercourse, they suggest that they get a similar kind of pleasure from these heroic acts as from the sex act, linking daring activity with sexuality (and hence an authentic masculinity).[8] All of these moments foreshadow the times in which Jack is actually violent. We expect Jack to triumph in each battle because—as the masculine symbols tell us—he is innately masculine and therefore innately violent. In other words, the film suggests that his violence ultimately is motivated by biology rather than culture. In this way, both the overwhelming spectacles of male violence (which escalate as the film goes on) and the plot (one man's attempt to stop a rampaging male criminal whose pathology is motivated by losing the recognition that Jack has throughout the film) attempt to define masculinity.

In his first act of violence, Jack shoots his partner Harry— wounding him in the knee—while Howard Payne (Dennis Hopper) holds Harry hostage. Because he has Jack's partner as a hostage, Payne assumes that he has the upper hand in this situation. This makes Jack's violent act all the more impressive. It allows him to turn the tables on Payne, transforming Payne's power over him into a deficit. Through his violent act, Jack finds a way out of a seemingly insoluble situation, thereby affirming his masculine prowess. De Bont shoots this scene in a way that affirms the masculinity suggested by Jack's actions. Jack speaks in a commanding voice throughout the scene and reduces his antagonist to whimpers. We see Jack remaining completely under control and calm, even in the direst circumstance. Jack's subsequent acts of violence in the film all follow the narrative and filmic model that this initial scene lays down.

Films like *Speed* presume that in order to embark on the project of establishing oneself as a "man," one must believe that there is a purpose to embodying multiple signifiers of masculinity, a goal of ideal masculinity that one might attain. But ideal masculinity is an ideological concept, and like all ideological concepts, it is hard to define because it feels natural to us. It is easier to point out some general elements that might make up an ideal masculinity, but it is not possible to add up all these individual signifiers to equal ideal masculinity (it is much more amorphous than just the sum of its parts). We often conceive of the President of the United States—the "leader of the world's only superpower"—as a man who should, as much as he can, embody masculinity itself; he should be an all-powerful patriarch. President Clinton's sex scandal in the White House was particularly revealing in this light. Although many people in the nation criticized him for this affair, much of the angst about the scandal could be linked to President Clinton's failure to have sexual intercourse with Monica Lewinsky. In effect, he played the feminine position of being elusive and devising other ways to interact sexually. This, coupled with his lack of military service (his avoidance of which indicates to much of America a lack of masculinity), does not coincide with the myth of the ultramasculine nature of the President of the United States. Clinton upset the public more by revealing the ideological nature of the presidency (by *not* having sex in the White House and by *not* involving himself with violence when he was younger) than by anything else. He revealed the ideological status of the ideal itself by making evident his own castration. William Luhr notes that since Clinton was in office there have been a significant number of films depicting a president becoming a warrior—taking up violence throughout the film to protect himself and his country (as in Roland Emmerich's *Independence Day* [1996] and Wolfgang Petersen's *Air Force One* [1997]). He suggests,

> While it is common for films to represent sitting presidents as courageous commanders-in-chief who are resolute in the face of national or even personal danger, those presidents are seldom depicted as actually shouldering weapons and triumphantly entering into battle. [. . .] Not since the era of Theodore Roosevelt has the notion of a warrior president, as opposed to commander-in-chief, been viable in popular narratives.[9]

Luhr claims that this depiction of the "warrior president" emerges in reaction to a crisis in masculinity. This figure develops out of a longing for a more traditional patriarchal authority. It is not surprising that to reinvent this presidential patriarch, films are relying on violence as the signifier that has the most direct connection to masculinity.

Turning to psychoanalysis here allows for a more detailed explanation of the relation between men and the ideal man (the position the president is supposed to come closest to). Psychoanalysis theorizes that men are subject to castration every bit as much as women, but that, unlike women, men are haunted by the (illusory) possibility of noncastration. As Bruce Fink says in *The Lacanian Subject*, "you can safely say that all people who are men, not in biological but rather in psychoanalytic terms, are castrated. But while men are wholly castrated, there is nevertheless a contradiction: that ideal of noncastration—of knowing no boundaries, no limitations—lives on somewhere, somehow, in each and every man."[10] Ultimately, then, this ideal masculinity, this all-powerful patriarch, is an impossible position, an unreachable ideal.[11] According to Joan Copjec, "no man can boast that he embodies this thing—masculinity—any more than any concept can be said to embody being."[12] It is in this sense that men are castrated: they can never fully embody the ideal that they nonetheless believe lies within their reach. They are limited on all sides by the symbolic order, yet they invest themselves in an ideal that has "no boundaries, no limitations," an ideal of noncastration.

In *Seminar XX*, Lacan describes this bind that masculine identity creates for subjects who attempt to take it up. He points out that "man as whole acquires his inscription" in the symbolic order only insofar as his identity "is limited due to the existence of [. . .] the father function" (which is to say, limited by the external ideal of noncastration).[13] For Lacan, men incessantly strive after an ideal that remains constitutively inaccessible for them. And this is the contradiction with which men must continually struggle. As Slavoj Žižek points out in *The Indivisible Remainder*,

> True, so-called "modern man" is [. . .] caught in the split between what (it seems to him that) the other (woman or social environment in general) expects of him (to be a strong macho type, etc.) and what he effectively is in himself (weak, uncertain of himself, etc.). [. . .] The macho image is experienced not as a delusive masquerade but as the ideal ego one is striving to become. Behind the macho image of a man there is no "secret," just a weak ordinary person who can never live up to his ideal.[14]

Despite intense striving to reach the ideal, the man never escapes the "weak ordinary person" that he feels himself to be.

Psychoanalyst James Gilligan's study on male violence revolves around discovering why the most violent men, those he studied in maximum security prison, reacted with *extreme* violence to seemingly insignificant events. Essentially, he suggests that this is just an extreme version of a common male reaction to castration. In other words, violence often erupts in response to an acute sense of castration, to an experience of the failure of ideology. We can see this clearly at work in the case of the Columbine school shooting. The two shooters, Dylan Klebold and Eric Harris, saw their attack as an act of revenge on the people who for them symbolized the origin of their castration—the jocks, the popular kids, and the minorities. Each of these groups seem to have "it"—the phallic signifier—and hence each embody the force that demanded Klebold and Harris's

renunciation of *jouissance*, their "acceptance" of castration. In reacting with violence, they are attempting to secure their masculinity
and their identities against all the perceived beatings it has taken by
those around them. Even now, after Klebold and Harris are dead,
"the jocks" continue to make evident that which Klebold and Harris
reacted against. Interviewed after the killings, Evan Todd, a football
player, said,

> Columbine is a clean good place except for those rejects. Most
> kids didn't want them there. They were into witchcraft. They
> were into voodoo dolls. Sure, we teased them. But what do you
> expect with kids who come to school wearing weird hairdos
> and horns on their hats? It's not just jocks: the whole school's
> disgusted with them. They're a bunch of homos, grabbing each
> other's private parts. If you want to get rid of someone, usually
> you tease 'em. So the whole school would call them homos, and
> when they did something sick, we'd tell them, "You're sick and
> that's wrong."[15]

Clearly, Klebold and Harris were not just paranoid; the other students did openly question their masculinity, and violence, as our
culture showed them, provided a way of recovering (or reestablish-
ing) it. Reacting with actual physical violence is an extreme response, an attempt to regain some sense of masculinity, to deny
castration and forcefully reimpose the ideals of ideology. Examples
such as these leads James Gilligan to proclaim that for men, "violence toward others, such as homicide, is an attempt to replace
shame with pride."[16] While this violence is a reaction to an individual's acute sense of castration, it often appears to erupt at inappro-
priate instances, when, for example, a boyfriend practically kills the
man with whom his girlfriend talks, or a man attacks someone who
looks at him the "wrong way." A look, a word, or a small incident
can trigger this anger and violence, but these insignificant moments
are just the triggers that reveal a building sense of castration. In a
way, this extreme violence found among prison inmates and often
depicted on film is *the* metaphor for every man's reaction to castration, because it indicates the everyday connections between violence
and masculinity.

If violence, the ultimate masculine signifier, is a way to combat castration, then it is also a symbol of this castration. In film, this double meaning is usually resolved by splitting the signifiers in masculinity (violence as masculinity on the one side, and violence as a desperate attempt to cover up castration on the other) and assigning them the protagonist and antagonist (respectively). Certainly, in *Speed*, Jack's violence embodies all that is lawful and masculine, but the violence of the criminal (often it is failed violence) operates as an indicator of his complete castration. Payne, we learn during the course of the film, used to be a police officer in Atlanta. He was on the force for many years (on the bomb squad), and all indications are that he was an excellent and highly skilled officer. We know for certain about his skill at building bombs, so we might infer that he excelled at dismantling them as well. When Jack and Harry examine the first bomb that Payne planted, they both note the expertise of its builder. We also find out that in the line of duty, Payne lost half of his hand. Throughout the film, when someone is injured in the line of duty, this injury adds to his masculinity. After Harry is shot, for example, the rest of the officers exalt him for his bravery.[17] Surely, Payne thought the same kind of thing would happen to him: he would be appreciated and lauded by his peers and the institution that he worked for. Instead, after his injury, the department laid him off and gave him disability pay. This one action stripped away many of the signifiers of masculinity that he had clearly worked all his life to attain, forcing him to experience his castration. The act of retiring him early suggested to Payne that the police force no longer supported him, nor thought him capable of performing adequately. From that point on, Payne vowed vengeance. He felt that society owed him his masculinity, which it initially promised and then stripped away. Payne felt a great sense of his castration, and in response he resorts to extreme and spectacular acts of violence to stave off the dissolution of his (masculine) identity.

Again, the film uses humor to demonstrate the connection between Payne's violence and his loss of masculinity. In fact, Payne's loss of face is emphasized throughout the film through jokes made at his expense. In the scene I discussed earlier, Jack and Harry joke about the sexual pleasure involved in their heroic rescue of the people in the elevator. Then, they proceed to insult the sexual prowess of Payne. Discussing the reason he might have triggered the bomb early (i.e., the reason his violent act wasn't completely successful), Harry says, "Maybe he couldn't hold his wad long enough. It's a common problem among middle-aged men. So I'm told." In this light, Payne's failed masculinity is also physically represented by the loss of half his hand, specifically his thumb.[18] In direct response to this sense of loss, Payne hopes, through his violence, to get revenge and to recover his lost masculinity.

According to what Payne says, however, his violent deeds are only an attempt to acquire a large sum of money. But in other dialogue he gives away his real concern, that is, his own masculinity. At the beginning of the film—after the elevator incident—Payne blows up a bus to get Jack's attention. While Jack is inspecting the bus, Payne rings him on a nearby pay phone and explains to him that there is a bomb on another bus that will blow unless Payne receives a certain amount of money. (The bus he just blew up was only meant to be an indication that he was "man enough" to go through with this next one if they didn't give him the money.) But it also seems as though Payne is targeting Jack, so Jack asks Payne why he chose him to target. Payne replies, "This is about ME"; in other words, Payne means for Jack to be merely incidental. The violent man is obsessed with—in his own terms—regaining self-respect, or attempting to nullify his castration. Thus, Payne's violence, which he uses to get revenge on police organizations and on Jack, has solely to do with regaining his lost masculinity.

These examples all deal with calculated violence in reaction to loss of masculinity. But *Speed* is also full of examples of more spontaneous reactions. At the end of the film, Jack has thwarted Payne's plans to some extent, but Payne still has ended up with the money. When he goes to inspect it, however, a paint bomb explodes all over him and the money. He realizes at this point that he has lost all possibility of regaining his masculinity. When he realizes this, he has a violent fit—punching, kicking, and screaming. He then runs after Jack to kill him, the only action which—or so he feels at this point—could lessen his sense of frustration. It is not, however, just the criminal who reacts in this way. Earlier on in the film, Payne informs Jack that a bomb Payne rigged has killed Jack's partner Harry. This news has the affect of stripping away some of Jack's masculinity because the criminal has killed Jack's partner and made him feel alone, possibly scared and extremely angry. Jack reacts to this news by having a very violent tantrum on the bus. This tantrum exemplifies how spontaneous outbursts of violence become a way of counterbalancing the shame and loss a man feels when his masculine signifiers have been ripped away. In other words, violence is a way of seeking some sort of justice for the injustice of masculinity's illusoriness.

What becomes apparent is that part of this process, this seeking of justice, almost always involves a relationship of reciprocity between men. In other words, it involves an exchange of violence between two men or two groups of men. Even in the relatively few examples from *Speed*, it is obvious that there is an exchange of violence between Payne and Jack (and the police force as a whole). This seems like a natural reciprocity—between criminals and cops—and indeed the law revolves around it. Exchanging violence for violence, that is, an economy of violence, in which each retaliation bolsters one man's masculinity and destroys the other's, has, such a film suggests, certainly thrived for a long time.

We know that violence often triggers retributive violence.[19] In *Violence and the Sacred*, René Girard suggests: "Only violence can put an end to violence, and that is why violence is self-propagating. Everyone wants to strike the last blow, and reprisal can thus follow reprisal without any true conclusion ever being reached."[20] Violent reciprocity attempts to destroy the masculinity of the other while protecting one's own. It is this continuous nature of the exchange that keeps society running smoothly and not destroying itself. At first glance, the idea of a continuous string of violent exchanges might seem contrary to a smooth running social system. Most people see violence as a barrier to social activity, which is why they clamor for more police on the street and support politicians who advocate a "crackdown on crime." In other words, we tend to believe that if violence is swept out of our community we will live safer, more relaxed lives and that society will function more optimally (children will be happier, work will be uninhibited, etc.). In reality, however, much of our society thrives on violence. For example, the very tranquil lifestyle of the American Dream is based on a certain system of violence and masculinity. In other words, few public voices suggest that the entire society is responsible for each crime committed because this would contradict our ideas of retribution. Instead, we rely on a more age-old understanding of crime and punishment—the idea that one violent act can only be annulled by returning the very same violent act (or some accepted lawful substitute). Seen in this way, a violent act always holds a kind of value, and one can always expect to have that value returned in one form or another. One might even say that the exchange of violence is capitalism *avant la lettre*. Thus, those who engage in violence engage in an accepted exchange that both mirrors and sustains capitalist society.

Moreover, capitalism has accentuated this function of violence because capitalism itself is based on a logic of exchange. Within this system, violence—like the rest of social relationships—becomes reified. People cannot understand violence, however, in terms of its relation to masculinity or to the social whole because capitalism works to prevent this type of reflection, which means that we continue to see violence as disconnected from larger social identities and relations.[21] We know violence on a visceral level, without the need for any mediation to help us comprehend it, because we see and experience it. This phenomenological experience of actual violence is an important influence on the kind of filmic techniques that developed to recreate this feeling on film. In other words, the filmic techniques themselves (cutting on action, cross cutting, shot-reverse shot, and so on) underscore the ontological status of violence simply by attempting to recreate it. This sense of having an immediate knowledge of a phenomenon (such as violence) is emblematic of reified consciousness. In *History and Class Consciousness*, Georg Lukács explains this process: "This approach makes of every historical object a variable monad which is denied any interaction with other—similarly viewed—monads and which possesses characteristics that appear to be absolutely immutable essences."[22] According to Lukács, capitalist society blinds us because it prompts us to see everything in isolation. This is especially true of the way we experience and perceive violence. By not seeing the role of violence in sustaining our ideas of masculinity, people encourage and indeed condone the very violence they say they are against. This is why masculine violence is usually not perceived as traumatic: it is part of the very system within which we live.[23] In this sense, capitalism cannot do without violence and its relationship to masculinity.

Even today, it is most often men who are expected to exchange violence. In other words, when a woman is a victim of violence, we still expected that her "man" will avenge this attack. The ostensible reason for the violence is the injured female, but, in actuality, she is

only a screen onto which men are able to project their own fantasmatic images. In other words, the wronged woman may seem like
the reason for the violence, but she really serves only to obscure the
real nature of the violence, which is the homosocial bond between
men and the demands of masculinity. Concepts of how violence operates are linked even here—or especially here—to concepts about
masculinity and femininity. And it is this dynamic, more than any
other, that can be found at the heart of American history and ideology and that is represented in American myths and films. In this dynamic, the man takes the role of the protector, and women and
children fall into the role of the protected: the male is active, and the
female is passive.[24] They seem to fit together like two pieces of a
puzzle, and this is part of the reason they feel as though they need
each other, that they are complementary. The woman needs her protector, and the man needs his woman to protect. This parallels the
very complementary nature of our ideas about masculinity and femininity. And it is within this relationship that violence seems to find
justification. In other words, here, in the workings of masculinity
and femininity, violence has a purpose. This is illustrated in a situation in which a man is protecting his wife and children; in this case,
his violence does not seem like something personal, irrational, or
evil. In fact, his violence seems justified because its purpose is to
protect. The woman's role is to necessitate—and to some degree
enjoy—male violence. Her role covers over the possibility that his violence is just an attempt to bolster his symbolic masculine status
through the exchange of violence with other men. She provides a
convenient justification for male violence that serves to obscure its
deeply homosocial dimension. If she steps out of her role, as the violent woman does, the ideological nature of his violence and his
masculinity would be revealed. Thus, masculinity is as dependent
on the existence of femininity as it is on the symbolic status of masculinity. Ironically, the man who protects often feels independent of
his "dependent" woman. But in actuality his identity—even his independence—is wholly dependent on the woman whom he is protecting and providing for. Thus, the protector/protected association
shapes masculinity as much as it does femininity.

This dynamic is reflected in the majority of films made today,
beyond simply action films. This protector/protected aspect to definitions of gender is a common part of most narratives where the

protector is violent and male and the protected is nonviolent and female. And if the male protects the woman, the film often rewards
him with her. In *Alice Doesn't*, Theresa de Lauretis explains this as a
general narrative form: "The female position, produced as the end
result of narrativization, is the figure of narrative closure, the narrative image in which the film, as Heath says, 'comes together.'"[25] In
the film *Speed*, Annie is one of the patrons on the bus, and when the
bus driver is accidentally shot, she takes over the driving. The rest of
the film is in many ways about the interaction between Annie and
Jack. It is clear from the beginning of this interaction that Jack's
place is to protect Annie and the rest of the bus patrons. Even
though this is obvious, Jack sometimes needs to be reminded of his
position in society. Such a moment happens directly after Jack's
violent tantrum at the news that his partner has been killed. He
seems to have given in entirely to his violent frustration at the death
of his partner at the hands of Payne, the criminal. In response, Annie
pleads with him: "Don't give up on me. We are really scared and we
need you right now. I can't do this by myself." In saying this, she
affirms the fact that he is the protector and she needs his protection,
as do the rest of the people on the bus, and that Jack must step up
and fill this masculine position. He answers her call for help and
through heroic actions saves everyone on the bus. Annie and Jack
are the last off the bus, and as a "reward" for his violent heroic masculinity, Jack ends up with Annie in his arms.

Of course, at the end of the film, Jack needs no reminders about
his masculinity. Not only does he kill Payne to save Annie (whom
Payne managed to kidnap), but also Jack puts his own life at great
risk to remain with Annie while she is handcuffed to a runaway
train. Just to reinforce the rewards the violent protector reaps, the
film ends with Jack and Annie kissing on the derailed train in the
middle of the city with many people watching them. The onlookers
clap as they see Annie and Jack embrace. In fact, the onlookers most
resemble a chorus that illustrates what the viewers should be feeling.
Through the use of violence, the male protector secures his complementary relationship with his protected female—and we applaud at
the stabilization of the social bond that this provides.

Throughout *Speed*, as in many action films, the hero is able to
use violence to overcome each new obstacle that is put in his path.
His relationship to violence is totally organic. He seems to have an

innate ability to be violent and never worries whether violence is the right course of action. To the action hero, violence is the proper and natural response to criminal activity or criminal violence. This ideological attitude goes hand-in-hand with him retaining a solid masculine identity, making it through very dangerous situations alive, and ending up with the girl. But as I've illustrated, violence is not just the requisite talent of a young, athletic Los Angeles police officer, nor a random criminal event that appears spontaneously, nor a quantifiable experience that needs no interpretation. It is nothing less than the foundation of our concept of masculinity.

CHAPTER 3

Female Murderers

America's Recurring Nightmare

According to Lacan, we know that an event is traumatic, not because we uncover a direct experience of the trauma, but rather through the ways that we react to the trauma. We recognize hysterical symptoms, for instance, and these point us in the direction of the traumatic event. Only through this kind of indirect route can we encounter a repressed trauma. The repressed makes itself heard, in the case of hysteria, through signifying on the body itself (in the form of the symptom), through the return of the repressed. Because this return of the repressed provides our only access to the repressed trauma itself, Lacan claims that "repression and the return of the repressed are the same thing."[1] Hence, in order to examine the status of female violence—in order to determine if it is traumatic for the social order or not—we must look not only at the way acts of female violence are represented but the public reactions to such acts. In these symptomatic reactions, we can discover the path that leads us toward understanding the relationship between narratives about female violence and the social order.

In contrast to male violence and masculinity, female violence doesn't fit conveniently into our ideas of the feminine, and, because of this, it has a disruptive and traumatic impact, as reactions to actual violent women in American history bear out. The overwhelming reaction to these violent women—hysterical questioning and then fantasizing—reveals the real threat that female violence poses to American society. Female murderers occupy an ambiguous place in society; we never know quite how to define them.[2] I will look at three of the more famous cases involving female murderers that reveal a range of public reactions. First, I will discuss two women from the past—Lizzie Borden (1892) and Ruth Snyder (1927)—and then move to a contemporary female murderer—Susan Smith (1990). My investigation of these public reactions will necessarily be an investigation of the media response to these female murderers because I am concerned with how these women and the public reaction to them are represented. Moreover, their representation in the media will provide an important context for understanding the way the media responded to *Thelma and Louise*—the first violent woman film to occasion a huge public debate about the place of the violent woman in society. Since the media response to *Thelma and Louise* so closely resembles the response to actual female murderers, it also has the status of a symptom. In this way, the real-ness of these women is only significant in terms of the narratives that are formed in reaction to them, in the effort to represent them.

The public discussion surrounding so many cases of violent women, both past and present, seems to be less about justice or the act in question than about what it is to be a woman—motherly, feminine, wifely, ladylike, and so forth. Nothing can bring up the discussion of proper womanly traits like a violent woman. The character of the media response to the violent woman is, in almost every case, hysterical. Hysteria is a neurotic reaction in which the subject constantly questions the desire and position of the Other, especially as the Other relates to the subject. In her essay, "Hysteria and Obsession," Collette Soler explains, "An hysteric is a subject who wonders what the Other desires or if the Other desires, a subject who questions the Other's desire."[3] For example, when confronted with a woman's violent act, we immediately begin to question her desire, to wonder why she acted violently. In the manner of the hysteric, the media asks again and again what the violent woman wants, while it also speculates endlessly about the definition of femininity. Obviously, the endless speculation about femininity is not only an attempt to define women, but also to define the relationship between masculinity and femininity.

This hysterical question regarding the violent woman is of course a derivative of Freud's famous question about female sexuality—"what does woman want?" The women that he originally based his question on were all hysterics; that is to say, they were constantly asking, "What does society want of me?" and "Why am I what society says I am?" But what is revealing for the cases that I am examining is that Freud's response to these questions was itself a hysterical question. In studying women's psychic place in society and studying particular women who constantly questioned this place, Freud himself was led to his own hysterical question, "what do these women want?" Like a good hysteric, Freud never finds a satisfactory answer to this question—and yet he continues its line of inquiry. Obviously, when the woman does not accept her traditional role—and instead questions it—the man's role is thrown into question as well. The most important aspect of Freud's approach to this question—and subsequently that of all of psychoanalysis—is that he attempted to struggle with it whereas normally when faced with such questions most respond with some sort of ideological fantasy.

The case of anti-Semitism provides us with a useful example. When confronted with the figure of the Jew and the ambiguity of this figure's desire in the mind of the anti-Semite, the anti-Semite has an hysterical moment. Face-to-face with this uncertainty, he or she quickly responds with an ideological—that is, anti-Semitic—fantasy that solves the enigma of this desire. In *The Sublime Object of Ideology*, Slavoj Žižek explains:

> In the case of anti-Semitism, the answer to "What does the Jew want?" is a fantasy of "Jewish conspiracy": a mysterious power of Jews to manipulate events, to pull the strings behind the scenes. The crucial point that must be made here on a theoretical level is that fantasy functions as a construction, as an imaginary scenario filling out the void, the opening of the *desire of the other*: by giving us a definite answer to the question "What does the Other want?", it enables us to evade the unbearable deadlock in which the Other wants something from us, but we are at the same time incapable of translating this desire of the other into a positive interpellation, into a mandate with which to identify.[4]

In other words, to clarify the position of the Jew in the symbolic world of the anti-Semite, the anti-Semite relies on an ideological fantasy (for example, using the terms "dirty," "lazy," "money hoarding," "stupid," etc.). This ideological fantasy answers the hysterical question by symbolizing the desire of the Other. That is, the anti-Semite fantasizes that the Jew desires to get ahead unfairly, undermine the social structure, and so on. This in turn allows the anti-Semite to construct a symbolic structure without gaps and allows him/her to hate and commit violence with impunity. Both the hysterical question and the excessive production of ideological fantasies in response to this question indicate an encounter with trauma. In the case of the anti-Semite, the trauma involves encountering the antagonism of his or her own social structure projected onto the figure of the Jew. Thus, it is important to analyze the excessive production of the ideological fantasy as well as the hysterical question. Both are certainly present in the case of the public's reaction to the female murderer.[5]

We deem violence so antithetical to femininity that when a woman murders someone it doesn't make sense within our symbolic system. Our reaction to the female murderer is hysterical because instead of trying to analyze her case or action, our encounter triggers the hysterical question, "What does this woman want?" This leads to an attempt, through ideological fantasy, to mold her back into what a woman should be. As happened in the Susan Smith case—in which Smith murdered her two children—the media headlines scream (whether explicitly or implicitly), "how could a WOMAN do this?" What the Smith case reveals is that the cases in which mothers murder their children seem the most traumatic because they so strongly go against our "idea" of the mother. When a mother murders her children, most people even find it difficult to describe her or how they feel about her. Instead, they continually ask, "What does this woman want? Why is she the way she is?" Of course, there is never any good answer, because the violent act itself continues to be traumatic and provoke the hysterical question, regardless of what particular answer the woman gives. For example, even after learning about Susan Smith's depression and the lack she felt in her life, we remain dissatisfied. This sense of dissatisfaction demands a fantasy construction in order to ameliorate it. In response to the trauma of female murderers, an ideological fantasy arises that works to cover over the trauma. Whereas hysteria allows the trauma to exist, fantasy smothers it. This fantasy gives the violent woman meaning and allows for her to have a "place" in the social order again. In the wake of a woman's violent act, a frenzy of symbolization occurs in an effort to lessen the act's trauma. This frenzy of symbolization works desperately to make her understandable, and after this reintegration, a more logical course of action can take place. For example, if we erect the fantasy of the "lady" in the place of the violent woman, we recognize that she is too dainty to commit an act of violence, and we acquit her. Conversely, if we fantasize that the violent woman is a "whore," we know she has no remorse or feelings, and we convict her.

Lizzie Borden's trial in 1893 is one instance of just such a frenzy of symbolization in reaction to a female murderer's violence. It not only gripped the public imagination at the time—throngs of people attended the trial each day and newspapers made huge profits reporting the case—but it also has fascinated people up to the present. Plays, films, songs, sayings, and dances have been inspired by Lizzie's story.[6] The simple facts of the case were that Lizzie's parents were found murdered in their home in Fall River, Massachusetts, on Friday, August 5, 1892. The assailant killed her father, Andrew Jackson Borden, with ten blows from a sharp instrument (most of them landing on his face) and killed her stepmother with twenty blows from the same sharp instrument. Investigators believed the instrument to be a hatchet. Lizzie Borden was at home at the time of the murders, but she claimed to be in the barn and unaware of what was happening. Despite this "alibi," the Fall River police did not believe her and charged her with the murder. The trial ended, however, on June 21, 1893, with Lizzie Borden's acquittal. During the trial, the whole nation seemed to rally behind Lizzie: nearly everyone believed her to be innocent. But after the trial ended, the townspeople—and eventually the nation as a whole—began to believe that Lizzie had murdered her parents, and today this belief has reached the status of an accepted fact.

Lizzie Borden was a spinster at the age of thirty-two and led a very respectable—albeit quiet—life. She was related to the most powerful family in Fall River (a small industrial city in New England). Her father was quite wealthy and felt that the Christian way was not to spend such wealth but to live frugally and save. Lizzie, however, disagreed with her father. She longed to be a part of the wealthy society life in which her relatives existed. Experts consider this Lizzie's ultimate reason for killing her father, and yet it was the one motive that people in the 1890s could not believe.

The reaction to Lizzie once she was arrested and put on trial was always one of respect: even if people thought her guilty, the newspapers represented her in ladylike terms. The press praised her "reserved demeanor" and her fainting spells, both of which were considered feminine traits. Besides the reporter commentary, the newspapers printed long and detailed descriptions of the trial. Both the prosecution team (led by Alfred Knowlton) and the defense team (led by former Governor Robinson) seemed to have worked to define Borden's actions within the construct of femininity. The papers reported that Knowlton concluded that a woman had to be the culprit because, "A man would have struck once or twice, perhaps three times, and have been contented with his work. Only a woman would make mincemeat of the head of Mrs. Borden and the face of Mr. Borden."[7] In this statement, the prosecutor suggests that a man who commits violence—and even murder—always acts within a certain masculine *ethos*, an *ethos* which has limits. But women, according to this logic, do not know what to do in violent situations because violence lies beyond their ken. And thus their violence is a priori excessive. With this comment, then, the prosecutor attempted to define how femininity and violence interact in order to sway the court. The defense also invoked femininity, albeit for an opposite end. Governor Robinson closed his arguments by saying: "We must conclude at the outset that such acts as these are morally and physically impossible for this young woman defendant [. . . it is] a contradiction of her physical capacity."[8] Appealing to popular conceptions of femininity, Governor Robinson defined females as generally incapable of violence as he talked specifically of Lizzie Borden. In other words, he invoked the universal feminine to aid Lizzie's particular case. The verdict bore out the wisdom of this defense, as the court ultimately acquitted Lizzie because obviously the jury could not imagine this "lady" wielding an axe over her head and having the strength to kill two people. That is to say, Governor Robinson, and the newspapers that agreed with and highlighted his representation, helped produce the ideological fantasy—the impossibility of a well-bred lady murdering anyone—in order to steer clear of the trauma of the murders.

Behind the propping up of the ideological fantasy lies the specter of the hysterical question. This image of Lizzie as a well-bred lady was constantly reinforced in the media as reporters described Lizzie being grandly escorted to and from the courtroom each day leaning on the arm of the City Missionary, Reverend Buck. She was also often described as carrying a bouquet of flowers in her hands and as gently dabbing tears away as she was fanning herself—with a lace fan that matched her outfit. On June 15, 1893, when the prosecution brought out the skulls of her father and stepmother, the media made careful note of the fact that the court excused Lizzie to another room because she had fainted the previous day at just a description of these very skulls. Certainly a lady who faints at just the mention of such violence could never commit it herself. As one well-known female novelist of that time, Anna Katherine Greene, wrote, after attending the trial for a few days:

> But for a girl of any education or training to bring down an axe again and again upon the unresisting form of a father, who, whatever his severity had been towards her, could have aroused in her no fury of antagonism which would not have been satisfied by his mere death, *is not consistent with what we know of female nature* [. . .] Cruelty and the shedding for blood's sake are a man's prerogative, or if they are ever found developed in a woman the cases are so rare that we may well afford to give Lizzie Borden the benefit of the doubt.[9]

Ironically, women filled the majority of the courtroom seats everyday at the trial, and the press often noted this in their description of the day's events. Clearly, this was an important case for women (and men) because it solidified the definition of femininity and reassured the public that things would not change. For if the public even entertained the idea that a woman could wield an axe and commit such a horrible crime just because she was unhappy, certainly the very structure of society was in danger.

During the 1800s, society could accept—and severely punish—one particular type of female murder: poisoning. Poisoning was acceptable because it was ladylike; it was (theoretically) nonviolent. The newspapers often wrote about a woman stirring poison into her victim's tea. This was something that the public could comprehend, and thus it was easy to charge and punish the women who were caught. These were feminine women gone awry, but their actions always stayed within the realm of the properly feminine. Of course, society can't have women killing their families even in the most feminine of ways. For this reason, newspapers often commented that these women needed to be made an example out of to deter other women from doing the same. The woman who poisons, however, is not traumatic to the social body in the way that the violent murderer is traumatic. In contrast, the violence of the Borden murder went entirely against everything that society expected of women; the very idea of a woman committing violence on this scale traumatized the society as a whole. Out of this trauma, therefore, arose the ideological fantasy that Borden was so dainty and feminine that she just couldn't have committed the murders. To do anything else—to accept that she might have committed the murders because of an underlying dissatisfaction—would mean opening up the traumatic questions: what does this woman want? how does her dissatisfaction reveal underlying social antagonisms? and, possibly most unsettling, how does what this woman wants reflect in some way what every woman might want? In the case of Borden, the courts and the papers immediately labeled her as the ultimate in proper femininity, which was all the alibi she needed. The local papers even reported this reaction from the bigger cities nearby: "A great deal has been said in out-of-town papers about the cruelty of detaining a finely bred and sensitive woman as Miss Borden is."[10] During the trial, the town rallied around Lizzie and supported her as the lady that the press presented her to be, but after the trial they punished her for what most suspected was getting away with murder: the town ostracized her completely, banning her from the upper-class society she so desperately wanted to be a part of. During the trial, however, the media suggested repeatedly that a lady could never commit these crimes and the courts obliged by acquitting her. But after this became official, popular myth and opinion held a different kind of court and punished Lizzie all the same for the violence they knew deep down she could—or any woman could—commit.

Just as Lizzie Borden had to live to quell the public trauma brought on by the idea of her violence, Ruth Snyder had to die.[11] The Snyder murder trial in 1927 was also one of those cases that captured the public's attention. On March 20, 1927, the murderer knocked Albert Snyder unconscious with a sash weight, smothered him with chloroform, and strangled him with picture wire in his own bed. The Snyder case has been dubbed the most important trial of that decade, and it provoked a hysterical frenzy of questioning and discussion about femininity. (In fact, a record number of newspapers with coverage of the trial were sold.) *The New York Times* considered the case so important that it published most of the court testimony alongside the paper's commentary on the day's proceedings. In this way, Snyder's act was publicly interpreted by the court's transcripts and the newspaper's commentary that ran alongside. This double inscription of ideology indicates how hard the media worked to explain Ruth Snyder's violence. As with the Borden case, the Snyder trial and the coverage of the trial attempted to repeatedly answer the questions: "What does Ruth Snyder want?" and "Why did she do what she did?" The ideological fantasy that emerged this time was not—as with Lizzie Borden—that Ruth Snyder was an innocent, ladylike angel who couldn't have committed murder; instead, it was that Snyder *did* commit the murder because she was a whore.[12] The story of Ruth Snyder and her lover, Henry Judd Gray, killing Ruth's husband, Albert Snyder, was turned into a fantastic, sordid sex scandal. The murder itself was brutal. It seemed that from the moment the detectives reached the Snyder home, to the trial, to the jurors' decision, to the story that lives on in most history books today, there was the general belief that Ruth had committed or had been the motivating force behind this brutal crime. The idea of a woman planning and committing such brutal and violent acts was only possible after the detectives, press, lawyers, and the media quickly turned her into a promiscuous, coldhearted, non-female monster. She was a devouring "serpent"—as Gray's lawyer was reported as calling her. No one could satiate her appetite for sex, drinking, smoking, and dancing. The judgment lingering behind these accusations was that this behavior could only end up ruining a good husband and family in a murderous rampage. Thus, the murder case enabled the media to paint the perfect picture of a woman: everything that Ruth Snyder was not. In other words, the ideological fantasy that covered the trauma of Snyder's violence involved her being a heartless whore, but this, ironically, also reinforced what a civilized woman really should be. As Ann Jones makes clear: "Before it was all over, avid readers knew that respectable women did not smoke, drink, dye their hair, cross their legs, lunch out with strange men, or feel ingratitude toward their husbands."[13] Of course, what was far more frightening to society—what produced the hysterical reaction in the first place—was that in reality Ruth Snyder was incredibly "average" by mainstream American standards in the 1920s.

Ruth Snyder was a white, middle-class woman who lived in suburbia—Queens Village, Long Island—with her husband, nine-year-old daughter (Lorraine), and her mother (Mrs. Josephine Brown). In many ways, her story was quintessentially American. Her parents were immigrants: her father (Harry Brown) was born in Norway and her mother in Sweden. Ruth's parents brought her up to be entirely American.[14] She worked for the telephone company and then as a secretary before she was married. When Ruth married Albert Snyder on July 24, 1915, she was only nineteen while he was thirty-two. Albert was striving to be more American and had his last name—originally Schneider—changed to Snyder. They lived in the city until Lorraine was five, and they had saved enough money to move to the suburbs where they bought a house. Albert was by no means well off; he only made $115 a week, just enough to create the atmosphere of prosperity. This narrative of immigrant to middle-class American family was common, which is one of the horrors of Ruth's story: it seemed as if it could have happened in any home in America. Part of the fantasy that arose from the media and the prosecutor, therefore, was that Ruth and her family were completely abnormal and that Ruth led a scandalous and dangerous life. In an attempt to counterbalance what was quickly becoming "fact" regarding Ruth's family life, her lawyer, Edgar F. Hazelton, made a point of asking Ruth a barrage of questions about her "wifely" duties. He had her explain that she always did all the housework, made all the curtains, made preserves, and did her own cooking. He also revealed that Ruth brought her daughter to Sunday school every Sunday, taught her hymns, and prayers.[15] Her lawyer tried to reverse the fantasy, which was quickly taking hold, by employing the more traditional image of femininity (the very image that got Lizzie Borden acquitted). Ruth had one problem, which she spoke about openly: her unhappiness and dissatisfaction with her life.[16] This fact, however, did not set her apart from the average American man or woman. Neither did her two-year affair with H. Judd Gray, a traveling corset salesman who was also married.[17] Indeed, this only made her more dangerously similar to the public that was so closely following the case.

Some of the stories told about Ruth in order to distance her from the average woman were extraordinary, and it is hard to believe that anyone would have accepted them. One of the first things reported about Ruth was that "Gray in his confession had said that Mrs. Snyder rubbed her hands on his cheeks and looked at him in a way which robbed him of his personal initiative, and that he was in this condition when he committed the murder."[18] The media presented this story as believable and they continually represented Judd Gray as an amiable, yet weak fellow.[19] It still seems hard to understand how the media could advance this initial description of Ruth's "power" over Gray (though this same "fact" was also used in court and seemed to have a powerful effect on the jury). On the other hand, the media was clearly drawn to anything that added to the ideological fantasy and relieved the trauma of Ruth's violence. The newspapers constantly reported that Gray got along very well with the detectives but that from the beginning Ruth had a difficult time with them. The newspapers also reported that the prosecutor, Richard E. Newcombe, was heard saying that he thought Lorraine (Ruth's daughter) to be a beautiful young lady and that he didn't understand how Ruth raised her. Insulting Ruth's mothering skills was an easy way to contribute to the idea of Ruth as a cold-blooded killer—because a "real" mother never could have committed murder. The insults and jibes at Ruth's motherhood were never ending. The lawyers and the papers constantly commented on the fact that she brought Lorraine with her on several occasions when she met Gray for lunch or dinner.[20]

The media response to Ruth is well-represented by playwright Willard Mack who wrote: "If Ruth Snyder is a woman, then, by God! You must find some other name for my mother, wife, or sister . . ."[21] With this comment, Mack is almost spelling out the problem of symbolization that the violent female presents. Once a woman commits such a murder—a woman who before the murder inhabited symbolic roles such as mother, wife, or sister—she throws into question all other women who come under that title. Thus, she must be distanced from these symbolic places as quickly as possible. Obviously, the ideological fantasy of her as a coldhearted whore symbolizes what she is safely distanced from the definition of a "good" woman. With all this against her, Ruth did not have much of a chance to defend herself during the trial or in the public realm. Even those facts which might have swayed the audience in the courtroom, such as her good mothering and well-performed wifely duties, only brought laughing and joking from the audience. The press noted that during Ruth's testimony the jury paid attention to this laughter. And by the end of the trial, the nation firmly decided that Ruth was the monster they believed her to be, and they cheered as Ruth Snyder and H. Judd Gray were found guilty and sentenced to death (and this death sentence was carried out on January 12, 1928). The jury not only found them guilty but also delivered verdicts on their different stories. As the *New York Times* reported: "The jurors were unanimous in disbelieving the story that Mrs. Snyder told."[22] They were also unanimous in believing that Gray "told the truth," but they felt that this still did not excuse him from the murder.

After one thoroughly examines all the transcripts and official documents, the Snyder trial still seems like an unsolved mystery. At the end of the trial, *The New York Times* summarized the difference between Ruth and Gray's stories:

> Mrs. Snyder's story is that she was dragged in afterward, partly under threats of death and partly because Gray convinced her that circumstances were so much against her that she would have to join him in trying to deceive the police. Gray's defense is that he was an automaton, that Mrs. Snyder's "magnetism" had benumbed his mind; that he was no guiltier than a hypnotic subject would be under the direction of a murderous Svengall.[23]

And although the state killed Judd Gray along with Ruth, the media emphatically represented Ruth as the one the public should fear, disparage, and condemn. Ultimately, Gray did not traumatize America, because no one was surprised that a man would commit violence. It was easy to consider him a criminal and be done with him. Ruth, however, was incomprehensible, and more often than not, Gray was used to oppose and contradict Ruth. At the beginning of the trial, when Gray's lawyer gave his opening statement, he commented that Ruth had had several affairs.[24] Hazelton immediately objected saying: "The defendant Snyder is not on trial for adultery."[25] But this initial small objection could not counteract the general feeling that Ruth *was* on trial for adultery, for promiscuity, for not being feminine enough, for wanting more than her "average" life provided, and for acting upon her desires—but most of all for traumatizing America with her violence.

The trial also made clear that even if she did not commit the crime—and her story was true—she still was guilty. Indeed, her behavior throughout the trial seemed to indict her more than anything else did. While Lizzie Borden had the cleverness to rely on the accoutrements of femininity, Ruth Snyder angrily and aggressively argued her point and attempted to present her side of the story and save her life.[26] When Gray said something untrue, and when his confession was read, she glared angrily at him. The newspapers reported: "Then with her eyes narrowed to slits and other features collaborating, she fixed her expression again on the back of Gray's narrow head with its neatly trimmed curly hair. No tears or outcries accompanied her passionate registrations."[27] Even when she did cry, the media suggested that she didn't cry correctly or at the right times. She only wept three times on the stand and two of them were not even related to the actual murder; instead, they were about her daughter and then about her husband's rejection of her daughter when she was first born. Her third short set of tears was related to coming into the bedroom during the murder and finding Gray on top of her husband bashing his head in. Yet one reporter even used this against her, as he reported that she cried at exactly the same point during the cross-examination, which to him indicated that Ruth contrived and planned her crying.[28]

Ruth was constantly being described as a "cold woman." According to one reporter: "Instead of growing agitated as she approached the details of the murder, Mrs. Snyder seemed to grow cooler than ever. [....] She held her composure for more than an hour, as she dealt with the ghastliest circumstances of the murder."[29] Clearly, the public and the press were aghast at the fact that Ruth was not a melodramatic female who might cry and fret over any mention of violence or unpleasantness. Ruth was not trying to make everyone like her; she was just trying to prove her story. And this is precisely what the media held against her. What also seemed to underlie many of the jibes at Ruth was that—even if she didn't commit the murder—she didn't seem all that sad that her husband was dead. When asked whether Gray terrified her after her husband was killed, she only said, "I was partly afraid. I saw what a terrible mess he had made of things, and I couldn't see any way out of anything other than to do as he asked me to do."[30] Had Ruth cried, fainted, dressed more plainly, presented herself as entirely distraught that her husband was dead, and so forth, the outcome of her trial might have been entirely different. The newspapers, however, only remembered this average housewife from Long Island as the "serpent woman" who used her powers to control men, as Gray's lawyer was often reported as saying: "[Gray] was in a web, he was hemmed in the abyss, he was dominated, he was commanded, he was driven by this malicious character. He became inveigled and was drawn into this hopeless chasm, when reason was gone, when mind was gone, and when his mind was absolutely weakened."[31] Using such words as "abyss" and "chasm" as dangers that exist in the terrain of femaleness capitalized on old but powerful fears of the ability women have to put men—such as poor Gray—into a complete stupor. Then, the damage they might do seems limitless. Clearly, the press had to depict Ruth Snyder as far from the average housewife in America as possible, yet the reason the press reacted this way was precisely because of her averageness.

Similarly, the media worked itself into a frenzy over—and represented the rather average Susan Smith as someone very out of the ordinary in—the 1994 *South Carolina v. Susan Smith* case. Susan Smith allowed her Mazda Protégé to roll into the John D. Long Lake in Union, South Carolina, on October 25, 1994, with her two children strapped inside. When she reported her children missing, she claimed a black man had carjacked her and kidnapped her kids in the process. Not surprisingly, the media was all too willing to believe this original story as it fed directly into racist stereotypes so often propagated by the media. But on November 3, Susan confessed that she had committed the murder, and from that moment on, the trial gripped the American public. The newspapers and magazines went over and over what it was to be a good mother, the proper way one acted as a single parent, what it was to be a good girl, and all the ways in which Susan Smith fell short of all these definitions. The moral of the story seemed to be that she should have sufficiently repressed any desire that might have gotten in the way of her motherly duties.

The murder that Smith committed is one that society fears the most: a mother killing her children. Smith's violent act became the nexus for a hysterical and constant discussion of motherhood and femininity. The nation's first reaction seemed to be one of shock. As one Union neighbor was quoted: "Being a mother myself, I couldn't have imagined anyone doing anything to their children."[32] And at the end of the case, *People* magazine presented its version of the public sentiment by asking the ultimate hysterical question: "How could any mother have committed such a terrible crime?"[33] One can clearly deduce, from these reactions, that part of the definition of motherhood is that a mother can do no harm to her children. By extension this means that a mother's gentle nature is a permanent part of her personality and should extend to not doing harm to anyone. Moreover, mothers are often praised if they do harm in order to protect their children, but even this can cross the line (as the many women in prison for protecting their children and themselves against their abusive husbands or boyfriends can testify). Within our very limited definition of motherhood, we need to believe that even if the mother may not be totally content, she is certainly happy and proud in raising her kids and providing a happy, loving, and safe home in which they can grow.[34]

Another move by the press, as with the Ruth Snyder case, was to portray Susan Smith as the antithesis of a "mother" and as far from average as possible. Susan had been voted the "friendliest girl" in high school; she worked at places like the Winn-Dixie supermarket; and she was devout in her commitment to religion. Clearly, these all are attributes that would usually categorize Smith as a good girl. At the time of the murder, she was working at a local textile plant, Conso, as a secretary and she was making $1,100, plus $115 in child support, a month. Even the owner at the local hamburger joint where she often ate commented: "She was clean [. . .] Almost everyone's got a little dirt on them, but she was clean."[35] But after the murder in her hometown of Union, the press depicted Susan Smith as somewhat schizophrenic: "Everyone talks about [Susan's constant] smile—it is as if there are two Susans. They talk over and over about what caused her to kill her own children, but nothing, for many people, will ever explain how this woman, who seemed to be a perfect mother and so hardworking and devout, could do such a thing."[36] The media developed a more traditional ideological fantasy: Smith was too promiscuous. *People*'s cover story on Susan Smith, "Does She Deserve To Die?", noted that although her family portrayed her as a normal young woman who suddenly snapped, "the reality is a good deal darker . . ."[37] And in another cover story, "David Smith: His Own Story," *People* wrote: "In the weeks, before she killed her sons, she frolicked nude in a hot tub with another man at the Findlay mansion. During the trial, Susan's psychiatrist said she also told him that around the same time she had even performed oral sex on her stepfather Bev."[38] One of the keys to the defense's case was the fact that Susan's stepfather, Bev Russell, had sexually abused her during her teen years on into her adult life— and this made her depressed and emotionally erratic. But most of the newspapers quickly secured statements that the sex Susan had with Bev was consensual and thus made even the sexual abuse she endured her own fault. *Time*, quoting a psychiatrist, explained that her "affair" with her stepfather, "had been going on since she was 15—one that she was happy about because she was jealous that her mother was getting all Russell's attention."[39] This statement indicates not only that Susan Smith was a terrible mother, but that she was also a terrible daughter. It seems Susan could not get any of the female roles right in the mind of the public.

Unless involved in a sex crime, a male criminal's sexuality rarely comes up, but the media almost always suggests that an admitted female criminal is also promiscuous.[40] It would be far more difficult to contain the threat of female violence if the woman involved fit into the proper definition of a "good" woman. It is understandable, then, that the press presented Smith as a sexually insatiable woman obsessed with sleeping with many different men. The newspapers reported that she cheated on her husband David before he cheated on her and that she slept with Tom Findlay (a young man from a prosperous family in town) and his father. Of course, no one paid much attention to the fact that many of these statements were just rumors or lies that Susan said she made up to anger people or make them jealous. Most importantly, however, no one thought to question why the media linked whom Susan slept with to her act of murder. The implication of this was the old admonishment: "You see what happens when you sleep with too many men." And the moral of the tale is that a woman should desire one man—preferably her spouse—or none at all. Even Tom Findlay told Susan that she was not a good girl in a letter he wrote her. In the letter, Tom says he's proud of her for going to night school and taking steps to "improve her life" but is upset about her "boy crazy" tendencies. He explains: "To be a nice girl, you must act like a nice girl, and that doesn't include sleeping with married men."[41] Instead of being perceived as jealous, misguided, and misogynist, or a typical product of the small upper class in Union,[42] the press perceived Tom Findlay as correct in his assumptions about proper female behavior.[43]

The prosecution, led by Sixteenth Circuit Court solicitor Thomas Pope, "painted Smith as a calculating, coldhearted woman who drowned her children to win the affections of Tom Findlay,"[44] and the press vilified her as a promiscuous and manipulative woman. Public sentiment was entirely against her: *The New York Times* reported that even grandmothers were demanding that the state execute Susan Smith. Further, just in case this wasn't enough condemnation, *People* conducted a poll, which indicated that 50 percent of adults believed that Smith should be executed.[45] So why wasn't Susan Smith given the death sentence? It had less to do with the fact that a woman hadn't been executed in South Carolina since 1947 and more to do with Susan's performance of femininity.[46] My interpretation of this cultural moment is that Susan was only given life in prison because she was too feminine to kill. Ruth Snyder calmly, and sometimes aggressively, tried to prove her innocence, but Susan did not make this mistake. Susan was excessively feminine at every moment of the trial. She cried at every mention of her children or the pain that her friends and relatives were going through. There were constant reports of suicide watches going on in her cell. Susan was a complete mess. It was even reported that she talked to the pictures that she had of her children. Ultimately, Susan Smith's courtroom hysteria convinced the jury that she was more female than her act of murder had indicated, and although the media would still vilify her and the jury would sentence her to life in prison, they also rewarded her femininity by not sentencing her to death. Smith claimed she did not know why she committed the murder: "'She cries out to me, 'Why?' says her brother Scotty Vaughn, 32. 'At times I get angry at her, but then I know that something went wrong and that the Susan I know is not to blame.'"[47]

Susan took on the role of the woman in need of help and protection. Had she seemed clearheaded, or calm, or not so sad, or less distraught, the jury would most likely have sentenced her to death.

Each of these cases captured the public imagination, and it is important to remember that the press coverage—especially the discussions of femininity—of these particular cases only mimics much of the rhetoric that occurs in every court case of a violent woman. The three cases I've discussed deal with the image of the female murderer that was created by the media—and what this revealed about femininity and society at the time. These real women killers are especially disturbing to society, because they suggest that other real women are capable of these acts. Filmic violent women create similar disturbances because their images are produced by cultural narratives that are struggling to make sense of an ideological failure that the violent woman represents (in other words, the failure of traditional femininity). The trauma caused by the filmic violent woman usually creates a reaction within the film itself through her representation and her role in the narrative. Rarely does American society react publicly to filmic violent women—except in one particular case: *Thelma and Louise*.[48]

The release of *Thelma and Louise* provoked media coverage that was amazingly similar to the coverage of the three real murder cases I've just discussed. The example of the media's reaction to *Thelma and Louise* warrants a comparison with the media's reaction to real female murderers because the comparison underscores the consistent cultural fantasies that are at play regarding violence and women. Such a comparison subsequently allows us to pursue the ideological purpose of these fantasies in relation to the violent woman in film. The similarity of the media's reactions suggests that the spectacle of female violence operates as a marker of ideological vulnerability. In other words, in the realm of ideological representation in the media, the representation of the violent woman confounds ideological norms regarding gender and violence.

Released in 1991, *Thelma and Louise* was the sleeper hit of the summer. The film is not about the conviction and trial of a female murderer (as might be assumed by its inclusion in this chapter); instead it is about what might have happened *before* the court case: the actual murder and the way this violence affected the women themselves. The film depicts two friends who head out for a weekend vacation but spend the majority of the film running from the law after Louise (Susan Sarandon) kills a man who has tried to rape Thelma (Geena Davis). The film became a cultural phenomenon, as it provoked huge debates and loud reactions from all parts of society about feminism and how a woman should act. While in the earlier cases discussed in this chapter real women were on trial in the media (and the courtroom), in the case of *Thelma and Louise* the representation of the violent woman was on trial. In this case, however, no official verdict was handed down. Instead several opposing views were consistently debated. Not surprisingly, each of the views mimics in various degrees the different media reactions to Lizzie Borden, Ruth Snyder, and Susan Smith. In some ways, then, these responses to *Thelma and Louise* could be seen as a meta-response in which the media reacted to its own contradictory depictions of the violent woman over the years.

The controversy of the violence in *Thelma and Louise* derives largely from the fact that Louise saved Thelma from rape by threatening the rapist with the gun but did not need to shoot him. No one would blame Louise for pulling her gun on Harlan as he was beginning to rape Thelma because she was protecting Thelma. But the meaning of the violence drastically changes into something completely unacceptable after they are safe and Louise pulls the trigger anyway, killing Harlan purely out of rage and anger. Such revenge killing gets little notice when committed by a male character, but when Louise pulled the trigger, it incited article titles such as *Newsweek*'s "Women Who Kill Too Much: Is *Thelma and Louise* feminism, or fascism?," *Time*'s "Gender Bender: A white-hot debate rages over whether *Thelma and Louise* celebrates liberated females, male bashers—or outlaws," and *Playboy*'s "Guerrilla Feminism." These reactions represent an hysterical questioning and redefining of what it is to be a woman that is characteristic of previous media representations of real violent women. And these varied reactions to *Thelma and Louise* are another example of society's need to create a sense of security when female violence erupts in order to stave off the ideological failure the violent woman reveals is possible.

A certain portion of the media's approach to *Thelma and Louise* was similar to the media's attempt to overly feminize Lizzie Borden, in order to make her violence impossible (and thus to make violent women an impossible idea). In reaction to *Thelma and Louise*, the news media presented the actresses themselves as completely feminine, nonviolent, and even nonfeminist in order to make their characters truly unreal—just as the media presented Borden as so feminine that it wished away the possibility of her violence. For example, newspaper and magazine articles often highlighted how sexy Susan Sarandon and Geena Davis were in this film. In *Los Angeles Magazine*'s cover story on Susan Sarandon, Rod Lurie writes: "Susan Sarandon definitely has a problem: She's too sexy for her own good."[49] It's her "va-va-va-voom" personality, Lurie explains, that makes people forget her "solid" performances and her political and social activism. Lurie's treatment of Sarandon elides her characters violent tendencies in favor of a sexy yet unthreatening figure. If a woman is seen as overly sexy, so sexy that it is a "problem," then her violence can be seen as part of this excess. Her violence is then contained and is far less threatening because its ultimate purpose is for the pleasure of the viewer.[50] *People*'s cover story on Geena Davis also uses such phrases as "a graceful former fashion model with glamorously chiseled features" to describe Davis as she appeared in the film.[51] Furthermore, this article's title, "Riding Shotgun: In the Battle of the Sexes, *Thelma and Louise*'s Geena Davis is Armed and Dangerous," might suggest a discussion of her violence but instead it centers—as does the portrait of Sarandon in the *Los Angeles Magazine*—on Davis's love life. Other articles also make it a point to discuss Davis and Sarandon's heterosexuality and the men in their lives. In a *New York Times* interview, Callie Khouri (the screen writer of *Thelma and Louise*) says that she does not hate men and that in fact she is married to a man whom she loves very much and who supported her on this project.[52] The fact that the press asked and published these types of questions and answers indicates that there was much concern about securing the fact that these three women were no threat to men.[53] Clearly, this way of representing these actors firmly positions them in the role of proper women and thus limits the threat the characters they played could have. But some writers went one step further and took away Thelma and Louise's agency in their violent acts all together. For example, in an article for *Maclean*'s, Fred Bruning said: "But what really can't be ignored is that Thelma and Louise are not strong or invincible, after all, but foolish and vulnerable."[54] All of these reactions fit into the ideological fantasy that was certainly clear in the case of Lizzie Borden: that these women are too ladylike, too feminine, to be the perpetuators of the violent acts carried out by their characters in the film.

But the opposite reaction (more akin to the media's attempt to paint Ruth Snyder as "not a woman"), that the violent woman is not a real woman and thus can't be threatening to society, can also be found in the media's reaction to *Thelma and Louise*. For example, according to Margaret Carlson: "The characters don't confide in each other as real-life women would."[55] Carlson then makes an observation that was also rampant among others responding to the film: "They are also free to behave like—well, men."[56] What this reaction suggests is that "real-life women" follow certain codes of behavior, codes that are implicated in Carlson's assessment of the actions of *Thelma and Louise*. Enabling people to distinguish between real women (who are nonviolent) and non-women (who are violent), Carlson lessens the threat of the violent woman and reinscribes the traditional definition of femininity. Commenting on these types of reactions to *Thelma and Louise*, Lynda Hart says: "The point here was to restore cultural confidence in *real* women's passivity."[57] Another way the press restored this "cultural confidence" was to critique *Thelma and Louise* for being antifeminist. Male and female journalists alike said, in the words of *Los Angeles Times* film critic Sheila Benson: "*Thelma and Louise* is a betrayal of feminism."[58] And, to the other extreme, several articles went on long diatribes on how this is "toxic feminism," and compared this "kind of feminism" with fascism and McCarthyism.[59] This debate about how the violence in *Thelma and Louise* might bear on feminism is a new addition to the previous media discussions of female violence. Certainly, even the contemporary example of the media representation of Susan Smith did not consider Smith's case to have any bearing on feminist issues. Instead, the media concentrated on how a "good mother" or a "good wife" should behave. As a fictional depiction of female violence, however, *Thelma and Louise* provides a narrative which depicts Thelma and Louise as liberated from their domestic and feminine restrictions (for example, Thelma is liberated from living her life according to her husband's desire, and both women are liberated from their jewelry, feminine clothing, and even their sexual submissiveness) because of this outlaw status. This narrative itself inflects the violent act which begins the film with these added layers of meaning to which the media then reacted to. Here, the media contradicts itself when reacting to the violent woman: Thelma and Louise are both too feminist and not feminist enough.[60]

Still, there were a good number of articles that championed the film.[61] Many writers felt that it was about time that this film came out and some even suggested it as therapy for women moviegoers. The majority of these reactions were celebrations of the film without much discussion about the violence in it, except to defend it by saying that it was less than what occurred in most actions films. To some, especially to some women, the violence, then, was exhilarating and fun—even if they couldn't put their finger on why. And it is no coincidence that those articles that criticized *Thelma and Louise* were not only reacting to the film, but also to this celebration and enjoyment of the film by so many women who watched it.

Peter Keough, film editor of the *Boston Phoenix*, said of the film: "Ten years from now it will be seen as a turning point."[62] And indeed it is. *Thelma and Louise* is one of the only films portraying violent women that received such public attention, most likely because it is a turning point, beginning the trend of violent women films in the 1990s. The media representation of *Thelma and Louise* falls into the same category as the past media reaction to female murderers: hysterical questioning regarding the woman and then ideological fantasizing to cover over the trauma of the violent woman (whether that be in the form of the overly feminizing, defeminizing, or politicizing of *Thelma and Louise*). Understanding the repetitive and historical nature of this kind of response reveals the deeply rooted fears and anxieties regarding the violent woman. Obviously, the content of the media representation depends on the sociohistorical fears and anxieties of the moment, but whatever the content of the representation, the form (the hysterical attempts to define femininity and its nonrelation to violence) have thus far remained the same. This curious connection—that is, the media representation itself—between the real female murderers and filmic depictions of violent women creates a road map of sorts to begin to understand the embedded fears and anxieties in contemporary films depicting the violent woman.

PART TWO

The Violent Woman on the Contemporary Screen

CHAPTER 4

Romancing Trauma

The Violent Woman in Contemporary American Film

The first time we see Sarah Connor (Linda Hamilton) in James Cameron's *Terminator 2: Judgment Day* (1991), she is in a mental hospital doing pull-ups while hanging from the end of the bed frame. As a mental patient with muscled arms and a well-toned physique, she has clearly changed a great deal since Cameron's first *Terminator* (1984) film. Indeed, these two *Terminator* films provide a strong example of the effect that the contemporary violent women trend has had on mainstream action films. It is no surprise that Sarah Connor, in the first film, is nonviolent because, as I have pointed out, in the early 1980s violent women mostly populated horror films. In the first *Terminator*, Sarah Connor looks like a woman who can't take care of herself. She needs a male hero for protection, and in fact the survival of the entire world depends on this hero protecting her because she will give birth—the quintessential "feminine" act—to the man who will save the human race in the future. Sarah and her protector also fall in love by the end of the film. In other words, Sarah's need for protection, her femininity (which Cameron emphasizes through the mise-en-scène: her trendy makeup, feathered hair, and style of dress), and the importance of her role as a mother are stressed in this 1980s film. By the 1990s, however, Sarah has lost her maternal femininity and instead adopts a more masculine persona (toting a gun with muscles bulging).

In the opening scene in *Terminator 2*, the camera directs our attention to Sarah Connor's bulging muscles as the doctor and interns look at her through a window in the door. Later, we see her attired as an outlaw handling a huge machine gun, seemingly more comfortable with the gun than with her own son. Most audience members would probably expect Sarah, once freed of the awesome responsibility of saving the world at the end of the film, to retreat back into her more feminine self. The film's narrative itself even suggests this at the end by showing Sarah finally break down and cry over her son. Does this imply that she will soon be setting up house again and allowing her body and mind to ease back into domesticity? Or will she continue as a violent female outlaw provoking more hostile reactions from society?

The struggle between these two possibilities can be found either implicitly or explicitly throughout all filmic narratives featuring violent women. As J. David Slocum says in a related context:

> The employment of narrative in mainstream cinema strongly inscribes and codes representations of violence, creating [. . .] ideological and formal frameworks for spectacles of destruction and death. When depictions of violence fall outside, run counter to, or exceed those normative frameworks, the acts mount both cultural and representational challenges.[1]

Falling outside ideological expectations regarding violence, the violent woman carries the burden of challenging cultural ideals and filmic traditions. Contemporary American films featuring violent women are especially complex and contradictory in terms of gender definitions. This contradiction manifests itself on the level of form and content. For example, filmmakers rarely choose to just depict the violent woman as completely masculine. Yet often directors do use some traditions from male action films. In this way, they make reference to masculine traditions without wholeheartedly adopting them. Similar to male action heroes, for instance, some such films pepper the heroine's deeds with comic remarks.[2] In *The Matrix*, for example, during the roof top battle, Neo, the hero, seems defeated until Trinity, his violent female partner, puts a gun to the enemy's head (an enemy who has previously dodged every bullet they have shot at him) and pauses to say, "DODGE THIS," before she blows him away, thereby saving Neo, providing comic relief, and proving her hero status by her ability to joke at such a moment. In choosing to mimic male violent traditions, however, the films also embed a marker of difference, a marker that *a priori* highlights sexual difference. This crisis of representation surrounding female violence is dealt with in myriad ways—for example, on the level of mise-en-scène, the twists of the plot, other characters' reactions to the violent woman, and the larger form of the film itself—which often both further confounds the crisis and serves to soothe ideologically the crisis by carefully defining why the violence is not a threat. In this chapter, I will consider these intersections between representations of female violence, film form, and narrative to reveal further the nature of the violent woman and her role in and relationship with film.

Investigating the contemporary violent woman in film is especially illuminating because of her proliferation across genres (as well as across mainstream and independent films). Because of this proliferation, it is vital to begin with a theoretical discussion of the relation between the realms of femininity and narrative. As the media reaction to female violence has revealed, the questions that most often arise in reaction to the violent woman are: Can this be a woman? Can femininity be corrupted by violence? Can femininity be attached to violence in any way? These hysterical questions are provoked, because the female violence in some way deeply threatens ideological definitions of gender that bind together and inform many other cultural ideals and ideological systems.

One of the most glaring similarities between contemporary films featuring violent women is that the almost requisite romantic union with which so many Hollywood films conclude *does not occur*.[3] Violent women are usually alive but left on their own at the end of these films. This suggests how difficult it is for Hollywood—the greatest of ideology machines—to integrate the violent woman into its typical narrative structure. This absence of romance, especially in so many mainstream Hollywood action films, is somewhat astounding considering the rate at which heterosexual couples usually end up in a romantic union in most Hollywood films. In *Terminator 2: Judgment Day*, for instance, Sarah Connor does at one point consider the Terminator (Arnold Schwarzenegger) as a possible father for her son—and hence as a mate for herself. Actually, her son gets along better with the Terminator than with her throughout most of the film. And Sarah Connor and the Terminator work very well together; we could imagine such a romance taking place. In the end, however, not only does a romantic union not occur, but the Terminator also descends into a pit of molten steel, killing himself and leaving little possibility for a resurrection. Although his motivation is to erase any possible destructive use of his advanced technology, his suicide also has the added advantage of neatly closing down the possibility of a love relationship with the violent woman.[4] At the end of the film, Sarah Connor stands alone with her son; it is difficult to imagine her reverting back to her more feminine 1980s self, and just as difficult to imagine her integrating into the community from which her violence has so estranged her. The failed romance in *Terminator 2*, and many other such films, suggests the extent to which male violence plays a significant part in the ideological construction of masculinity and femininity, while female violence dwells in this construction as such.

One of the main clues to how narrative film relies on this construction—and how violent women interact with it—lies in what makes the relationship between masculinity and femininity ideological. Psychoanalysis—picking up on a discussion that has often run throughout the history of philosophy—suggests that this ideological relationship is dependent on the concept of the complementarity of opposites. For example, in the realm of the action film: the man protects or attacks, and the woman is protected or is attacked (which leads to her need for protection, thereby completing the circle). Thus, when the woman is violent she eliminates the need for the male protector, thereby disrupting this complementary relationship. The notion of complementarity has a long history and is deeply entrenched in our concepts of love and sex, as well as masculinity and femininity. The social structure itself has its roots in the idea of the complementary couple (which usually manifests itself as heterosexual and monogamous, though this is by no means requisite).[5] As psychoanalysis and Marxism point out in their own ways, complementarity is the most important motivating force behind the ideological support of the social order because it masks antagonism and makes the world seem whole. In her discussion of sexuation, Joan Copjec addresses this:

> Rather than defining a universe of men that is complemented by a universe of women, Lacan defines man as the prohibition against constructing a universe and woman as the impossibility of doing so. The sexual relation fails for two reasons: it is impossible and it is prohibited. Put these two failures together; you will never come up with a whole.[6]

Just as the sexes are barred from knowing themselves as subjects, they are also barred from knowing each other as sexed beings. In other words, if as psychoanalysis suggests, the symbolic cannot fully understand itself, and the subject is barred from ever completely knowing itself, it follows that the subject cannot rely on the relationship between masculinity and femininity to provide such meaning and wholeness that cannot be found elsewhere. Of course, this originary failure is exactly what ideology elides through the idea (or ideal) of complementarity.

Although heterosexual complementarity has for centuries maintained ideological hegemony, it did not always predominate, as the proliferation of the idea of homosexual complementarity in ancient Greek society suggests. Regardless of the sexual pairing, what is important is the *complementarity* that alleviates or represses a sense of antagonism. This idea extends back to Plato's *Symposium*, where the character of Aristophanes gives it voice, offering the archetypal articulation of the idea of complementarity.[7] He envisions love as the reunion of two complementary parts that were long ago divided. As a result of this prior division, Aristophanes suggests, "'Love' is just the name we give to the desire for and pursuit of wholeness."[8] The love relationship makes each feel whole, which is to say, free from alienation and complete. Aristophanes makes clear that the function of complementarity is to create satisfied subjects eager to do the work of the social order. He claims that Zeus separated beings into halves in order that "relationships would at least involve sexual satisfaction, so that people would relax, get on with their work and take care of other aspects of life."[9] In short, complementarity allows the smooth working of society to continue. The idea of complementarity allows the individual subject to feel that she is not alone, or alienated, because there is someone out there to complete her, namely, her complementary other. The social order requires the ideology of complementarity because the social order itself is too tenuous and delicate to withstand acts that bring to light its seams (i.e., its antagonisms). In other words, the idea of complementarity—and all the narratives that reinforce it—is one of the most powerful ways that ideology covers over antagonisms. Our unending appetite for romantic narratives, as well as the structuring nature of the romance in other genres (the contemporary action film, for example), provides clear evidence of our concern for reinforcing the possibility of a complementary relationship. Lacan suggests that our constant discussions, both in popular culture and in analysis, of our inability to find the right mate also reveal our reliance on complementarity for a sense of meaning in the world. Lacan captures the essence of this when he says, "What constitutes the basis of life, in effect, is that for everything having to do with relations between men and women, what is called collectivity, it's not working out. It's not working out, and the whole world talks about it, and a large part of our activity is taken up with saying so."[10] In complaining about our inability to find romance—or in complaining about the romance that we have found—we are both revealing the impossibility of complementarity and reinforcing our belief in it.

In *Three Essays on the Theory of Sexuality*, Freud addresses complementarity when he himself recounts Aristophanes' famous creation story: "The popular view of the sexual instinct is beautifully reflected in the poetic fable which tells how the original human beings were cut up into two halves—man and woman—and how these are always striving to unite again in love."[11] The act through which the two halves unite in love represents the imaginary unifying of the social whole—the reconciliation of the social antagonism. Complementarity allows us to believe in the social order precisely because the opposition between male and female stands in for the social antagonism. As Slavoj Žižek points out: "What we experience as 'sexuality' is precisely the effect of the contingent act of 'grafting' the fundamental deadlock of symbolization on to the biological opposition of male and female."[12] Thus, much more is at stake in the idea of complementarity between male and female than just an individual sense of completion. The coherence of the social order as a whole rests on this idea. Which is why the popular view leads us to believe that we could not survive—either emotionally or physically—if it weren't for this complementarity.

This is a belief that is played out time and again in film. In Cameron Crowe's popular *Jerry Maguire* (1997), Jerry's (Tom Cruise) life remains unfulfilled until he finds the woman with whom he belongs. He professes his love to her with the words of complementarity, proclaiming, "You complete me." The film depicts the highest compliment, or the emotional feeling that is more deeply rooted than any other, as telling another person that she makes you feel whole. Love promises a wholeness that fills in the lack in both partners. In *Sublime Object of Ideology*, Žižek notes that "the operation of love is [. . .] double: the subject fills in his own lack by offering himself to the other as the object filling out the lack in the Other—love's deception is that this overlapping of two lacks annuls lack as such in a mutual completion."[13] This sense of mutual completion is the one ideological bond that allows people to ignore the fundamentally alienating experience of being a subject in society. What Žižek calls "love's deception" is thus at the root of the amelioration of the social antagonism.

But there is some level—the unconscious level—on which all subjects know that finding someone to *complete* them is utterly impossible. That is, despite our investment in the fantasy of complementarity, we remain aware of the underlying Real antagonism. Commenting on this in his *Seminar XX*, Lacan notes: "'We are but one.' Everyone knows, of course, that two have never become but one, but nevertheless 'we are but one.' The idea of love begins with that."[14] We perceive love as a "natural" feeling or impulse, but as Lacan is explaining here, it is wholly based on our ideas of masculinity and femininity and their complementarity—the idea of the *one*. This is to say that ultimately love is ideological because complementarity is impossible.[15]

Psychoanalysis explains that the sense of a complementary relation always involves the mediation of a third party—the Name of the Father. The Name of the Father, the fundamental social Law, acts as a mediator between the antagonistic positions of male and female, making it appear as if a sexual relationship does exist. As Bruce Fink puts it, "nothing that would qualify as a true relationship between the sexes can be either spoken or written. There is nothing complementary about their relationship, nor is there a simple inverse relationship or some kind of parallelism between them. Rather, *each sex is defined separately and with respect to a third term*."[16] This third term is the fundamental signifier of the symbolic order, that quilting point of the symbolic order that anchors all meaning but ultimately is an empty signifier in and of itself. Because the sexes only relate to each other—and only experience love—through this third term, the love relationship is necessarily ideological, accomplished through the mediation that ideology provides. As Lacan explains at the conclusion of *Seminar XI*, "any shelter in which may be established a viable, temperate relation of one sex to the other necessitates the intervention— this is what psychoanalysis teaches us—of that medium known as the paternal metaphor."[17] This means that the existence of romantic love relationships—the products of the paternal metaphor's mediation—serves to mask a fundamental impossibility: the impossibility of male and female relating directly to each other. It is this impossibility that leads to Lacan's famous dictum—what is perhaps the fundamental claim of psychoanalysis—"there is no sexual relationship."[18] And while film has an overabundance of romantic plots, it also at times looks directly at the impossible nature of a sexual relationship. This is why we see in Stanley Kubrick's *Eyes Wide Shut* (1999), for instance, the inability of male and female sexuality to coincide harmoniously: the more Bill Harford (Tom Cruise) strives to discover the secret of feminine *jouissance*—by visiting a prostitute, by attending a secret orgy—the more it absolutely eludes him. Kubrick's film reveals perfectly what Lacan calls "the radical heterogeneity of male *jouissance* and female *jouissance*."[19] The illusion of the sexual relationship is also exactly what films featuring violent women expose when the violent woman does not often end up in love, because she has shattered the fantasy of complementarity on which love rests.

Theoretical debates about the relationship between masculinity and femininity have a long history, but it is the theoretical emphasis that psychoanalysis places on this relationship that reveals what is at stake in it and provides a complex way of understanding how cultural gender definitions are both intimately tied to yet also relatively indifferent toward masculinity and femininity (sexual difference). While Freud does believe in sexual difference, he does not believe, as is popularly thought, that sexual difference can be reduced to any positive gender characteristics. In trying to explain this he says: "For distinguishing between male and female in emotional life we make use of what is an obviously inadequate empirical and conventional equation: we call everything that is strong and active male, and everything that is weak and passive female."[20] In other words, Freud finds men and women to be more complicated than their traditional definition and yet realizes that these definitions have a most powerful influence. He realizes that the terms "active" and "passive," because they were complementary opposites, do not fully represent sexual difference, but he also knows that no terms exist that could communicate adequately the relationship between masculinity and femininity. For Lacan, Freud's dogged refusal to accept fully the terms "activity" and "passivity" stands out. According to Lacan, "activity and passivity are only substitutes, about which, each time that he would employ them, Freud emphasizes that their character is—I will not say inadequate—suspect."[21] The problematic status of these substitute terms—"activity" and "passivity"—indicates that masculinity and femininity cannot be brought into relation with each other. Cognescent of the radicality of this insight, Lacan says, "Is it not absolutely fabulous that we could not, in absolutely any case, render an account of a link between these terms that justifies taking one for the inverse of the other[?]"[22] What Lacan finds "absolutely fabulous" here is precisely the way in which the (failed) relation between male and female reveals the underlying social antagonism.

Building on Freud, Lacan recognizes that what was being hidden by gender definitions was that masculine and feminine positions are not complementary, that in fact there is no such sexual relationship, and that it is ideological gender definitions that smooth over this antagonism. Masculinity and femininity are two fundamentally different ways of experiencing the symbolic order, and these two positions reflect the underlying antagonism that splits the symbolic order itself. According to Lacan, these masculine and feminine positions are neither complementary nor binary opposites. In fact, seeing them as opposites would obviously still constitute them as in some way complementary. Instead, he theorizes they are supplements to each other: neither dependent on each other nor completely independent of each other. Exploring this supplementary relationship reveals that antagonism arises in the most unclear and ambiguous spaces. It does not necessarily arise in spaces of opposition, which can at least rely on some logic to their positions. This idea leaves us far more empty-handed than one would expect. Where can you go from here? It is certainly not a prescriptive theory that suggests how theorists or nontheorists should approach or reform gender. As Joan Copjec says: "*Male and female* [. . .] *are not predicates, which means that rather than increasing our knowledge of the subject, they qualify the mode of the failure of our knowledge.*"[23] That is to say, the more you understand the constructed nature of gender, the less you know about masculinity and femininity. This does not, however, as it would seem, result in a dead end. Psychoanalysis suggests that this failure of knowledge actually provides a new opening. It is the moment of realizing the true nature of sexuality—the moment of a traumatic encounter. Such moments occur when we experience the social antagonism that ideology otherwise obscures: at these times, we come face-to-face with the nonexistence of the big Other, with the fact that there is no ground for our symbolic identity.

The question is, of course, the extent to which films elide antagonism and ideologically smooth over these traumatic moments. The violent woman, for example, provokes traumatic moments that are more difficult than most to symbolize. Violence functions primarily within ideas of complementarity insofar as men are violent and women are spectators and guarantors of violence. When women react with violence toward the loss or threatened loss of their femininity, they do not regain their femininity, but instead position themselves even further from that femininity and their complementary relationship with masculinity. There are times when a woman's violence might protect her symbolic position, for example, protecting her children and thereby preserving her status as mother, or enhancing her evil image and securing her status as a bad girl. Even these quite rare instances of violence that enhance feminine positions are not cases in which violence is intimately linked to femininity. They are singular cases, whereas the link between violence and masculinity exists on a much more general scale. This is because women function as the victims of violence, both literally and metaphorically.[24] Male violence often has its justification in the fact that men are violent to *protect* women (or destroy another man's masculinity). And this is the traditional relationship that the woman has to violence—as the one *protected* from it.

Reinforcing the idea of complementarity (as in the way that violence structures our ideas about gender) is one of the most powerful ideological ways to minimize contradiction and trauma, and thereby reduce the possibility of revealing the alienated and noncomplementary nature of both subjectivity and the social order itself. This is why real female murderers provoke such exaggerated attempts to define femininity: their violence disrupts this sense of complementarity and throws off (or unsettles) all the cultural nuances that define the media's traditional ideals of femininity at that historical period. Fictional violent women in film similarly disrupt a sense of complementarity and unsettle not only the narrative (in its trajectory toward a romantic union), but also all the cultural nuances and gender definitions that film normally relies on. Violent women create a moment in which the trauma of sexual antagonism is revealed, and provoke a rash of "meaning making," that is, trying to redefine gender, which thus opens up possibilities for change. In other words (as I argued in the introduction), violence can either aid ideology or reveal the antagonism that underlies narrative. In the case of the violent woman, the narrative often goes to great lengths to cover over the trauma of noncomplementarity that female violence amplifies. Moreover, it is the tension between violence (of the woman) and narrative (especially of the romance plot) that produces evidence of the traumatic nature of the violent woman.

One of the best examples of this occurs in John Dahl's *The Last Seduction* (1993).[25] Dahl's film not only explores the crimes of a violent woman but also how the violent woman destabilizes femininity. The violent woman makes the complementary relationship impossible, but the disruption manifests itself in other ways as well, ways that reverberate throughout the plot and mise-en-scène and that further reveal the antagonism that underlies ideological fantasy. One particular manifestation of the trauma of the violent woman in *The Last Seduction* is the way in which she thwarts man's constant attempt to feminize (i.e., define) her by both challenging some male expectations of femininity and overemphasizing others. Bridget Gregory (Linda Fiorentino) and Clay Gregory (Bill Pullman), her husband, live in New York City where Bridget has masterminded a drug deal in which they will make one million dollars. But after the conclusion of the deal, Bridget decides to take the money and keep it all for herself. On the advice of a lawyer friend, Bridget interrupts her flight from Clay and stays in Beston, a small town in New York, where she stopped to get gas. There she meets

Mike Swale (Peter Berg). Mike has recently had his masculinity threatened during a brief stay in Buffalo, where he unknowingly married a transvestite. He has landed back in Beston, nursing his damaged masculine pride. When Bridget walks into the neighborhood bar, Mike is immediately intrigued. His friend asks him: "What do you see in that city trash?" And Mike replies: "Maybe a new set of balls." From the moment they meet, then, Mike depends on Bridget to reestablish his masculinity. What is important to him is that she is not from Beston and that she is beautiful and sexy in a feminine—if not glamorous—way. He continually tries to put her into the feminine roles he wants her to play, that is, into a complementary relationship with him. But other than just a sexual relationship, Bridget won't allow him to force her into acting "properly" feminine because she does not occupy the traditional feminine identity. She does not care what others think about her and will use violence at any moment to get what she wants. She gets what she wants from society by using femininity (in every possible manifestation), but in actuality she is complementary to no one. Femininity is usually depicted as requiring a kind of "application": women apply makeup (as in the old saying, "I never leave the house without putting my face on"), do their hair, wear clothes more for looks than comfort, and even surgically alter parts of their bodies according to the current feminine trends. In many ways, Bridget uses femininity as a mask to operate in a society dominated by feminine stereotypes. Throughout the film, she deploys femininity as masquerade. In her discussion of the nature of masquerade in film, Mary Ann Doane says: "The masquerade, in flaunting femininity, holds it at a distance. Womanliness is a mask which can be worn or removed."[26] This sense of feminine masquerade often becomes exaggerated when combined with female violence.

Their violence aside, women in such films seem relatively similar to the majority of other nonviolent female characters in film, except for this more overt sense of masquerade. Most violent female characters are more aware of their appearance, or are forced into situations in which their female identities or their identities in general are revealed as utterly contingent. For example, after Thelma and Louise commit one violent act, they spend the rest of the film shedding their femininity. The film represents this through their discarding some female articles, like rings and lipstick, and donning a few masculine ones, such as a cowboy hat. In Ridley Scott's *G.I. Jane* (1997), after being inducted into the rites of violence of the Navy Seals, Jordan O'Neil (Demi Moore) symbolically shears her long hair. And Angela Bennett (Sandra Bullock), in Irwin Winkler's *The Net* (1995), loses every bit of her identity within the symbolic and is forced into using violence in order to survive. And in *Terminator 2: Judgment Day*, Sarah Connor was willing to shed her femininity, which is so present in the first *Terminator*, and create a muscled body in order to embrace violence and save her son and the world. Each of these cases reveals feminine identity as something that can be removed because it is not intrinsic to the characters. Nowhere is this sense of masquerade more present, however, than in *The Last Seduction*. Everything about Bridget seems slightly off, or faked, because she *employs* her femininity. That is, her femininity does not seem "natural" but applied. Representations of masculinity seem more tied to the ideal of a natural body, which is not supposed to be altered or enhanced but just "is." In this way, masculinity seems more innate, less ideological (which is, of course, nonetheless wholly ideological). As Slavoj Žižek points out in *Indivisible Remainder*: "Behind the macho image of a man there is no 'secret,' just a weak ordinary person who can never live up to his ideal."[27] Thus, masculinity is, of course, as constructed as femininity but part of its construction lies in creating the appearance of not being constructed.

In *The Last Seduction*, Bridget understands this dynamic and uses it, but unlike most women who go to the same lengths that she does, she seems uninvested in the feminine mask as an integral part of her identity. Indeed, she seems to use femininity in an almost violent way, by, for example, using it to distract someone before she commits violence. (She kills both a detective and her husband in this way.) As in all films featuring violent women, violence and femininity so contrast with each other that together they highlight the contingency of feminine identity, and therefore the contingency of the masculine identity as well. This sense of contingency permeates the whole film and Bridget's feminine identity, and it is the relationship to contingency that allows Bridget to expose the nature of subjectivity itself. As Žižek says,

> It is precisely in so far as woman is characterized by an original "masquerade," in so far as all her features are artificially "put on," that she is more subject than man, since [. . .] what ultimately characterizes the subject is this very radical contingency and artificiality of her every positive feature, that is, the fact that "she" in herself is a pure void that cannot be identified with any of these features.[28]

Bridget is this pure void for whom every identity that she takes on functions as a tool that she can use to manipulate men; in this sense, she is the perfect female subject, the one who betrays absolutely no investment in the masks that she wears because she recognizes the contingency of every one of them.

This grasp of the contingency of every positive feature of identity is apparent throughout the mise-en-scène of the film. It begins with Bridget's actual physical appearance, which remains almost exactly the same throughout the film. Bridget has long brown hair parted on the side, which she continually plays with. Throughout the film, she wears some variation of a black miniskirt, a white dress shirt tucked into the skirt, black pantyhose, and black high heels. And she always carries a fashionable purse and jacket to match. But more than this "feminine" costume, it is her actions that seem to deploy femininity. Upon first entering the neighborhood bar in Beston, she tersely asks for a drink and is not served until Mike comes over and orders for her (saying "please"). She says: "Oh, so that's the game, I have to say 'please.'" Upon deciding to stay in the town of Beston, she applies for a job. To make sure her husband doesn't find her there, she tells her employer she's been abused "savagely" by her husband and must change her name. The employer naively believes her and is very sympathetic. Unlike the woman we saw in the bar, here she acts submissive (looking down a lot) and nervous, which makes her seem more vulnerable and feminine. This discrepancy clearly reveals that what we assume to be typical feminine behavior is, for Bridget, simply a guise that she adopts when it is useful for her.

Not only does Bridget employ femininity to get what she wants, but she uses it to reveal the masquerade itself. In one scene, Mike is getting tired of only having sex and no other kind of interaction with Bridget. Figuring that she is resisting more commitment because she is afraid of being hurt, he asks: "What are you so scared of?" Looking puppy-eyed and sincere and talking in a sweeter, softer voice, Bridget replies: "I don't know. I guess it's because I've been hurt before. I don't want to get close to anyone right now. You're different than the others, Mike. I feel like maybe I could love you." Mike is listening intently and believing every word, as if he has finally discovered the real feminine side that he knew she had. Then Bridget finishes sarcastically with, "Will that do? Fucking doesn't have to be anything more than fucking." This exchange reveals the eagerness with which Mike wants Bridget to be traditionally feminine and vulnerable. It also depicts the way in which his own masculinity is riding on the belief that beneath all her sarcasm is a femininity that needs him and his masculinity. But instead, at every turn, the film reveals Bridget's femininity to be a masquerade, which is further emphasized by even smaller details about Bridget, for example, she changes her name to Wendy Kroy (which is a version of New York spelled backwards), she has a knack for writing upside down, and she also writes letters you can only read in a mirror. These details emphasize the way in which she knowingly plays with symbolic constructs. Thus, she continually mystifies Mike, but he has a history of being mystified by femininity. Mike was married for a brief time to Trish, a man who dressed and acted like a woman. What made this masquerade even more disturbing to Mike was that he thought Trish was really female. The trauma here comes from the idea that a masculine man is supposed to be able to "recognize" a feminine woman. But Bridget provides him with no solace because she may look feminine and be female, but she is far less complementary to him than Trish was. She makes evident to Mike—and to the viewer—the failure of the sexual relationship.

At the end of the film, even Bridget's husband—who supposedly knows her true nature—tries to seduce her back into their "complementary" sexual relationship. She responds by kissing him, but then pries his mouth open and sprays pepper spray down his throat, killing him. She then coerces Mike into raping her while she calls 911 to record the rape. This tape, and the charge that he killed her husband, puts him in jail for life. As the film concludes, Bridget walks away with all the money from the drug deal that opened the film. The ending emphasizes that her motives were purely selfish, just in case the viewer had any lingering ideas that she may have done all this to escape from an abusive husband and that, after this, her true, kind self would surface. Instead, the end reveals that she has easily forgotten that she killed two men and put another innocent man in jail for life: she is depicted already happily enjoying the money she made off with (as is evident by the limousine she leaves in and the smile of contentment on her face). The film is an excellent example therefore of the way in which female violence acts as a provocative metaphor for the lack of a sexual relationship and the constructed nature of femininity.

The Last Seduction is a classic example of one of the chief effects that a violent woman has—her effect on the narrative. Narrative itself works to create complementarity. Teresa de Lauretis points out that "the work of narrative, then, is mapping differences, and specifically, first and foremost, of sexual difference into each text; and hence, by a sort of accumulation, into the universe of meaning, fiction, and history, represented by the literary-artistic tradition and all the texts of culture."[29] But I would expand this definition even further: narrative not only maps sexual difference, but also works to transform the antagonism of sexual difference into complementarity. By making the male/female relationship seem a complementary one, narrative allows us to believe in the possibility of overcoming antagonism. In many ways, Hollywood succeeds best at producing sexual difference as complementary—in other words, at producing romance and romantic endings. One might even say that this is the fundamental ideological task of Hollywood film, at least in its contemporary manifestation. As I pointed out before, even an action film, which seems to have nothing to do with romance, will typically end with a romantic union. For example, in John McTiernan's *Die Hard* (1988), John McClain (Bruce Willis) fights to protect a building full of people (and his estranged wife) against terrorists, and his reward for winning the fight is a romantic reunion with his wife. Another unlikely example is *Independence Day* (1996), in which two very different men come together to save the world (from attacking aliens), and the film rewards both of them in the final scene when their two romantic partners run to meet and embrace them. And in Michael Bay's *The Rock* (1996), a scientist turned action hero saves San Francisco from destruction, and the end of the film depicts a reunion between the scientist and his girlfriend-become-wife. In each case, the romantic ending solidifies the story as ideological, as it reinforces notions of complementarity and the protector/protected dynamic; in short, the women stay in the background while the men violently save the day. Complementarity—the love relationship depicted in film—functions as an ideological fantasy, which always reinforces the idea that things fit together smoothly, that society functions without an impassable hurdle. In this way, films deliver the fantasmatic goods, and audiences are continually awash in dreams of complementarity. No one can deny the seductive power that James Cameron's *Titanic* (1997) had on millions of women and men—and thirteen-year-old girls—due to its romance, which neatly obscured the trauma of its story. Indeed, the film ends leaving the impression that though thousands tragically died when the Titanic sank, true love can conquer even this trauma of death.

The disruption that the violent woman has on the more typical male/female relationship is evident in Steven Soderberg's *Out of Sight* (1998). *Out of Sight* stars George Clooney and Jennifer Lopez, two actors who embody contemporary ideals of masculinity and femininity. Clooney and Lopez do not end up in a romantic embrace at the end of the film; instead, the law stands between their relationship. If ever the casting of a film signified an eventual romantic union, it is here. And, in fact, the idea that there should be a love relationship between these two is a constant tension in the film. This tension between the possible love relationship and the disruptiveness of the violent woman is mirrored in the tension between Karen Sisco's (Jennifer Lopez) looks and her job as a federal marshal. The film begins when Karen happens upon Jack Foley's (George Clooney) jailbreak attempt, which she tries to prevent. She pulls out a shotgun and tries to arrest him. The image of her pulling out a shotgun is immediately incongruous with her dress and appearance because, even though she is going to the prison for work-related reasons, she is dressed in a short miniskirt and her hair and makeup look flawless. The incongruity strikes Jack as well, who says to her, "Girl, what do you do for a living, packing a shot gun?" She answers that she's a federal marshal. Jack replies: "Why would someone like you become a federal marshal?" Thus, right from the beginning of the film the contradiction between femininity and violence is raised on the level of both image and dialogue.

Jack is immediately attracted to Karen and hopes to impress her, even though he's a criminal and she's trying to put him in jail. Jack's relationship to Karen parallels society's typical reaction to the violent woman. On the one hand, Karen's violence makes her more attractive: she represents the possibility of a wholly new kind of relationship, a relationship of antagonism rather than complementarity. The sense of antagonism that she evokes intrigues Jack, leading him to pursue her later in the film even at the risk of incarceration. Karen, as a violent woman, has something that other women don't have: she completely uproots Jack's symbolic identity, allowing him to experience a *jouissance* that has hitherto seemed impossible. But on the other hand, precisely because Karen signals the possibility of this *jouissance*, she represents a danger to Jack. These two faces of the violent woman produce our ambivalent reaction to her: like Jack, the viewer is drawn to the antagonism that she opens up, but also recoils from the trauma of experiencing this antagonism. In order to avoid this trauma, the film stresses the violent woman's femininity, in hopes that this will obscure her violence.

We can see this focus on femininity clearly in the case of Jack. While Jack enjoys the threat that Karen's violence provides, at the same time he wants to eliminate it.[30] He continually thinks that she will react to him from the standpoint of her femininity rather than with violence, and each time she corrects him by pulling a gun on him and ordering him under arrest. But the film works to reassure both Jack and the viewers of Karen's femininity. Karen is not your average looking woman—and therefore not your average looking female federal marshal—because she is always dressed up and shot very seductively. Indeed, she comments to Jack that he is ruining her nine-hundred-dollar dress when he throws her in the trunk of a car. Even in the trunk, as throughout the film, her hair and makeup are perfect and her clothes are stylish. The contradictions between her heightened femininity and her violence are used both to intrigue viewers and comfort them. Clearly, the film highlights this intentional discrepancy between her femininity and her violence, but by drawing attention to Karen's glamorous and sexual appearance the film also emphasizes that this could not be an average woman and that her glamorized looks tend to constantly supercede her violence. Throughout the film, the characters and camera take notice of this discrepancy between Karen's femininity and her violence. During one scene—presented through a classic shot-reverse shot—early on in the film when she is having dinner with her father, he gives her a gift for her birthday. The camera angle while she opens and admires the gift prevents us from identifying the gift until the reverse shot reveals it as a gun. Clearly, this sequence of shots works to surprise the viewer, because the gun is an instrument of violence, which is not what a father typically gives to his feminine little girl.

Even though Karen and Jack begin a relationship during the film, not surprisingly, they do not end up together at the film's conclusion. Karen shoots Jack during a robbery and turns him in, sending him to jail. The ending suggests that she hopes he'll find a way to escape, but this *suggestion* of a romance in and of itself does not make for a "typical" Hollywood romantic union. The film does, however, try to deal with this possible romance in one scene in which they have sex. Throughout the scene, they discuss wanting to take a "time-out." Karen says to Foley, "I just kept thinking— what if we took a time-out?" This question is provocatively symbolic when we consider what the time-out offers respite from. In the film, it is clear that the time-out is from their roles vis-à-vis the law: she is a police officer, and he is a criminal. In the larger scope of the social order, however, it enacts the film's acknowledgement of the threatening aspects of female violence to complementarity. The antagonism that has been exposed through her violence is what they want to take a break from. And indeed they do for one night, but the next day they are both compelled to resume their previous roles. To take a total break, one of them would have to give up their current identity, because a violent female police officer and a violent male criminal cannot "fit" together.

In other words, in order to "fit" together, women must be complicitous in the idea of protector/protected complementarity. As Martha McCaughey, in *Real Knockouts: The Physical Feminism of Women's Self-defense*, says: "Keeping women away from violence, or denying the aggressive potential in them, preserves the association of violence and masculinity, and upholds a false similarity within the category 'women.'"[31] When a woman becomes her own protector, she disrupts this cycle. This is why there are hardly any dramatic scenes in all these violent women films in which the strong male hero is present but the strong female heroine takes care of the situation, using violence to protect them both.[32] This is not only too threatening but unthinkable to filmmakers and film audiences alike in the 1990s or 2000s. Even the impressive Sarah Connor in *Terminator 2* is out of bullets at the end of the film, and the good Terminator must take the final, lifesaving act (which kills the evil Terminator). Being out of bullets is a wholly contingent predicament, but I would say that in this case it is not only predictable but required in order to privilege the Terminator's masculinity (especially because the Terminator is played by one of Hollywood's most masculine-identified actors) and Sarah Connor's—albeit somewhat hidden—femininity.

One way films do explore the possibility of a woman saving a man is through comedy, as in Richard Donner's *Lethal Weapon 3* (1992).[33] Lorna Cole (Rene Russo) is a police internal affairs investigator, who is immediately at odds with the film's heroes, Riggs and Murtaugh (Mel Gibson and Danny Glover). Cole is authoritative and calm at the beginning of the film, but it is not until she and Riggs are each checking out different parts of a warehouse that we see her ability to be violent. As the criminals surprise Riggs and begin to strangle him, Cole walks in with her gun and orders them to drop their prisoner. A man surprises her from behind and tells her to drop her gun—the typical representation of the female police officer who cannot handle herself in a life-threatening situation. However, just as she drops her gun, she raises one eyebrow at Riggs, whips around, and beats up the man behind her and two others who rush her. She then steals a truck by kicking the driver in the face and knocking him out of the seat. Ostensibly we have here a scene in which the female protects the male hero on her own. And on its own it stands as one of the only scenes in popular film where this occurs.

Not too many scenes later, however, Cole, Riggs, and Mutaugh are interrogating a suspect when the suspect's friends arrive and begin to cause trouble. Cole approaches them, telling Riggs and Mutaugh that she can handle it. When Mutaugh suggests that he help her, Riggs says (with a bemused and cavalier look on his face), "No, don't. Watch this. She's got a gift." What was previously a serious act of competence is now turned into a joke and a metaphorical striptease in order to limit the impact of this powerful woman. This scene also forces the viewer to reread the earlier scene and view that violence as comic as well. After we witness the second scene, the violence in both scenes takes on the function of striptease: Cole performs the violence for the enjoyment of the men who watch her. And as Linda Williams comments about the striptease in *Hard Core: Power, Pleasure and the "Frenzy of the Visible,"* "The artistry of performance comes to compensate for what is missing in discursive exchange between partner and audience."[34] In this case, what is missing is the traditional role of the female, and so it is reinvented in the "striptease" of Cole's violence, in the form of Riggs's joke about the novelty in her ability to handle herself. At the end of the scene, Cole herself contributes to the making light of her violence; she says, "This PMS is murder." Murtaugh replies, "Yeah, I know what you mean: I've been married twenty-five years." With this comment, he then deals the final blow by symbolizing, interpreting, and containing her violence within the typical joke about "bitchy" women and PMS.

Lethal Weapon 3 must go to such extreme lengths precisely because of the disruption that the violent woman occasions. To be violent, the violent woman must move away from traditional femininity, and in being violent, she further unravels the accepted definitions of masculinity and femininity as well as the possibility of these coming together in romance. This is why the violent woman seems to threaten the family. She may be committing violence to save her family, but in the process she disrupts the complementary relationship upon which the family is based. The root of social life is the family, so when the family is threatened, the very fabric of the social order is threatened as well. As McCaughey points out: "Because men's aggression is taken for granted as natural, women's seems threatening to society in a different way. The fear that women's rebellion will cause social life to crumble still exists."[35] Ironically enough, this is also the appeal of the violent woman: she does represent the possibility of a total breakdown of traditional values and relations. The violent woman is the ultimate radical in this sense. She is fighting not only against the situation she is in, but—metaphorically—against all social traditions as well. Of course, the audience would not get much pleasure out of seeing society actually crumble, so the violence of the woman must have reasons and justifications. In this way, the viewer has both the enjoyment of the possible breakdown of society (through the violence of the woman) and the fantasy of a completely harmonious and stable society satisfied within the same viewing experience. This was not the case, however, with some films that upset many of the audiences that saw them, such as *Thelma and Louise, Fatal Attraction*, and *Basic Instinct*. As the 1990s wore on, these ideological subversions were covered over with more integrated reasons and justifications and no violent woman has quite sparked the same intensity of reaction as the women in these films.

Feminine violence disturbs us because it is extralegal while masculine violence is an integral part of the legal system (if not its very raison d'être). Masculine violence fits into a system of exchange: we expect masculine violence to trigger an appropriate compensation, whether through retaliation or punishment by the state. Psychoanalysis discusses masculine subjectivity as existing in reference to a certain limit, and I would suggest that it is illuminating to see masculine violence in this same way. We know that masculine violence—even the extreme violence of a serial killer—will always remain within this limit. Why is this? Male violence respects a limit because male subjectivity is structured in reference to a limit. Psychoanalysis theorizes that this limit is the primal father—the ideal man that knows no barriers or limitations. Male subjectivity has a wholeness or an essence because it is structured in reference to this limit. As Bruce Fink puts it: "Man can be considered as a whole, because there is something that delimits him."[36] No man attains ideal masculinity—or the position of the primal father—but this is precisely why this ideal can serve as a point of reference for all men. Furthermore, we can know and define male essence because we have a limit point beyond which male identity cannot go. For Lacan, the man, in contrast to the woman, does exist, which means that he can be wholly apprehended through the signifier. The same is true of male violence. Like male subjectivity, male violence exists in reference to an ideal—the macho primal father with no chinks in his armor. Hence, every actual act of male violence—that is, every act that falls short of the ideal—necessarily exists within our symbolic universe, where we can readily make sense of it.

But female violence, like female subjectivity, is not beholden to such a limit. Whereas we can isolate male subjectivity and locate it definitively within the symbolic structure (precisely because it occurs in reference to a point outside of that structure), we cannot localize female subjectivity in this way. Female subjectivity lacks a corresponding reference to an ideal, omnipotent female figure.

Thus, women have no limit against which to define themselves. They are not continually striving toward an ideal femininity in the way that men are striving toward an ideal masculinity. In her outstanding commentary on sexual difference in *Read My Desire*, Joan Copjec makes clear what this implies:

> Woman is there where no limit intervenes to inhibit a progressive unfolding of signifiers, where, therefore, a judgment of existence becomes impossible. This means that everything can be and is said about her, but that none of it is subject to "reality testing"—none of what is said amounts to a confirmation or denial of her existence, which thereby eludes every symbolic articulation. The relation of the woman to the symbolic and to the phallic function is considerably complicated by this argument. For it is precisely because she is totally, that is, limitlessly inscribed within the symbolic order that she is in some sense wholly outside it, which is to say the question of her existence is absolutely undecidable within it.[37]

One can never define completely female subjectivity, Copjec claims, because it lacks the externally located ideal that informs male subjectivity.[38] The ideal allows men to be whole, but this wholeness comes with a price: complete subjection to the signifier. In contrast to males, according to Serge André, "the reality of the female sex [. . .] is what appears as a lacuna in discourse, a hole in the signifying fabric."[39] As a "lacuna in discourse," the female sex does not suffer from the signifier in the same ways that males do. Women escape the male's complete subjection because they are not-whole. As Lacan puts it: "There's no such thing as Woman, Woman with a capital *W* indicating the universal. There's no such thing as Woman because, in her essence [. . .] she is not-whole."[40] The not-whole status of female subjectivity allows women to act in a way that breaks from the symbolic order, a way that cannot be completely contained within the structure of that order.

This psychoanalytic understanding of femininity is essential to my argument about female violence, and it is especially here that I think psychoanalysis can help expand current discussions of the violent woman within film studies. What makes female violence so threatening then is precisely this "not-whole" nature of female subjectivity. Because female subjectivity does not operate in reference to a limit, there is an element of the uncontainable within it. It is this element that female violence engages. Female violence disturbs us—and our filmic narratives—because it takes place without reference to a limit. Once a woman embarks on violence, we have a sense that she may never stop, and our fear of this possibility manifests itself in the relationship between violence and narrative. This becomes quite clear in the case of *Thelma and Louise*, which implies that once an average woman reacts with violence to a threat she encounters, she is doomed to a life of crime, a life separated from her family and former feminine self. If an average man reacted in violence to protect himself (or even in anger after he was attacked), he would not be so doomed. But one violent act on the part of the average woman indicates that she—for that moment—broke from her femininity, her position in the social order. Female subjectivity lacks the limit that would rein it in, and hence we fear that nothing can stop female violence once it begins. The moment itself is crucial because if Louise had pulled the trigger during the rape, she might have had a hard time in court, but the public would be more accepting. Violence in this kind of moment helps to keep the woman safe so she can continue her role as the protected subject. Louise's violence, however, was done purely out of anger; Thelma was no longer in danger. While we can accept female violence (when she is protecting her role as the one protected), we have no way to make sense of the kind of violence that Louise exhibits in this circumstance. And if this is the case, then it cannot be avenged or punished in the same way as masculine violence. We cannot pin Louise's violence down; it exceeds the logic of the signifier.[41]

In contrast to male violence, female violence doesn't occur against the background of the big Other. While legitimate male violence (that of the police) is the instrument of the big Other, criminal male violence defines itself in relation to the big Other as well—as rebellion. Whenever a man acts violently from the male symbolic position, he necessarily acts for the Other. Female violence omits this frame of reference. It takes place with complete indifference to the big Other. Beginning with its tagline, "Murder isn't always a crime," Bruce Beresford's *Double Jeopardy* (1999) seems to literalize this idea. In the film, Elizabeth "Libby" Parsons (Ashley Judd) finds herself in jail for the murder of Nick Parsons, her husband. Although she did not commit this murder, she cannot convince the court system of this; she serves her sentence until receiving parole for good behavior. Before she gets out, Libby discovers that Nick is alive and is raising their young son to believe that Libby is a murderer. A jail mate tells her that she cannot be tried for the same crime twice and suggests she gets even with her husband. While extremely angry with Nick, Libby intends only to retrieve her son. Nick, however, decides to kill Libby, who will certainly foil his current schemes. The climax of the film occurs in the final battle in which to save herself (and her ornery yet endearing parole officer) Libby has to shoot Nick. This violent act exists outside the law and beyond possible punishment since one cannot murder the same person twice. Libby is angry, determined, unstoppable, and violent throughout this film, and thus it is no surprise that she does not end up in a romance at the end of the film. Just as Libby spends most of the film creeping through shadows and around buildings while on the run, the female violence in *Double Jeopardy* is so outside the social norm that the law itself cannot recognize it.

The same type of indifference toward the big Other animates feminine *jouissance*: both female violence and feminine *jouissance* share a self-sufficiency that male violence and phallic *jouissance* lack. This indifference to the Other manifests itself most emphatically in the case of the femme fatale. As Renata Salecl claims: "A *femme fatale* enjoys her own self-sufficiency, which is why we cannot simply say that she needs men as relays to her *jouissance*. Of course, she wants to catch and hold the gaze of men, but she is attractive because she quickly turns around and shows very little interest in her admirers."[42] The indifference of the femme fatale—and the violent woman in general—to the Other makes her violence seem more dangerous. Once she begins, the violent woman has no reason to stop. One has precisely this sense while watching *Thelma and Louise*: after beginning on the road to violence, there is no viable way that Thelma and Louise can turn back. The film suggests that when ordinary women turn to violence, they lose all grounding in the restrictions and limitations of the social order.

This is also the premise of F. Gary Gray's *Set It Off* (1997). Set in Los Angeles, *Set It Off* tries to discover what would happen if four average, working-class women responded actively—to the point of violence—to the injustices in their lives. Besides Kathryn Bigelow's

Strange Days, this is one of the few violent women films featuring violent African-American women, and *Set It Off* explicitly explores the way that racial issues are intimately linked with issues of femininity and cultural definitions of violence.[43] American film has often used aggression as a characteristic of black femininity in order to contrast with the idea of passive white femininity. In "Waiting to Set It Off: African American Women and the Sapphire Fixation," Kimberly Springer explains this historical tradition and considers the implications of this history on the contemporary violent black woman. She argues: "In U.S. cinema, the violence of Black women always seems a result of their being Black, while the violence of white women is often celebrated as liberatory."[44] In general the stereotypical depiction of a black woman fell into various types that either left out sexuality, such as the mammy or maid character, or overemphasized sexuality, such as the sapphire or mulatto characters. These oversexualized characters were the ones most likely to use violence, which would usually hasten their tragic end. Clearly the Blaxploitation heroines were very sexualized but their characterizations were far more complex and thus began to move away somewhat from the Classical Hollywood stereotypes. The image of the contemporary violent black woman, then, has this history to contend with, but like the violent white woman, her violence also works to destabilize traditional ideas about femininity. Certainly, films no longer portray white women as passive or pure, especially in the case of the violent heroine. Thus, it is difficult to entirely condemn the image of the violent black woman as completely relying on racist traditions of aggressive black femininity when violent white femininity today more and more signifies power and strength. Also not willing to completely dismiss black female violence on film, Springer says: "I believe that a celebration of the violent African American woman on-screen is contingent upon the outcome of that violence."[45] Whether or not he is completely successful with *Set It off*, F. Gary Gray does at least attempt to carefully navigate these contemporary issues regarding black femininity and violence.

In the beginning of the film, Gray provides detailed reasons why these average women are so angry. In general, he tries to show that these four women turn to violence, not because it is somehow intrinsic to their racial identity, but instead he shows that the violence is a reaction to racial and class injustices. Furthermore, the violence is an anathema to the majority of the women. Frankie (Vivica Fox), for example, loses her job when the bank she works for is robbed, and because the bank robber grew up in the same area as she, the bank makes the blatantly racist assumption that Frankie was in on the robbery. Stony (Jada Pinkett) is forced into having sex with a man she hates in order to get enough money for her younger brother to go to college, and then the police brutally murder her brother in a case of mistaken identity. Tisean (Kimberly Elise) loses her son to child services because they feel she left him in an unsafe environment when she brought him to her janitorial job at a large office building (because she couldn't afford a babysitter). And Cleo (Queen Latifah) is their tough friend who wants more money and respect in life.

The four friends respond to this violence very differently. In fact, their varied approaches to violence represent a majority of the ways that violent women are depicted in film. Tisean is scared and timid even during their gun practice. She recoils from violence and handles a gun tentatively. As she experiences the violence and the money it brings them, however, she becomes more sure of herself. During one robbery she discovers a bank customer with a gun and disarms him. And eventually when a man they know steals their money, Tisean kills him because he is holding a gun to Cleo's head. While she is the most reluctant to take up violence—because she has always been a more passive person—she embraces violence in the end as the only gesture that can appropriately express her anger and bring about changes in her life. Tisean thus embodies precisely what is most horrifying about the idea of a violent woman. Once she becomes a little violent, there seems to be no stopping her, no point at which her increasing violence ends.

Frankie also illustrates the danger of the woman who turns to violence. Unlike Tisean, Frankie takes up her violence against banks with glee because of the way her former employer treated her. Her violence is aimed solely at institutions (like banks and government bureaucrats) and thus seems much more political rather than personal. Through Frankie's story, the film supports Springer's observation that "the capitalist, white patriarchy provokes them to commit a bank robbery by pushing them over the

edge of social disenfranchisement."[46] Cleo seems to really enjoy
the violence and the power that comes with it. Her *jouissance* is
obvious in one scene when she dances around with her gun after
their first robbery. It is only through Cleo that the film investigates the possibility of a woman enjoying aggression. It is no surprise then that Cleo's character is also totally embedded in
various stereotypes which work to explain and thus contain this
jouissance. First, Cleo is the only woman of the four involved in
the gangsta street life that is often depicted as the environment
within which they all live. Cleo seems to emulate the male
gangstas, and indeed it is Cleo who has the contacts to help them
find guns and learn to use them. Cleo is masculinized in various
ways. She dresses in a masculine way, is heavier than the other
women, and speaks more crudely. She is also a lesbian, which the
other women spend some time discussing and commenting on.
Thus, her violent *jouissance* is not threatening when presented
within this entire image, which positions her far from the average
heterosexual and feminine woman.

Questions of the violent woman's sexuality often work toward
this kind of containment. Films featuring violent women investigate—at the level of form and content—the complexities of many
American cultural tensions, such as representations of race and
gender, but they also just as often rely on stereotypes in an attempt
to contain the trauma of the violent women. Lynda Hart convincingly details in *Fatal Women: Lesbian Sexuality and the Mark of Aggression* the ways in which lesbian representation is so often
combined with out-of-control aggression and vice versa. Hart suggests that the representation of the violent lesbian woman, "functions [. . .] as a specialized and hence containable category."[47] Most
of the mainstream films featuring violent women, which I discuss,
do not explicitly depict lesbian sexuality. Even still, there are a few
that do refer to lesbianism as a reason for aggressive behavior, such
as *Basic Instinct*, *G.I. Jane* and *Courage under Fire*. *Bound* is the only
film with violent women that depicts a lesbian relationship and
does not explicitly link the female violence with lesbianism. Instead, it could be argued, in *Bound* the female violence is more
linked to the history of the femme fatale as the narrative and mise-
en-scène are steeped in the traditions of film noir. Patricia White's
argument that lesbianism can be read in many Classical Hollywood

films through the depictions of out of the ordinary women as well as through the excessive glamorization of the female star can be expanded here to also encompass films depicting violent women. Many viewers and critics, for example, read *Thelma and Louise* as a love story even though this was never explicit. In *Thelma and Louise* when two women commit violence together it seems to bring them closer and express underlying sexual tension. Seen in this light, Cleo's lesbian identity in *Set It Off* may also prevent the other women from forming these close bonds. In this way, Cleo's clearly defined sexuality, which is stereotypically coded as masculine and aggressive, stands in contrast and thus defines the other heterosexual women.

Cleo's violence, however, is not wholly unthreatening. Consequently, the police brutally kill her at the end of the film—as she is making her getaway from the last robbery. Her death reassures audiences that such a woman will not live or threaten people for very long. Frankie and Tisean also die in a similar manner.

Stony is the one woman who escapes successfully to Mexico. She is able to live, I would argue, because she was the one who least enjoyed the robberies and desperately wanted to raise herself to a middle-class status. Unlike the other women, she doesn't seem headed down the one-way street of female violence. During the film she meets an upper-class banker, Keith (Blair Underwood), who falls in love with her. Even though Stony avoids the destruction that befalls her friends, this romance does not work out in the end—her violence precludes the possibility. But for the failure of the romance, the ending of this film mirrors almost precisely Delmer Daves' *Dark Passage* (1947), which also depicts a fugitive involved in a romantic relationship. In the film, Vincent Ferry (Humphrey Bogart) eludes the police by getting on a bus headed out of town (as does Stony in *Set It Off*). The last scene of *Dark Passage* depicts Irene Jansen (Lauren Bacall), his love interest, meeting him at a café in Mexico in an impossible yet utterly predictable reunion. In other words, it seems like fate for the violent male protector to be romantically united with the woman he protects. Even though Bogart is a fugitive, the film rewards him with Bacall's love. Stony, however, must brave it alone, because no matter how wonderful Keith is, the film cannot conceive of him meeting her at a café in Mexico to live happily ever after. *Set It Off* ends with a last phone call that Stony makes to Keith from Mexico, in which silence is the prevailing form of communication. Within this silence lies the impossibility of their relationship—their noncomplementarity. Keith loves her but does not know how to proceed because their relationship seems utterly impossible. Similarly, the violent woman intrigues contemporary American filmmakers, but they do not have an easy time inserting her into the traditional narrative: she throws a wrench into the cogs of narrative by disrupting the very complementarity upon which it is based. Stony drives off in a jeep in Mexico, Bridget rides through New York City in a limousine, and Karen drives her would-be lover to jail. All remain on the move precisely because the narrative cannot find a way to integrate their violence.

CHAPTER 5

Violent Women in Love

There are exceptions to violent women being automatically barred from romance in Hollywood films. There are a handful of films that conclude with the violent woman in a romantic union, but what one immediately notices is the great lengths to which these films go in order to unite the violent woman and the male hero romantically. In the films that yoke the violent woman with a romantic interest, the circumstances surrounding the woman's violence and the constitution of the romantic couple indicate the effect that a violent woman has on a film: often the traditional Hollywood film form is disrupted, traditional gender roles are completely reversed, or the woman's violence is split from her femininity. The films I will discuss in detail—Oliver Stone's *Natural Born Killers* (1994), Kathryn Bigelow's *Strange Days* (1995), the Coen Brothers' *Fargo* (1996), and Roger Spottiswoode's *Tomorrow Never Dies* (1997)—share a fantastical edge, a separation from normal everyday life, that allows respite from the trauma of the violent woman. In a fantastical context, films can address and experiment with social contradictions without implicating viewers in what results. This kind of exploration—regardless of how it is shrouded in fantasy—allows these films to reveal further the significance of the violent woman. Each one opens up myriad issues that surround the violent woman and her impact, both filmically and culturally.

One of the most outlandish romantic unions in any Hollywood film can be found in Oliver Stone's *Natural Born Killers* (1994). The film was controversial both because of the extreme violence it depicts and because of its unconventional style. The plot has its origins in the story of Bonnie and Clyde. This story first entered the public imagination in the early 1930s, when the real Bonnie and Clyde became notorious criminals and eventually died at the hands of the police. *Natural Born Killers* follows a similar story line, like other films modeled on the exploits of this couple: Fritz Lang's *You Only Live Once* (1937), Nicholas Ray's *They Live By Night* (1948), Joseph H. Lewis' *Gun Crazy* (1949), and Arthur Penn's *Bonnie and Clyde* (1967). In each case, the couple goes on a crime spree and engages in escalating violence as the film progresses. In the depiction of this crime spree, the films distribute the violence almost equally between the woman and the man. Most importantly, each film ends with the police shooting the couple to death. *Natural Born Killers* follows this narrative line very closely—albeit modernized for the 1990s—except for the ending in which the couple escapes from the police and walks off together in the romantic union that concludes so many Hollywood films. This initially seems like a radical departure from the earlier versions of the story—a departure that indicates a massive change in thinking. But this ending does not indicate that America in the 1990s—unlike in earlier decades—could accept the idea of the violent woman in a complementary love relationship. Instead, the romantic ending is possible because of the very form of the film itself, that is, the wild, postmodern-style editing (which includes noncontinuity editing, random switching between black and white and color film, using cartoon and other films to represent the state of mind of the characters, and so on). But before explaining this, it is important to understand more completely the influence of the prototype: the actual Bonnie and Clyde story.

Bonnie and Clyde burst into the public eye during the bleak years of the Great Depression in February 1932, gaining notoriety for a series of crimes that the press reported with great zeal. (Every film about the couple repeats this last aspect of the story.) The public during this time was caught up in the exploits of several famous criminals, such as John Dillinger, Baby Face Nelson, Machine-Gun Kelly, and the Barker Gang. At the same time, the gangster film was one of Hollywood's most popular genres. In "Bonnie and Clyde: Tradition and Transformation," John Calwelti points out the clear link between these phenomena: "Public fascination with Bonnie and

Clyde, and with the other rampaging criminal gangs of the late-1920s and early-1930s, helped to make the gangster film one of Hollywood's most important and typical creations."[1] The original films based on the real Bonnie and Clyde were not as controversial as later ones (such as Penn's *Bonnie and Clyde* and Stone's *Natural Born Killers*). The original films (*You Only Live Once, They Live By Night,* and *Gun Crazy*) came out during a time when gangster films proliferated, and thus the audience understood them as embedded in this genre. Of course, the real Bonnie and Clyde did capture the public's imagination, as the public both feared Bonnie and Clyde and adored them as celebrities. This fascination with Bonnie and Clyde indicates both people's need to be diverted from daily hardships and people's desire for a kind of symbolic allegiance with Bonnie and Clyde as outlaws rebelling against the banks and police. I would like to suggest, however, that by hysterically discussing and reporting their exploits, the society at the time also displaced the anxiety that the violent woman fomented, as it tried to discover or invent an agreed-upon symbolic position for Bonnie and Clyde's violence.

When Arthur Penn's *Bonnie and Clyde* generated controversy and debate in 1967, the story became important again. This film fascinated the general public, and it did well at the box office, even though initially critics panned the film. The loudest criticism focused on the violence. Even today, many critics contend that *Bonnie and Clyde* is one of the films that pushed film to an entirely new level of violence. In *A Cinema of Loneliness*, Robert Kolker claims: "Penn showed the way. *Bonnie and Clyde* opened the bloodgates, and our cinema has barely stopped bleeding since."[2] The violence of *Bonnie and Clyde* traumatized its audiences while at the same time mesmerizing them. Arthur Penn filmed violence more graphically and more realistically than previous filmmakers. Kolker points out that this new type of graphic violence concentrated on depicting anatomical detail that could evoke a sense of immediacy and provoke a physical reaction in the audience. But it is not just a coincidence that one of the major films credited with changing the violent nature of cinema featured a violent woman. I would contend that it was Bonnie's violence that pushed the violence from disturbing to traumatic. Although unfamiliar with Penn's new filmic approach, viewers were certainly used to Clyde's male violence, but Bonnie's violence represented an imbalance in the normal relationship between masculinity and femininity. In the film, Bonnie is unafraid of shooting a gun, just as involved in the bank robberies as Clyde, and is clearly not remorseful about her violent activity; in fact she appears to have enjoyed them. Her violence increases the tension in the couple's romance because it emphasizes the noncomplementarity between masculinity and femininity.[3] By contradicting femininity, Bonnie's violence disrupts the status of masculinity. Thus, we experience the film's graphic violence not only as more visceral and gruesome, but also as violence that undermines our traditional understanding of masculinity and femininity.

Stone's *Natural Born Killers* clearly owes a debt to Penn's film. In Stone's film, female violence also heightens the tension and the trauma of the plot. Clearly, female violence is not the only reason for the impact that this film had on its viewers, but I do believe that the female violence pushes the narrative tensions to a much higher level. Like *Bonnie and Clyde*, the violence in *Natural Born Killers* is extremely graphic and frequent. With *Bonnie and Clyde*, Penn's film critiques the relationship between film and television viewers and violence. He was also making reference to violent events that the public had recently experienced, such as the Kennedy assassination. Similarly, Oliver Stone's film captures America's involvement in and relationship with violence on television and in film. He was also making reference to—both metaphorically and literally, through actual news footage at the end of the film—recent violent events that had gripped the nation, including the Menendez brothers' killing of their parents, Tonya Harding's attempt to eliminate her competition in the skating world, the Rodney King beating, the Los Angeles riots, and the O. J. Simpson case. Penn—heavily influenced by French New Wave filmmakers—approached his critique through unconventional narrative and filmic styles that heightened the extremity of the violence and further implicated the viewer in this violence. Stone also looked toward recent, albeit more popular, media styles—specifically the editing and camera work from MTV music videos—to help underline his critique and intensify the experience of the violence.[4]

The experience of the film owes much to the film form itself. In order to understand the possible impact of the violent woman on film form, I believe it is not only productive, but also essential to introduce the psychoanalytic concept of psychosis into this discus-

sion. The filmic form of *Natural Born Killers* provides a compelling
example of how psychosis can manifest itself on the level of form.
Indeed, it would be hard to find a better example of a psychotic film
form than that of *Natural Born Killers*. According to Lacan, psychosis
involves the foreclosure of the Name of the Father. That is to say, in
the case of the psychotic, the symbolic Father does not lay down the
Law successfully, which leaves the psychotic not fully integrated
into the symbolic order, stuck in the realm of the imaginary. The
psychotic subject thus has a different relationship to language, to the
signifier, than the "normal" subject. In his *Seminar III* on psychosis,
Lacan says, "compared to you the psychotic has this disadvantage,
but also this privilege, of finding himself a little bit at odds with,
askew in relation to, the signifier."[5] For nonpsychotic subjects, the
signifier represents the signified, but these subjects also understand
that while the signifier allows you access to the signified—what is
meant—it also acts as a mediator and thus as a barrier to the signified. In other words, it is understood that we can't ever "know" the
signified, but our solace is that at least we can interact with each
other and the world through the signifier (language), even though
this *lacks* immediacy.[6] Thus, nonpsychotic subjects relate to the signifier, not to the meaning of the signifier (the signified). Psychotics,
however, are not fully integrated into the functioning of the symbolic order and thus feel as though they relate to the meaning or the
signified directly—and therefore have an ambiguous relationship to
the signifier. For psychotics, language is elusive. Signifiers seem to
slip and slide off their objects because there is no Law to anchor
them, no Name of the Father to act as a quilting point.[7] In his *A Clinical Introduction to Lacanian Psychoanalysis*, Bruce Fink recounts a
psychotic patient's comments:

> "Words frighten me. I've always wanted to write, but couldn't
> manage to put a word on a thing. . . . It was as though words
> slipped off things." Of course, Roger never manages to "pos-
> sess" them all—that is, stop them from "slipping off things"—
> for there is no anchoring point for him that could ever tie word
> to thing, or, more precisely, signifier to signified. In the absence
> of the fundamental button tie that links the father's name or
> "No!" with the mother's desire, words and meanings, signifiers
> and signifieds, are condemned to drift aimlessly.[8]

Although this example pertains to writing, it is translatable to cinema. The multiple images employed in *Natural Born Killers* (one action is often repeated several times in different angles and colors), for example, seem to slip off their signifieds. These repetitions do not clarify the action, nor do they purposely depict another person's point of view of the action. Instead, the repetitions seem arbitrary and disorienting, as if the film can't quite secure what it wants to say, what it wants to signify. It is as if the action exists, but the film has trouble representing the action—the signifier keeps slipping off the signified. This is apparent in the very first scene of *Natural Born Killers*. The first few shots of this scene are not traditional but by no means signal anything totally atypical. These shots merely set up the environment: a black and white shot of the empty Texas road, a rattlesnake flicking its tongue, a red-toned shot of a train riding by, and an establishing shot of the name of the diner where Mickey (Woody Harrelson) and Mallory (Juliette Lewis) are eating. In the diner, the film uses a typical shot-reverse shot sequence to depict the conversation between a waitress and Mickey. The first indication of a break from traditional Hollywood film form occurs when, following a question by the waitress, there is a repetition of that same question in black and white in a shot that is done slightly closer and with a lower angle. This repetition is clearly part of the filmic form but not part of the linear time within the narrative—that is, part of the discourse but not part of the story. This is the first sense we have that the signifier is not sure of its signified. We are shown a different version of the signified, but it is not another point of view (from a character's perspective, for example). It registers, instead, as extra signifying. This process continues throughout the scene. Mallory leaves Mickey in order to dance in front of the jukebox, and as she passes one of the booths, a man sitting there stares at her and then disappears into thin air. After she has also passed a truck driver who leers at her, Mallory begins to dance, and Mickey—in a black and white close-up—turns in slow motion to look at her proudly. The nonrealistic events (such as the man disappearing), the black and white shots mixed with the color shots, and the slow motion shot are indicative of the kinds of disruptions of form that escalate throughout the film.

The ambiguity and the slippery nature of the signifier is obvious in the way that Stone edits together the action sequences as well. As the first scene progresses, Mallory battles with the two hunters who have come into the diner. After arriving, they begin to taunt her and make sexual passes at her. The camera angles and color change wildly and rapidly. This section of the scene is also a good example of how the film depicts Mallory's violence (and the pleasure she obtains from it).[9] The young hunter behaves lewdly toward Mallory, and Mallory replies, "Are you flirting with me?" A juxtaposition of differently colored and angled shots follows: starting with a color close-up shot of the record changing, then cutting to a black and white close-up of the younger hunter drinking, smiling, and finally appearing stunned when Mallory punches him in the face. The next shot is a low-angle, color shot that finishes the motion of Mallory's punch. Finally, we see Mallory's face as she laughs with pleasure and punches him again. There is a wildness about Mallory in this scene. She seems to be completely fearless and enjoying this violence. The young hunter says, "You want a piece of me darlin, do ya?" And she retaliates in a black and white medium-long shot, punching him again and then stepping back, spreading her arms wide, shaking her hips, and shouting, "Your move, your move, fucker," as she laughs and laughs. The young hunter hits Mallory in the face, and she responds by punching and kneeing him. Provocatively, the black and white and color, as well as the different camera angles, seem to be battling each other as much as the people are battling each other. The viewer understands the fight is happening and understands the progression of the fight, but can't obtain a good grasp on what it actually looks like. We are oddly both too close to the action (in the ever changing close-ups from different angles) and too far from it (the disconnectedness alienates us from the signifiers themselves). This puts us precisely in the position of the psychotic. As Slavoj Žižek explains in *The Indivisible Remainder*, "psychosis is characterized precisely by the paradoxical coincidence of over proximity and externality."[10] Thus, this wild editing and shooting brings a psychotic dimension to both the scene and Mallory's violence.[11] This psychotic form functions as a defense mechanism to the violent woman in love, or, one might even say, the violent woman provokes it. In other words, *Natural Born Killers* depicts the love relationship between a violent woman and man as disrupting the traditional film form and manifesting itself in a turn toward psychosis.[12]

Moreover, the film also indicates to us on the level of narrative and mise-en-scène that we are not supposed to take this couple seriously, which is best underscored in the first scene of the film. At the end of this scene, Mickey and Mallory kill all the people in the diner except for a truck driver. After they have killed all the others, the camera turns to the truck driver who begins to back away looking extremely nervous. Mallory says to him, "When those people come here and they ask you who done this, you say Mickey and Mallory Knox did it. All right, say it." The truck driver understands that he is to live and—looking nervous—repeats this phrase. Mallory exclaims again, "Mickey and Mallory Knox did it," enjoying the feel of those words. She then jumps on Mickey saying, "I love you Mickey" and he returns, "I love you Mallory." The film then cuts to a close up of the truck driver who, looking at this display of affection, leans back and opens his eyes wide completely terrified at what he sees. He is most terrified when he sees them attempt to be a loving couple, rather than when he wasn't sure if he'd live. At this point, the truck driver *knows he will live*, and yet he is nonetheless completely overcome with horror. He has this reaction—the reaction we as audience members are meant to identify with, or at least understand—because Mickey and Mallory's complementarity seems impossible. In other words, the film presents the coupling of a violent male with a violent female as wholly terrifying, destructive, and uncontrollable, both through the story line and the film form. At this point in the scene, the music changes from hard rock to soft romantic music, and the film changes to color, as Mickey and Mallory spin around and around in each other's arms. The lighting fades and they are backlit until the scene fades into fireworks. This over-the-top mise-en-scene seems to indicate further how ridiculous and impossible this couple actually is. Their love becomes comical.[13]

Natural Born Killers takes place in a psychotic world; the violence that the film depicts is as extreme as its characters are fantastical. There are, however, less extreme films where the violent woman ends up in a romance. I will now turn to two of these films which—although very different in every other regard—depict the violent woman, in relation to masculinity and femininity, in a similar way: Kathryn Bigelow's *Strange Days* (1995) and the Joel Coen's *Fargo* (1996). Both films are able to depict the violent woman in a romantic union because they enact a symbolic reversal of roles that the characters take up. Not only do the violent women in these films occupy masculine roles, but their male partners also take up feminine positions. Reversing the roles in this way allows the relationship to be complementary because symbolically the biological woman who is violent is actually occupying the structural position of the violent male protector; this is validated because she has a feminine, nonviolent male who needs protection. This reversal, which functions as a mechanism of defense on the part of the narrative itself, indicates the traumatic status of the violent woman who necessitates it.

In *Strange Days*, the violent woman literally occupies the position of protector. Mace (Angela Bassett) is a bodyguard and protects her friend Lenny (Ralph Fiennes) throughout the film. Lenny, an ex-cop kicked off the force, sells virtual reality clips of "real life" on the street. These clips allow people to experience what the person who recorded an event experienced—as Lenny explains it to a client, "pure and uncut straight from the cerebral cortex." In the film, Lenny is akin to a drug pusher, both in the way he has to sell the clips (making deals in alleys and in the back rooms of bars) and in the flashy yet tacky clothes that he wears. Far from being ultramasculine and violent, however, Lenny escapes difficult situations through charm. He is totally emotional (especially about an ex-girlfriend who no longer wants to see him) and is not aggressive. Throughout the film, a variety of characters easily knock him around—and do not seem to exert much energy when they do so. At one point in the film, Lenny tries to act heroically (i.e., in a masculine way) when he attempts to save his ex-girlfriend Faith (Juliette Lewis) from her current boyfriend, Philo Gant (Michael Wincott).[14] Lenny's attempt to be a "man" prompts incredulity on the part of Faith, who says to him, "What are you going to do? Protect me? You're a talker. You don't even have a gun." As Faith walks away, Lenny protests by saying that he has a gun now, and he mutters under his breath that it's under his bed. But clearly, whether or not Lenny actually had a handgun would not matter to Faith. What Faith is really saying is that Lenny does not have the phallus—he is not masculine enough—and therefore he cannot protect her. Instead, he has the stereotypically feminine "gift of gab," which does on occasion get him where he wants to go, but more often than not gets him into more trouble.

On this particular occasion, when Lenny tries to save his ex-girlfriend, he winds up in trouble: led to a basement where a group of Philo's bodyguards are waiting. Lenny does not put up a struggle. They easily hold him while a female bodyguard pummels him, and the two male bodyguards joke about this reversal. Mace, however, has been waiting for Lenny and suddenly appears on the scene to save him. In a dramatic close-up that emphasizes her strength and agility, Mace catches the female bodyguard's hand before she is able to throw a punch. Then, Mace very quickly and violently demolishes all three bodyguards. Lenny recovers from his beating and manages in the end to crash a chair over the female bodyguard before she attacks Mace. It is obvious, however, that Mace could have handled it on her own, since she has just incapacitated the two large male bodyguards. As they run out, Lenny stops and runs back to kick one of the male bodyguards in the stomach. This gesture emphasizes Lenny's awareness of his lack of masculinity, as well as the comic contradiction between Mace's bravery and Lenny's timidity. These scenes are shot and directed, however, in such a way that the comic aspects of his lack of masculinity come across as endearing rather than as farcical. This is significant because rather than create a reversal of roles which seems over the top or too obvious, the film shows the complexities of these characters and presents them as alternatives to the more traditional action heroes.

Kathryn Bigelow seems to be constantly working toward such complexities—all of which, I would argue, are attached to or provoked in one way or another by the violent woman. For example, just as Arthur Penn unfolds the Bonnie and Clyde story in front of the hardships of the Great Depression, Mace and Lenny's story is inextricably tied to the racial strife and tension that had its apotheosis in the 1992 Los Angeles riots. Christina Lane first suggests this in her "The Strange days of Kathryn Bigelow and James Cameron," when she points out that "if extreme racial tensions served as *Strange Days'* backdrop when Lenny first acquaints us with his millennial milieu, they prove to be the ultimate source of conflict in this world of virtuality, violence, and paranoia."[15] As in the case in both Penn's *Bonnie and Clyde* and Stone's *Natural Born Killers*, the violent woman—a mélange of cultural meanings that threaten either the complete destruction of or the complete re-commitment to the social—seems an unsurprising response. On the verge of social destruction, whether through class or racial antagonism, these films turn toward exploring sexual antagonism through the violent

woman. These films suggest that, in the face of class or racial antagonism tearing apart the social, it becomes easier to focus on sexual
antagonism. As such, they are evidence of Hollywood's specialty in
overcoming such difference through romance. The execution of
Bonnie and Clyde and the uniting of Mace and Lenny momentarily
divert the trauma of the more immediate sociohistorical traumas.

Mace certainly embodies many of the traits of a traditional action
hero. Her body is physically athletic and muscled. She does not show
nor discuss her emotions easily but instead communicates through
action. She is in love with Lenny but will not tell him, especially because she sees he remains obsessed with Faith. She manages, however, to rescue him out of every difficult situation he gets into and is
willing to help him at every moment. She doesn't offer this help
readily but just "happens" to be there to save him each time. As most
action heroes do, Mace also approaches difficult situations with complete calm and often wit. At one point, Lenny and Mace are trapped
inside a burning car. Mace plunges the car into a river. Lenny franti-
cally remarks that she is out of her mind, and Mace calmly replies,
"The fire's out isn't it?," before she gets them out of the car to safety.
Similar to the traditional action hero, Mace is—besides being witty—
attempting to protect Lenny, who is flustered and in danger. Since
this kind of suave punch line is usually reserved for male heroes
such as Bruce Willis or Arnold Schwarzenegger, here it suggests a
kind of retelling of cinematic history. Mace's comic lines and violent
actions resonate in multiple ways: they point out the absence of black
heroines in the history of cinema, call for more such roles in the future, complicate the plethora of white heroines on screen, all the
while continuing to further complicate general gender expectations.

The reversal of gender roles in this film is not just limited to
Mace's work as a bodyguard. On one occasion, Lenny needs to retrieve a "virtual clip" from his car that has been repossessed. To
reach the car, they need to break into a fenced area. It is Mace who
uses her strength to cut the lock to the fence and then incapacitate
the guard dog while Lenny stands by and waits. Thus, even in the
nonviolent circumstances, Mace takes up the more typically masculine activities and Lenny takes up the feminine. One could imagine
Lenny acting like an equal partner in these adventures, but instead
he steps back and lets Mace do all the physical work.

In addition, the film portrays the characters as fully aware of their roles. In one particular scene, two corrupt police officers attack them, and Lenny begins to protest as he and Mace make a difficult escape. But Mace says to him, "Calm down baby, this is what *I do*." Later, Mace wonders how they will get into the most elite New Year's Eve party—in order to save Faith and themselves—and Lenny says, "Don't worry, this is what *I do best*." Lenny's skills clearly lie in charm and talk, and these more feminine traits are emphasized throughout the film. This in turn serves to emphasize the complementary relationship between his feminine attributes and Mace's masculine attributes.[16] The violent woman with male characteristics protecting a nonviolent man with female characteristics creates a sense of complementarity and can thus be seen as a defense mechanism that ensures that the woman's violence does not disrupt the complementarity of the love relationship.

Just such a defense mechanism is also apparent in *Fargo*, an offbeat noirish comedy about a man who has his wife kidnapped in order to procure a large sum of money from her father. The kidnapping plan goes awry when the kidnappers end up killing a state trooper and a couple (who by chance saw the state trooper killed). In the end, the wife, the wife's father, and one of the kidnappers are also murdered. It is Marge Gunderson (Frances McDormand), the Chief of Police in Brainerd, Minnesota, who is in charge of solving the case and apprehending the kidnappers. Marge seems in every way to be an average woman, except that she is a police chief and seven months pregnant. Otherwise, her hair and clothes reflect the styles of a stereotypically average white middle-class Midwestern woman. Yet, she takes up the masculine position within her marriage. Marge's husband Norm Gunderson (John Carroll Lynch), a painter who stays at home and cooks all the meals, clearly takes up the feminine position in this relationship.

The first time we see Marge, a phone call wakes her in the early morning, summoning her to investigate the triple homicide. Her husband makes a big deal about making her breakfast before she leaves. This is a clear reversal from most relationships in film and television, in which the husband is off to work and the wife is in her nightgown making breakfast, sending kids to school. In this case, Norm makes breakfast, and later he brings Marge's lunch to work. He seems generally uninterested in her police work and more interested instead in taking care of her. He also seems more excited than Marge about the baby who is about to be born. At the end of the film, he pats her pregnant belly and says, "two more months," while she reassuringly touches his arm.

Throughout the film, Norm is the one who displays the most typical feminine emotions. Marge, on the other hand, seems wholly unafraid of violence and death, and she is very capable of dealing with difficult situations in a very determined, business-like manner. She is also concerned that Norm is happy and encourages him in his painting, but in the way that one encourages a child to continue a hobby. The most dramatic scene, which depicts her calm approach to violence, is the one in which she apprehends the killer. She discovers Gaare Grindrud (Peter Stormare) shoving body parts into a wood chipper. The film reveals no shock on her face; instead, she draws her gun and calmly approaches. Grindrud throws a piece of wood at her and runs. She shoots once and misses, but then shoots him in the leg—at which time she deftly arrests him. This calm and efficient demeanor in the face of the most vicious violence and depraved criminal activity typically characterizes the male hero, but here it is part of the personality of a seven-months-pregnant female police chief. Marge's pregnancy is a constant physical intrusion into every scene, and it is present even though it is not an important part of the plot. Indeed, her pregnancy neither affords her special privileges, nor does it stop her from doing anything (including apprehending the most vicious criminal). It is, however, always present, and as Carol Dole notes, in her essay on the "female lawman," "The image of a uniformed police officer holding a gun above her swollen belly complicates gendered categories."[17] Similarly, Norm Gunderson, while a painter and a caretaker, also enjoys fishing, which can be seen as a traditionally male characteristic. The complex combinations of the male and female characters in these two films come out of the films' attempt to both allow for complementarity which includes the violent woman and to still keep the characters within more traditional roles. And although the more obvious result is a reversal of gender roles, the overall outcome is far more complex and provocative than most other depictions of violent women.

Andy and Larry Wachowski's *The Matrix* (1999) provides a similarly complex example of gender relations. Neo (Keanu Reeves), the violent hero, and Trinity (Carrie-Anne Moss), one of his violent comrades, fight evil enemy agents throughout the film as equal partners. Throughout the film, each feels an attraction to the other, but they do not become lovers. *The Matrix*, however, unites the violent woman and man by the end of the film rather than barring them from romance. The defense mechanisms in *The Matrix* are similar to *Strange Days*: *The Matrix* takes place in a science fiction future in which very little is "real," and the enemy is more akin to lines of computer code than to actual aliens. Obviously, this futuristic vision allows the viewer distance from the figure of the violent woman. But the most interesting defense against the trauma of the violent woman is the status of Neo in relation to masculinity. By the conclusion of the film, Neo learns that he is "the One." That is to say, Neo is the savior who will rescue humanity from its thralldom. In the climactic battle of the film, Neo gains the ability to defy space and time, to dodge bullets and move effortlessly.

As "the One," the savior of the world, Neo is not subject to castration; he doesn't experience the lack that constitutes us as subjects. Instead, he is the ideal man, the exception to the Law of castration against which every other man measures himself. Because he occupies this position outside the symbolic Law, Neo *can* achieve a romantic union with a violent woman such as Trinity. He is "the One," or so *The Matrix* implies, who has the potency to handle the violent woman. Hence, even though *The Matrix* seems to testify to the possibility of the violent woman's reinsertion into a complementary relationship, it actually illustrates most powerfully our inability to conceive of such a relationship. It is possible only with the man qua exception, the man not subject to castration.

Andy and Larry Wachowski's *The Matrix Reloaded* (2003) continues this investigation, presenting Neo and Trinity now as lovers. Until the end of the film, Trinity actually has much less involvement in the action than she does in *The Matrix*. Instead, the film presents her love as that which sustains Neo's strength and sanity—that is, she provides the savior of the world with a reason to live rather than actually being the savior herself. Indeed, throughout the film Neo dreams repeatedly of Trinity's death at the hands of one of the agents, an event which traumatizes him and motivates his actions. In the end, the film reveals that Neo's status as the One was a creation of the very symbolic structure (the Matrix) that he thought he was contesting. Neo discovers that the Matrix needed and depended on Neo occupying an outside position. When the prophecy turns out to be orchestrated in this way, Neo's potency seems undone. At the same time, however, it allows him to save Trinity from the death he had been foreseeing. I would argue that Trinity's diminished role in the action (though she still does have some involvement in the violent battles) is due to the films attempt to conceive of Neo and Trinity as a permanent couple. By the end, *The Matrix Reloaded* keeps the violent couple together, and yet the final frame (which reads: "To be concluded") contradicts the importance of this ending by suggesting that this story is not over and that perhaps this couple will not be able to endure—and indeed it cannot, as Trinity's death before the denouement of *The Matrix Revolutions* (2003) attests.

Because of its daring attempt to truly bring the violent woman and man together in a realistic love relationship, Karyn Kusama's *Girlfight* (2000) is perhaps the most intriguing depiction thus far of a violent woman in American film. Diana Guzman (Michelle Rodriguez), a working-class angry teenager, takes up boxing as a way to release her anger, find self worth, and ultimately discover a profession.[18] While training, Diana falls in love with Adrian (Santiago Douglas), a young male boxer, and their relationship is put to the test when they must fight each other in a professional fight. Diana wins the fight; and this puts an end to their relationship until the end of the film when they reunite. The last scene is emotional, as they each struggle to get beyond the gender definitions that have previously kept them apart. Their split, and all their previous difficulties in their relationship, revolves around Diana's boxing. Unlike Adrian's first girlfriend in the film, who seems far more feminine than Diana, Diana's violence (and more masculine appearance) threatens Adrian's masculinity. Nonetheless, the film makes it clear that these are also attributes that he loves about her. In the end, Diana has—through boxing—worked through her personal anger and now continues to box as a professional athlete. Similar to a policewoman or a government agent, a professional athlete embraces aggression (and sometimes violence) as a means to an end—in this case, as a way of advancing in her sport. Thus, Diana's violence becomes, by the very end of the film, folded into the definition of the professional athlete. This de-emphasizes the trauma of her violence, which throughout the majority of the film threatened to tear apart almost every one of her relationships. Karyn Kusama's complex ending and sincere depiction of the struggles of an average woman with aggression and violence makes *Girlfight* one of the only films that comes close to uniting the violent woman and the violent man.[19]

I would now like to turn from these more complex violent women in *Fargo, Strange Days, The Matrix*, and *Girlfight* to the far more one-dimensional violent women in James Bond films. Violence and women can scarcely be discussed without at some point mentioning the Bond films. The most well-known characteristic of a Bond female character is her sensuous sexuality. But she is also often one of the villains who try to kill James Bond. Typically, of course, Bond sleeps with her and then either incapacitates her or woos her over to his side (at least long enough to save his life and complete his mission). Certainly, there is one guarantee about James Bond: he will always be with a new female—or two—in the next James Bond film. The audience knows this because of Bond's track record in the twenty films that have been made. Bond also spends a good amount of time in his films protecting innocent women (and entering into sexual relationships with them either before, during, or after protecting them). In this way, he plays out the traditional role of the masculine protector, and illustrates that this is tied to masculine prowess. In a recent Bond film entitled *Tomorrow Never Dies* (1998), however, Bond (Pierce Brosnan) encounters Mai Lin (Michelle Yeoh), a different woman than James Bond usually encounters. She is an undercover agent for the Chinese government and is on her own independent mission. She demonstrates throughout the film that she is fully capable of violently protecting herself and accomplishing her mission. In the last scene of the film, they kiss, and the film indicates that they are about to slip away for a lover's holiday after their exhausting mission. How is it that this romantic ending, this suggestion of complementarity between the violent woman and the violent man, can come about? I would suggest that here the defense against the trauma of the violent woman has everything to do with the form and tradition of romance in the James Bond film, as well as an emerging professionalization of female violence.

In the last half of the film, Bond and Lin have worked together to topple a criminal mastermind (by blowing up his ship), and they end up aboard a large piece of floating wreckage in the middle of the ocean. In typical Bond style, when the rescue boat comes close enough to hear them, they nonchalantly ignore the rescuers and begin to kiss. Although other Hollywood actions or dramas that end with a kiss indicate the beginning of a love relationship, this kiss is ambiguous for several reasons. The most obvious has to do with the formula of a Bond film—or what the audience has learned to expect from a Bond film. Like a genre unto itself, Bond films have an expected plot, familiar icons, and recurring characters. One of these expected traits is the way Bond romances women. The films depict Bond as irresistible to every woman he encounters (both good and evil). In general, however, Bond films create a split between sex and love. Love is tied to a complementary relation between the sexes and promises a sense of eternity. Bond's encounters with women, however, are clearly only sexual and temporary.[20] The sure indication of this is that these women he becomes involved with—even at the end of the film—never show up in the next Bond film. Indeed, no woman that Bond has a love relationship with has ever reappeared in another Bond film.[21] In this light, we know that Bond and Lin's love relationship is most likely only sexual or, at the very least, only temporary and further, it is pointedly *not represented* as the film fades to black before we witness more than a kiss. And this temporality is further emphasized by the fact that they are floating on a piece of wreckage in the middle of the ocean when they kiss. This is not the kind of mise-en-scène that foreshadows a stable and grounded love relationship. Instead, it suggests the adventure-like quality and temporality that characterizes their mission and Bond's past involvement with women. If that is not enough proof of temporality, this encounter filled with cleverness and witty dialogue is also contrasted with an earlier love scene from the film.

Earlier, the film depicts Bond reuniting with his one true love. Inconveniently, she is also married to Bond's criminal antagonist. Bond and she were lovers "long ago," but he walked out on her without even saying goodbye. She indicates that he left because she got "too close." In other words, this was the one woman with whom Bond fell in love, his complementary other. But he couldn't handle this and left. It is possible that to Bond a complementary other would seem to compromise his ability to be a spy, a fighter, or a nation's protector. It is also possible that England *herself* must remain his only complement. In *Tomorrow Never Dies*, when he reunites with his true love (in the first half of the film), he is visibly touched by their lovemaking. Instead of engaging in a playful or simply sensual sexual experience, Bond seems emotionally impacted by her caresses and suggests that he help get her out of the country. In this way, he hints that he would like to try their relationship again, that even Bond is seeking complementarity. Her husband kills her, however, soon after this in an attempt to trap Bond. It is important that Bond's true love is present in the same film in which he ends up kissing his violent female partner at the end of the mission. His true love exists to provide a contrast between the two encounters. The first encounter is the real thing—a union with his one complementary other—while his second encounter is playful and seems more a romantic interlude between friends (or coworkers). The true relationship between Bond and Lin seems to me to lie in their professional or work relationship.

Bond and Lin are agents for different countries going after the same target. Each is independent and accustomed to doing things his and/or her own way, but they find themselves forced into the same situations time and again. They also find that they are a good team, especially when it comes to violently making their way out of a dangerous situation. The film has a great deal of humor and clever dialogue that highlights the nature of their entanglement, especially the tension between his masculinity and her violent femininity. In one scene, they are making an escape on a motorcycle while handcuffed to one another. After both vie for the position of driver, they agree to share and each hold onto a handlebar. When they are being particularly harassed, Bond yells, "Get on the back of the bike." Lin replies sarcastically, "What are you trying to do, protect me?" Bond replies, "No, I need to balance the bike." This dialogue indicates the awareness on the part of the film—and the characters—of the traditional relationship that men and women usually have in such scenarios. The dialogue also suggests that this relationship is different because Bond is not trying to protect her. He doesn't try to protect her because she doesn't need his protection. In a dazzling display of Lin's physical capabilities in a later scene, she disables five or six attackers on her own. Bond happens to come in at the last minute and kills the last one. He then says, "Lucky for you I stopped by." To which she replies, "I could have taken care of him." And then subtly, Bond says under his breath, "Yeah, but you didn't." This scene is somewhat ambiguous because although he does save her in the end, it is clear that she could have handled the situation on her own. In many ways, the banter between them throughout the film can be compared to the banter that takes place between male partners in action films. Often called "buddy films," they are characterized by two, often opposite types who must work together to solve a crime. Throughout their adventures, the two grow to appreciate and even love each other. Much work has been done on the underlying homosexual tones in these films.[22] But the heterosexual makeup of this duo in *Tomorrow Never Dies* allows these mainstream action "buddies" to finally consummate these sexual tensions at the end of the film.

I do not intend here to suggest that Lin is thus just occupying a male role. In fact, unlike in *Fargo* and *Strange Days*, I would say that—outside of her career choice—Lin is much more feminine than Mace or Marge. Lin's petite body, long hair, and pretty face suggest femininity. Her lithe yet violent athleticism contrasts but does not overpower her appearance. Instead, I would suggest that what begins to occur in this film is the professionalization of female violence. In other words, one of the mechanisms of defense this film employs (to defend itself against the threat of the violent woman) is to split the violence from the woman's femaleness.[23] Her violence is just part of her career choice, as government agent, not part of her femininity. *Tomorrow Never Dies* gives us just a taste of the professionalized violent woman. She appears in full flower in the films that depict women in the military.

CHAPTER 6

Femininity on the Front Line

Portrayals of Violent Women in Recent Military Films

The history of American military films is heterogeneous. There are few similarities between the celebration of individual heroism in *Sands of Iwo Jima* (1949), the depiction of allied ingenuity in *The Great Escape* (1962), the recollection of war's psychological toll in *Apocalypse Now* (1979), and the illustration of battle in *Saving Private Ryan* (1998). Nothing but the military experience itself seems to link these films. However, there is one element that unites military films throughout the history of Hollywood: a strong link between masculinity and violence. American military films almost unanimously equate manhood with violence, with the ability to endure violence, and with victory in battle.[1] Despite the transformation of the image of masculinity in military films—from the hyper-masculinized image of John Wayne to the more sensitive and intelligent images of George Clooney, Tom Hanks, and Matt Damon—masculinity's monopoly of violence continues unabated. The salient feature of *Courage Under Fire* (1996) and *G.I. Jane* (1997) is their ability to break this monopoly and associate military violence in some form with femininity.

American military films have a long history of depicting a symbiotic relationship between violence and masculinity, and this is especially so because of the connection between masculinity and violence in the military itself. Yet, more than any other social institution, it is the military that has to deal with the possibility of violent women every day. Instead of a smooth integration, women in the military have provoked questions at every level—from questions about the definition of masculinity and femininity to questions about the very structure and purpose of the military itself. The debate surrounding the role that women should play in the military almost always asks: how can we send our women into the path of fatal violence? The answer from the American public is generally a resounding cry against having women in combat. In truth, however, women have often played some role—albeit unacknowledged—in war (as nurses, transport drivers, test pilots, etc).[2] When these women became involved in combat, the military simply claimed that they weren't, that it was impossible because women weren't allowed in combat. However, this problem became more pronounced in the early 1970s, when the military began the integrated all-volunteer force, which was primarily an attempt to save the military and its depleted numbers (after the cessation of the draft). Women, indeed, did save the military at that time by signing up in large numbers, and presently the military could not operate without its women. Since the beginning of the all-volunteer force, however, the military has faced a conundrum. On the one hand, it needs women to fill positions that would otherwise be empty, but, on the other, women often prove an obstacle to the military's smooth functioning, insofar as that functioning depends upon an investment in patriarchal ideology.

In order to ensure its efficiency, the military needs cohesiveness, and to facilitate this cohesiveness, it has always relied on certain notions about men and women. In this regard, the most important strategy for the military is its reliance on ideas of hyper-masculinity to create a strong homosocial bond between (male) soldiers. This bond forms because women are not allowed and are unable, according to military ideology, to do what the men can do. Women cannot fight, and thus masculinity in the military depends on the exclusivity of men's fighting capabilities. This is perfectly articulated in a 1979 testimony by retired Army Chief of Staff General William Westmoreland, during a bid for a repeal of the law against women in combat: "No man with gumption wants a woman to fight his nation's battles."[3] The image of the man fighting the nation's battles

and protecting the woman at home (who is unable to protect herself) is the image of a complementary relationship between the
sexes, in which each has a particular role to play. That is, the military attitude relies on the image of a complementary female at home
who both supports the male in the military and needs his protection—an image shattered by women in combat. As Cynthia Enloe
concludes in *Sexual Politics At the End of the Cold War*, "women are
voluntarily constructing a feminized 'home front' to complement a
battle front that—thousands of American women soldiers notwith-
standing—is thoroughly masculinized."[4] This is a dichotomy that
the military cannot do without.

The women in the military, however, have complicated this
once unquestioned structure. In the end, the military both cannot
survive without women and yet still feels threatened by their presence. This conflict has only gotten worse as time has passed, because
women in the military have systematically disproved all the reasons
that military ideology has assembled to keep women out of combat.
Women have proven themselves physically, thereby debunking the
idea that women are too weak to be in the military. They have sur-
vived all the most extreme military training, including the rigorous
S.E.R.E. (Survival, Evasion, Resistance, and Escape) Training. And
during the Gulf War two women became the example that proved
that being a female POW is no more horrifying than being a male
POW.[5] Military women have through their actions, successfully re-
futed all of the arguments against allowing women in combat, and
yet the law against it still stands. Currently, the argument for this
law contends that women in combat are a risk to national security
because men themselves cannot emotionally handle women in combat with them. This attitude is exemplified in the president of the
Center for Military Readiness Elaine Donnelly's comment: "The
concept of equality does not fit in combat environments [. . .]
Women in combat units endanger male morale and military performance."[6] Today, then, the only reason women aren't in combat is
because of cultural traditions and stereotypes, not because of biological inadequacies.

This deep-seated fear of women in combat is made explicit—
even on the level of form—in Edward Zwick's *Courage Under Fire*.
The film depicts the military leadership trying to figure out whether
or not Captain Karen Emma Walden (Meg Ryan), who was killed in

the line of duty, deserves a Medal of Honor, or if she actually hindered her crew's valiant attempt at a rescue. (She will be the first woman to win the Medal of Honor if the investigation finds her deserving.) Both the story and the form set out to question the nature of the violent woman in the military. The story is told in a *Rashomon*-like way (in which several renditions of the same event are depicted), as the investigator of the case, Colonel Nat Serling (Denzel Washington), hears the different versions of the story from the men who experienced the event with Walden. The fact that the film relies upon the form made famous by Akira Kurosawa's *Rashomon* (1951) reveals much more than the story itself about a violent woman because *Rashomon* is the quintessential example of the way form can articulate a subject matter as much or more than the film's narrative content. In *Rashomon*, it is the very nature of female desire that seems to provoke the film into depicting multiple versions of the same event, into an investigation about the truth of a woman's rape. That is to say, the form seems driven by the question, "what does woman want?" and how this will affect the men who encounter this desire. Similarly, *Courage Under Fire*'s form seems driven by the same question with a slightly different emphasis: "what happens to society when woman is violent?" The different versions the men describe are depicted visually as well, so that the viewer can see this woman having several reactions to violence. These reactions vary from crying, hysteria, and an inability to decide, to complete calm and the ability to make the right decision. Each man's different story is not only representative of various common beliefs about women and violence, but also serves to illustrate the man's crisis about his own masculinity. Thus, each version asks a different question: Are violent women just faking it, and ultimately will they crumble under the actual pressure of war? Will a woman's violence erase all the other things we like about women? Will men be able to get over their urge to protect women when in war with a violent woman?

The different reactions represent the thoughts of each man in Walden's unit. Thus, the film attempts to suggest how different versions of masculinity would react to the violent woman. Not surprisingly, the man (Manfriez [Lou Diamond Phillips]), who tells the most accusatory story about Walden, is also presented as the most masculine. In each of his appearances in the film, Manfriez's masculinity is continually on display. For instance, Serling conducts the interviews in different spaces (usually wherever he can find Walden's crew), and Manfriez's interview takes place in a boxing gym. As Manfriez tells his version of the story, he is punching a heavy bag or jumping rope. In this ultramasculine environment, Manfriez paints a picture of Walden as a weak, incapable female whose presence put the whole crew at risk. He also manages to make it look as if he was the one who saved the crew. The contrast between masculinity (strong, protective) and femininity (weak, needing to be protected) seems the greatest in Monfriez's version. It is also in Monfriez's version that male and female are the most complementary. In other words, men and women in his story fit into the most traditional stereotypes. It may conflict with the other versions, but it appears the easiest to believe because it conflicts least with traditional views of femininity and violence.[7]

Colonel Serling's relationship with the deceased Walden also works in the service of restoring ideology. In his investigation, Serling concludes that Walden deserves the medal. The investigation also redeems Serling himself, who had been feeling guilt for his actions in the Gulf War. This guilt estranged him from both his family and the United States Army. After the investigation, however, he returns to his family and his military duties, free of the guilt that had plagued him. [8] And Serling also concludes that Walden—although violent—is a good mother, daughter, and caring person who performed heroically in combat. The conclusion of the film reassuringly suggests that the trauma both black masculinity and violent white femininity can pose to society does not really exist, and this is conveniently concluded by the very people who embody those positions.[9]

Thus, the film begins with questions about the violent woman in combat and when these issues are nearly resolved, it reveals that not only was she a good soldier, but also at home Walden was an exemplary mother and daughter. In the space between this question and the eventual answer, however, lies the majority of the film and its insecurity regarding this woman. Often, the ambiguity of the violent woman reveals itself in Walden's own image. For example, when Serling interviews Walden's copilot Rady (Rim Guinee), Rady's girlfriend complains about Walden being too "Butch." At first, Rady chastises his girlfriend, because Walden saved his life, but then he looks at Serling and says—with a knowing wink—that Walden really was very "Butch." According to this account, her violence and valor only make sense if she is not feminine. The film uses what are now typical ways to indicate her nonfemininity. When Walden is depicted as the most masculine—when she is actually rescuing the trapped soldiers—she swears more frequently and is unconcerned with what the others think of her. In her most feminine moments, however, she is unable to make decisions and she starts to cry at the drop of a hat. In this discussion with Rady, however, the filmic image clashes resolutely with his words because Meg Ryan plays Walden. As Rady discusses Walden, the film cuts to an image of her which is meant to confirm the claim that she is "Butch." Meg Ryan is, of course, a petite, pretty blonde with a "girl next door" image, embraced by both Hollywood and America as a leading romantic actress. Even when she is trying her hardest to be "Butch," Ryan's image continues to resonate with the residual signification of her roles in films such as *When Harry Met Sally* (1989) and *Sleepless in Seattle* (1993). Hence, *Courage Under Fire* is ambiguous and contradictory about the violent woman not only on the level of the multiple versions of her actions, but also on the more basic level of matching image with description.

Although Serling ultimately approves issuing to Walden the Medal of Honor, the film still seems relatively ambiguous about women in combat. The film does nonetheless have the virtue of illustrating that the violent woman in combat is a site of crisis for the military and for America, precisely because violence is a masculine business and the military relies on this association.[10] *Courage Under Fire* indicates this crisis on the level of form, content, and image, and points to the initial traumatic moment that the violent woman provokes.

Films such as *Courage Under Fire*, depicting violent women in the military, attempt to deal with the trauma of the violent woman in a way that *Tomorrow Never Dies* merely touches on: splitting the woman's violence from her femininity. Splitting, as a form of ideological assimilation or reconciliation of the violent woman, is often utilized as a way for contemporary society to contain the trauma of the violent woman. In almost all discussions of actual military women, it is apparent that a splitting is at work, a splitting that functions as a mechanism of defense against the trauma of the violent women. This mechanism of defense allows for the complementarity between masculinity and femininity to continue by splitting the woman's violence from her femininity. To accomplish this, the split allows us to accept the violence of a woman as attached to her job rather than her femininity, and therefore society can still believe that her violence in no way disrupts the definitions of masculinity and femininity.

This move in Hollywood film is most likely influenced by the real military's own attempts to deal with the cultural clash between the ideological definitions of femininity and of violence. Most obviously, at least during the most intensive parts of their training, the military tries to avoid this clash by stripping women of most monikers of femininity: requiring women to cut their hair, wear army fatigues, and so on. Somewhat similarly, men must strip any signs of individuality when they enter the military in order to suggest on the surface the uniformity they are meant to achieve. The difference here, of course, is that the military uniform, hairstyle, and mannerisms men take on, as they shed their own styles, are meant to accentuate their masculinity. Thus, when men enter the military they give up much of their individuality, but they receive in exchange a sense of increased masculinity. Women in the military, however, must not only shed their individual styles but also their femininity. When they put on the military uniform and its accoutrements, they are clearly "wearing" the military's masculine codes as well. This application of masculinity is needed to erase any obvious difference between the women and the men. Women can be taught the skills needed for combat readiness—that is, the skills they need to be violent—only when much of the sexual difference is erased.

In a blatant contradiction, however, the United States military— while it attempts to make violence nonfeminine—also tries to encourage its women to be more feminine when they are not involved in training exercises, in order to prove that they are still women. This may have been one of the reasons that while during the past twenty years women have been proving their strength, they have also worked hard to prove their femininity. In *Ground Zero*, Linda Francke explains that the United States Army hires the most attractive and feminine officers to work and teach at West Point, in order to act as an example for the young women officers. These top female officers, who have already proven their strength and combat readiness, come dressed in skirts, wearing perfectly applied makeup and well-coifed hair everyday for work. For them, this is a survival mechanism in the military, a mechanism which stems the tide of chides and taunts about their femininity. As Francke's study makes clear, establishing femininity is an important part of a woman's military training: "'Women Marine recruits receive instruction in hair care, techniques of makeup application, guidance on poise, and etiquette,' read a Marine recruit training manual for women in the wake of the Gulf War. The corps even issued an official Marine lipstick to its female recruits in boot camp."[11] Although it is hard to imagine stranger bedfellows than Maybelline and the Marines, it makes perfect sense when you recognize that the military depends upon traditional gender definitions as heavily as does the rest of society. The military cannot have the tens of thousands of enlisted women be totally exempt from these definitions. The military works hard to defeminize violent women when they are involved with violence, but it also works to feminize these same women when they are not training or in combat. In this way, the feminine woman is split from her violence, which is instead aligned with her military job. The effect this splitting has is to make the woman's violence more palatable and less traumatic.

The way the splitting of violence from femininity in these films functions as an ideological process can be explained through both reference to its sociological functions (as reification) and its psychic manifestations (as a form of disavowal). On the subject of the splitting at work in a capitalist society, Georg Lukács makes clear in *History and Class Consciousness* that it creates a division between who one is and what one has done. Lukács says, "a man's own activity, his own labour becomes something objective and independent of him."[12] In other words, this splitting alienates the subject from his or her work. This, in turn, makes the capitalist economy seem entirely dehumanized—reified—as if it functioned on the basis of its own autonomous laws rather than on the activity of subjects working within this economy. Lukács points out that in a reified environment all jobs and relationships are affected. The military, of course, is no exception. Work in the military has many different facets, but ultimately it relies upon violence: violence is the ultimate work of the military.

Faced with the trauma of the violent woman, as well as the need for women to bolster sagging enlistment, the military has attempted to "capitalize" on this process and produce a similar splitting for women—taking one attribute or skill and isolating it. Lukács makes explicit how this could be possible: "Not every mental faculty is suppressed by mechanization; only one faculty (or complex of faculties) is detached from the whole personality and placed in opposition to it, becoming a thing, a commodity."[13] Once violence becomes a thing, rather than something a woman *does,* it can be made to seem as if it is disconnected from the woman herself. This one part of the woman's personality is separated or split from her and seen not as something that *comes from her* but rather something randomly *attached to her* because of her job. This process of isolation prevents the violence of the woman from encroaching on her femininity. Her violence then amounts to no more than a skill that she would acquire on an assembly line. While reification also separates individual men from their violent acts—which is why we don't see soldiers as murderers—it does not enact this separation as rigidly as it does with female soldiers. The more violent a male soldier is, however, the more masculine he becomes. But because of the way that reification works with violent female soldiers, this violence remains separate from their femininity.

In the terms of psychoanalysis, we can see this process of splitting in another, related way—as a kind of disavowal. It is obvious to everyone that the woman is violent, but because this violence is isolated from who the woman "really" is, we can still believe she is not really violent. In *For They Know Not What They Do*, Slavoj Žižek points to the statement: "I know that it is so, but nevertheless I can't believe it"[14] as the exemplary utterance of disavowal. He goes on to explain, "This kind of gap between knowledge and belief, in so far as both are 'conscious,' attests to a psychotic split, a 'disavowal of reality'."[15] In other words, we see the non-traditional woman, see that she exists, that is, "that it is so," but nevertheless we don't believe it—and instead choose to believe something more ideological. The United States military hopes that we will look at the woman in combat but not believe that the violence she commits is in any way attached to her identity. This psychic defense mechanism clearly works hand in hand with reification: both function on the basis of a process of splitting that isolates the violence of the violent woman. These mechanisms have worked well for other ideological purposes, so it seems possible that female violence in combat can be stripped of femininity while the appearance and characteristics of women in the military can be pointedly feminine.

In actuality, however, the disavowal of the violence of the violent woman in the military is extremely complicated and not completely successful. This can be attributed partly to the multiple contradictions that must occur to achieve this disavowal. In a way, the military tries to treat the violence of a woman as having no impact on her femininity and instead treats her violence as purely connected to her professional responsibilities. In other words, during the instant she is violent, she is not a woman. But this does not totally circumvent the trauma, because the woman must also exist in the military on a day-to-day basis as a woman. The military is, after all, one of the oldest purveyors of traditional gender roles. As I have pointed out, it relies on them to construct its masculine battlefront and feminine homeland, which it is protecting. It cannot, therefore, have thousands of military women deny their proper feminine role. Thus, it issues lipstick and demands the application of femininity. In this case, the military looks at the violent woman and says that she is really not violent. These contradictions create a continuous cycle. In this way, then, the multiple, conflicting perspective of the narrative form in *Courage Under Fire* perfectly captures the spirit of the confusion that the violent woman creates. The military is constantly oscillating between trying to integrate women into the masculine military and sustaining them as the feminine object that the military exists to protect. Once it moves too far to one side, the military seems to compensate on the other. But there is no way out of this quandary. The difficulty involved in successfully splitting violence from the violent woman becomes fully apparent in *G.I. Jane*, a film that places the violent military woman in the foreground.

Ridley Scott's *G.I. Jane* responds to *Courage Under Fire*'s questions about how to deal with violent women, Scott's film enacts an even more radical attempt to split the female soldier's violence from her femininity. *G.I. Jane* tries to facilitate camaraderie between men and women who are violent together in the military and a sexual complementarity between the violent woman and her mate. The film imagines the first woman legally trained for military combat as both violent and involved in a traditional love relationship. Through form and content, *G.I. Jane* tries to split the female soldier's violence from her femininity—thereby creating a palatable version of the violent woman. The film begins as Senator Lillian DeHaven (Anne Bancroft) pulls a political coup at a Senate Arms Committee meeting, where she sneaks the issue of women in combat into the appointment of the Secretary of the Navy.[16] She will not support the Navy's candidate unless they begin to integrate women into combat positions. Outside of the public eye, the two sides strike a deal, and the military agrees to conduct a test case for integrating women into these positions (in return for the senator's approval of their candidate). The Navy decides to put the first test case through the Navy SEALs because, as one top aide says about this training, "No woman's gonna last a week. I don't care who she is." Senator De-Haven chooses Lt. Jordan O'Neil (Demi Moore) to enter this program (due explicitly to the fact that she is tough, beautiful, and heterosexual).

The film attempts to secure the woman in combat as ultimately nonthreatening by emphasizing the professional ambition of the woman—and making clear that this ambition is as unambiguous as possible. Throughout the film, Jordan repeatedly reassures the people around her that she only wants to be in combat positions because of the career advancement opportunities that this would allow her. She has been barred from these opportunities because they are only offered to those who have served in combat positions. As she tells her long-time boyfriend, "Royce, we're the same age, we entered the Navy the same month, and which one of us is wearing more ribbons?" Royce (Jason Beghe) suggests that it is just because he got lucky during the war. Jordan agrees, "operation experience is the key to advancement. Yet anyone with tits can't be on a sub, can't be a SEAL . . ." She also repeats that her decision and desire to be in the Navy SEALs is not a feminist move, when she says, "I'm just not interested in being some poster girl for women's rights."[17] This combination of concern for career advancement and disdain for political motivations is just the right combination to make her unthreatening. This way she does not desire involvement with violence per se, her decision is justified by the military's own structure vis-à-vis job advancement. Learning to be violent, then, can be just a job-related skill, which does not symbolize any change in her femininity.

When we first see Jordan, she is working at the NIC (Naval Intelligence Center) as a topographic analyst. She fits the military's idea of a service woman: neatly dressed, with several hints of femininity. Her long hair is pulled into a bun at the nape of her neck; she is wearing pearl earrings and makeup. To be accepted as a possible

Navy SEAL, however, Jordan goes through the process of systematically stripping herself of aspects of femininity. She does not try to become male, nor does she give up her femininity entirely; instead, she erases certain aspects of femininity (specific aspects of difference) in order to be accepted—not necessarily as one of the guys, but as one of the team. This elision of difference allows the men to see her accomplishments without being upset by her femininity invading their all-male environment. One of the first major symbolic erasures of difference that Jordan employs is shaving her head.

During exercises at the beginning of "hell week," Jordan's long hair repeatedly comes undone and gets in her face. It is also an obvious marker of sexual difference among the group of male SEAL candidates whose heads are shaved. After encountering fierce resistance to her presence among the male trainees, Jordan heads to the barbershop, finds it empty, and commandeers one of the clippers to get rid of her hair.[18] Scott shoots this scene slowly and carefully because it is her first step toward integration. The film dwells on all angles of her clipping and on her long hair falling to the ground. After this haircut, Jordan receives the first friendly word from one of the other candidates, when he calls to her and motions that he likes her haircut. Immediately prior to this, Jordan pleads with the commander of the base that she be treated equally and that they remove the military's "gender norming" rules (which allow Jordan extra help with things like the obstacle course). Once the commander accepts this—and after she shears her head—Jordan decides to move into the men's barracks. This change in her living environment is another symbolic erasure of difference. Another change, which is not planned nor is it publicized (but which is nevertheless important) occurs after the first few weeks of training when Jordan does not get her period. The nurse explains that her body fat has fallen below the female norm, and this has caused her periods to stop. The nurse informs her that it will return after the intense training is over, indicating that the absence of femininity is only temporary. Menstruation is one of the most obvious markers of difference between the sexes. Yet, while in training—while on the job—Jordan stops menstruating, which indicates the completeness with which she has been integrated into this male space.

After all these physical differences have been elided, however, there is one more barrier: the social behavior of the men in the Navy

SEALs. Jordan is tough throughout the film and although she eventually becomes integrated on the level of the job, the men do not accept her socially. This is problematic for a military unit because it means she has not gained the individual trust of the men with whom she is working. Clearly, the military's success during its missions relies heavily on its men—and women—trusting each other. As I explained earlier, the military man's inability to trust a woman in combat (as well as his inability to put down his desire to protect or save the woman) is one of the last—and, according to the military, most important—reasons why women are not allowed in combat. In the last training exercise in *G.I. Jane*, however, there comes a turning point after which Jordan becomes more integrated into the social fiber of her team by gaining her teammates' approval and confidence. During a S.E.R.E. (survivalist training) exercise, the drill instructors (posing as the enemy) brutalize the trainees in a mock interrogation. The Master Chief (Viggo Mortensen) especially brutalizes Jordan to prove to the rest of the men (and Jordan) that women do not belong in combat positions. He even indicates that he will rape her in order to get the other men to give up information (because part of the object of the survival training is to learn to resist interrogation and keep all information from the enemy). But she (even though her hands are tied behind her) fights back and begins to injure the Master Chief with her blows. All the men cheer her on, and at one point after being taunted by the Master Chief, she screams, "suck my dick." Hearing this, all the men scream and cheer for her. And it is at this moment that they most fully accept her onto the team. During this fight, not only does she prove her strength and determination, but also she uses a masculine insult toward the Master Chief—"suck my dick"—which mobilizes the men's trust by further erasing any difference between her and them.[19] After this exercise, the men on Jordan's team invite her out for a drink, which is a more formal sign of their acceptance.

To complete the split, however, Jordan also must be feminine at home, and the film attempts to show this as well. We must see that there are no similarities between Jordan the violent soldier and Jordan the woman at home. While the film begins with Jordan and her boyfriend Royce working together at the Navel Intelligence Center, after Jordan enters the Navy SEALs her time and the mise-en-scène is split between SEALs training and her time at home with Royce. In other words, once she enters the Navy SEALs, she and Royce are only depicted together in the frame in a domestic space, rather than a work or military space. Thus, the film keeps the two realms very separate: Royce does not, for example, visit her at the base (even though his military position would allow him to).[20] The first time we see them at home, they are in a bubble bath together. Here, Scott depicts a very feminine and sexual space as the room is lit only with candles and Jordan's long hair is down. We next see them interact when Jordan calls Royce from the base. She begins to cry a little about the difficulties of her experience at the base at the end of the phone call, and at the moment when she is clearly giving in to this feminine impulse, she hangs up so as not to become too emotional while at the base. This is the first and one of the only times we see Jordan cry, even though she has been through things in training that made the men cry.

Thus, her crying, which is stereotypically considered, of course, a female attribute, is depicted as linked to her life outside her job. Her emotional attachment to her boyfriend is what brings out her femininity. This further suggests the separation between job and home life: when the woman is home, she takes up her feminine position. Moreover, this film clearly depicts heterosexuality as the key to Jordan's continued femininity. Here the film presents a common homophobic way of defining femininity (which also serves to hide the trauma of the violent woman). This is made more explicit when the military (purposely) charges Jordan with being a lesbian in order to have her kicked out of the military. Indeed, the military's refusal to legally allow gay or lesbian soldiers bears a marked similarity to its rule against women in the military in that both antiquated rules clearly still exist because of rigid gender definitions that depend on such prejudices. While much could be investigated in this arena, the film presents this charge as just a brief stumbling block. Indeed, it is also a moment when Jordan and her boyfriend can bond and work together to help her career (i.e., in this case, the mystery surrounds proving the military's complicity in creating the lie that she is a lesbian). When Jordan is accused of being a lesbian and is kicked out of the SEALs, she goes home to her boyfriend. There they reunite and smooth over any difficulties they were having over her decision to join the SEALs. After embracing Royce, she begins to cry a little again and finds great comfort in his arms.

Again, this is a completely different depiction of Jordan than when she is with the SEALs. There she doesn't need comfort or help from anyone; when she is at home, however, she returns to the feminine role of needing help and protection from her boyfriend. After having sex, they sit around in their bathrobes and underwear and discuss how to fix her problem. This "leave your violence at work" policy allows the complementary relationship to endure between the man and the woman. In addition, once she proves her ability to fit in with the SEALs, to remain feminine, to interact with violence as a professional skill, and to pull her own weight in a moment of crisis, she is then accepted by those men around her and promoted as a graduate of Navy SEALs training. Furthermore, after an actual mission that she and her team successfully complete, one of the men says, "Hey, O'Neil, I'd go to war with you any day."

Of course, regardless of what the film attempts, it remains filled with ambiguities. For example, even though Jordan says she's not joining the SEALs for feminist causes, her own achievements and the successful integration of the SEALs do further feminist causes by creating equal opportunity for women in combat positions previously closed to women. This is clear when Jordan is talking with the nurse (the only other female on base that Jordan has contact with):

> Nurse: Lieutenant, why are you doing this?
> Jordan: Do you ask the men that same question?
> Nurse: As a matter of fact I do.
> Jordan: What do they say?
> Nurse: Because I get to blow shit up.
> Jordan (laughs): Well, there you go.

When Jordan laughs and answers as she does, we know that she is joking, that is, that she does not want, unlike her male counterparts, just to blow things up. She has said many times throughout the film that she is there so that she may advance in her career, not because she is excited by the thrills involved in military violence. The carefree attitude that the men display with their comment indicates that regardless of their desire for career advancement, they accept being a navy SEALs as another way to enhance their masculinity. For Jordan, however, it means having the world open up to her in a way that it never did before. Her being there has a political effect on her own career and on the lives of all other women. Furthermore, she may strip much of her femininity to be accepted on the job, but ultimately she is still a woman and, especially when played by Demi Moore, she does not lose very much of her femininity. Moore, after all, has posed pregnant on the cover of *Vanity Fair* and has appeared as an exotic dancer in Andrew Bergman's *Striptease* (1996)—foregrounding her femininity in the most explicit of ways. Even during the moments when the film depicts Moore committing violence, she still looks like a beautiful woman. While on the level of narrative, *G.I. Jane* suggests that violence can be split from femininity (and thus women should be allowed in combat), on the level of the image it refutes the idea that this split is possible. So although *G.I. Jane* attempts—and to some extent succeeds—to take a stand on and answer the questions brought up in *Courage Under Fire*, it is still ambiguous in both its content and form regarding the violent woman in combat.

The very nature of this struggle on film and in the military indicates the peculiar trauma that the violent woman causes American society. Though recent military films such as *Saving Private Ryan* and *The Thin Red Line* (1998) break from traditional depictions of masculine violence, they do not break the link between masculinity and violence. As long as this link continues to exist, the status of the violent woman will continue to be traumatic. Disturbing the complementary nature of the male/female relationship, the violent woman will continue to be a volatile nexus for many unanswerable contradictions in society—contradictions evident in the structure of both *Courage Under Fire* and *G.I. Jane*. Thus, even though we see more and more women entering the military, their sheer numbers do not in any way put us closer to a resolution of the antagonism that the violent woman brings to light. She does not offer resolution but something more important: she continues to do us the service of laying bare our wounds.

CHAPTER 7

Conclusion

The Long Kiss Goodnight

Of all the recent films depicting violent women, Renny Harlin's *The Long Kiss Goodnight* (1996) is in some sense the most revelatory. It most dramatically depicts the contradictions inherent in both the violent woman herself and in all attempts to incorporate her into the filmic form. In this way, the film itself struggles with all the ideas that I have discussed thus far. One of the main reasons, however, that I have chosen to conclude with this film is because of its failure. That is, it is exemplary more for its failure to deal successfully with the violent woman than for the way in which it actually does so. For although the film tries to bring together femininity and violence, it fails to do this convincingly, and this failure is manifested on the level of both form and content throughout the film. Through the failure of *The Long Kiss Goodnight* to integrate femininity and violence—despite its near-Herculean efforts at just such an integration—we see most clearly the precise nature of the disruption that the violent woman occasions.

The film begins by introducing Samantha Cain (Geena Davis), a single mother and schoolteacher who has amnesia and can only remember the past eight years of her life. As she works through her amnesia with the help of private investigator Mitch Henessey (Samuel L. Jackson), Samantha Cain must confront the fact that she used to be a hired assassin for the United States government. In the end, it turns out that Samantha Cain was only a cover during a mission in which she was shot in the head and flung into the ocean. Her real name is Charlene (Charly) Elizabeth Baltimore. During the eight years she has been missing, however, her boss in the CIA, Mr. Perkins (Patrick Malahide), has been organizing terrorist activity in the United States in order to scare Congress into giving the CIA more money to support antiterrorist efforts. Since Charly would uncover this new alliance of Mr. Perkins with old enemies, numerous people are trying to kill her. In the end, Charly and Mitch stop the CIA/terrorist activity, and Charly must struggle with the identity she has occupied for eight years: Samantha.

The question that predominates throughout the film concerns the identity of the character that Geena Davis plays: is she Samantha or is she Charly?[1] From its opening, the film introduces Samantha as an exemplar of white bourgeois femininity. And following from this, she is also a good example of a perfectly complementary subject who can take part in a love relationship and be a member of the community. She is pretty, has long hair, and wears a little makeup; she wears loose dresses and stylish outfits. All of these are, of course, characteristics of "proper" femininity. In addition, the film begins with images of Samantha making Rice Krispie treats, taking care of her daughter, interacting with the community, and walking with her boyfriend—all the activities of a good mother. In the voice-over, she not only explains her situation (that she has focal retrograde amnesia), but she also explains that she really likes her life as it is. She is—or so she says—content. In this way, the film demonstrates that an identity that fits into a complementary position of femininity—like Samantha's at the beginning of the film—is able to smooth over the trauma of being alone. Seen metaphorically, Samantha's amnesia is a void that leaves her alone and bereft of a symbolic identity. But one cannot function in society without such an identity.

After she recovered eight years earlier, she could not simply choose to go on as an identity-less being, without any symbolic designation; she was forced—if she was to enter into the social order as such—to assume an identity, even if it wasn't who she "really" was. Taking on an identity at this late age makes more obvious the ideological nature of both gender and identity. In other words, she must pick and choose her identity as if she is picking out a new hat, revealing the way in which identity is something that one takes up according to the dictates of ideology.[2] Her choice is obviously random—based upon the tiniest fragments of memory that she chose to focus on—and, it is clear, she could very well have chosen a different one. This assumption of an identity paves the way to Samantha's happiness. Even though, eight years earlier, she was all alone in the world with no memories, she now seems always cheerful and happy. Samantha—the ideal mother, girlfriend, community member, and all around feminine woman—lives in a nice big house in a suburban town. Renny Harlin goes to considerable lengths to emphasize that, at the beginning of the film, Samantha is the embodiment of traditional female subjectivity (but for her amnesia). Samantha conveniently chose the role that was most attractive—that is, the role of the feminine woman, of the complementary other half—an identity that could easily cover over the trauma of being alone and completely lacking any identity.

When Charly (a totally violent and nontraditional woman) begins to surface (as Samantha's amnesia clears), this ideological scene of harmonious existence undergoes a violent revolution. A killer, who is after Charly, destroys her perfect house; another group of killers threatens Samantha's daughter Caitlin's (Yvonne Zima) life and endangers the community at large. Hal (Tom Amandes), Samantha's boyfriend, used to be able to take care of Samantha; he supported, loved, and helped her through her worries about her amnesia. He also helped her become more fully integrated into the community. When the man who thought he had killed Samantha eight years earlier comes to Samantha's house to finish her off, we quickly see the limits of Hal's protective abilities.[3] Hal tries to defend Samantha, but the killer easily throws him aside and reveals him to be rather weak. Thus, he can no longer protect Samantha and becomes somewhat feminized, because, after this appearance of the killer from the past, she must protect *him*. In addition, Hal is visibly distressed by Samantha's newly emerging violent skills. In short, Hal is unable to take up a masculine role around Samantha once Charly begins to surface. Relying on a theme I have discussed before in the case of *Strange Days* and *Fargo*, *The Long Kiss Goodnight* reverses the roles between masculine and feminine once the violent woman appears, as the woman takes up the role of the violent protector and the man the nonviolent protected. Samantha leaves Hal behind to take care of Caitlin (which, the film shows, he is very good at, because he is kind and warm with her), while she, taking up the role of the traditional hero, must leave her domesticity behind to save herself, her family, and ultimately a whole city of people.

Rather than pair her with a strong male character who can help save her, the film pairs Samantha with two men who are not very masculine. Hal is kind, understanding, and good with Samantha's daughter, but because of his inability to be violent and protect those he loves, he does not measure up to Hollywood's traditional ideal of masculinity (especially in an action film). Her private detective, Mitch, though he is the only person who manages to help Samantha navigate her two identities throughout the film, is nonetheless also depicted as a failure at traditional masculine activities. He has failed as a cop (spending time in prison) and as a husband (he is divorced and his wife will not let him spend time alone with his child). In taking her case, Mitch hopes to help Samantha restore her identity and at the same time restore his own masculinity.[4] Mitch tells Charly, "I never did one thing right in my life, that takes skill." Even at the end of the film, when he charges out to save Caitlin (hoping that he can finally do one thing right), he is riddled with bullets and unable to save her.

It is also Mitch, however, who provides commentary to the viewers about this strange predicament regarding Samantha's two identities. Mitch makes comments (often in the form of humor or sarcasm) about her changing femininity/identity, her class status, and her whiteness.[5] It is no coincidence that Mitch's character is African American. Often in films about violent women, the problem of the violent woman is more easily explored in interracial relationships because the way this pairing is depicted heightens the sense of antagonism at work. Though it seems counterintuitive to suggest that mainstream Hollywood films would attempt to heighten antagonism, it is, in actuality, a commonplace. It is not unusual precisely because even the most ideological film works to create an antagonism that it can then solve—and the greater the antagonism, the greater the strength of the ideology that is able to solve it.[6] In other words, films try to heighten the antagonism in order to heighten the ideological work that they do in its resolution. In films with violent women, not only does this interracial pairing create tension in the film, but it also allows for a greater sense of resolution. In his essay "The Black Image in Protective Custody," Ed Guerrero elaborates on this notion in terms of interracial buddy films:

Hollywood well understands that the biracial buddy film represents a proven formula for meeting first its material but also ideological needs. For the buddy formula is able to attract the demographically broadest possible audience while negotiating, containing and fantastically resolving the tangled and socially charged issue of race relations on the screen.[7]

Similarly, the films starring an African American man and a violent white female—films that at first glance seem to be exploring possible disruptions of ideology—often end up soothing any possible trauma by showing that the disruption is not as bad as we fear. That is, violent woman films often pair violent white women with African American males—a seemingly radical pairing—thereby heightening the antagonism, in order that the resolution depicted in the films reinforces the status quo.

White violent women are often either finding friendship only with African American men, being at odds with African American men in their quest for an identity, or being investigated by African American men. In *G.I. Jane*, the only African American male in Jordan's team, McCool (Morris Chesnut), is the most supportive and accepting of her presence in the Navy SEALs. In one scene, he explains to her and the other white men present that his grandfather couldn't fight for his country during World War II because the military said that "Negroes" had poor night vision. In a moment where the film equates female and African American integration of the military, McCool explains that he knows where Jordan is coming from, and he concludes by saying, "you're just the new nigger on the block." In this case, black masculinity and violent white femininity line up against white masculinity (the military). Similarly, although in a much smaller (and completely stereotypical) role, a Rastafarian cyclist—who blows marijuana smoke into the trunk of a car where Thelma and Louise have trapped a police officer—is the only man who is truly aligned against white masculinity with the two violent white women in *Thelma and Louise*.[8] Of course, this opposition is depicted as humorous and ultimately feckless, undermining any kind of power this allegiance might have had. But both these films suggest that there is an innate sense of solidarity between the violent white woman and the African-American man, a solidarity that is informed by their combined oppression by the white male.[9] In *The Last Seduction*, on the other hand, the African American male who investigates the violent white woman is her adversary. In their main scene together, the woman gets rid of the detective by invoking racist slurs (about the sexual prowess of African American men) in order to distract him long enough to kill him in a car crash. Even though these two characters do not achieve any kind of solidarity (as in, for instance, *G.I. Jane)*, the film does nonetheless depict an African American man investigating the violent white woman—suggesting a connection between them.

Similarly, in *The Long Kiss Goodnight*, Mitch investigates Samantha, who is a violent white woman. In this case, however, the violent woman herself is the one who initiates the investigation. Mitch represents Samantha's last hope for uncovering her past identity. In the process of investigating the mystery of Samantha's identity, Mitch attempts to restore his own identity. Indeed, it is by helping to save Samantha and Caitlin and by helping to change the violent Charly back into the socially acceptable Sam (an uncomfortable amalgamation of Samantha and Charly) that Mitch regains his masculinity and his place within society.[10] In this film, violent white femininity and black masculinity subdue the white male criminal (Mr. Perkins and his crew) and restore white male democracy. In doing so, they prove themselves to be unthreatening to society (by aiding the government, giving up violence, and taking up more law-abiding roles within the community). Still, Mitch is not presented in a totally serious light at the very end of the film. Due to a request from Sam, Larry King has Mitch on his show and announces to the world Mitch's role in stopping the CIA conspiracy. Mitch responds to Larry King by telling a joke, which makes Mitch look somewhat silly. This ending seems ambiguous because it doesn't secure Mitch's identity in the same way as, for example, *Courage Under Fire* secures Serling's identity. Mitch does reclaim his masculinity. He also helps to tame the violent woman. His silly joking at the end of the film, however, suggests something extra that remains unsubdued in the process of reclaiming his masculinity. This "something extra" can be understood, I believe, as a kind of *jouissance* that Mitch obtains from his jokes. This is true for him throughout the film. His jokes are often a combination of goofiness, politics, and wit. Even though, therefore, he is situated in a more acceptable social position in the end of the film, he still resists some of this symbolic anchoring through his humor.

Sam has a similar moment at the end of the film, when even though she has given up her CIA job and become a schoolteacher again, she has an uncontrollable urge to throw a knife into a nearby stump. In this scene, her knife throw is depicted as involuntary and one which gives Sam a moment of *jouissance*—as we can see from the wry smile on her face. This action seems to hint that a violent woman can never totally give up her violence, precisely because it is a source of such *jouissance*. That is to say, once a woman has experienced violence, it will forever seduce her.[11] The film attempts to work out this enigma from the moment Charly's inclination toward violence begins to bubble up in Samantha's behavior. The first time we see Samantha commit any kind of violence is when her amnesia begins to breakdown. This occurs for two reasons: she is sexually harassed, and she experiences a traumatic car crash. While driving a guest home from her Christmas party, the guest makes lewd comments to her and then he attempts to touch her breasts. Shortly thereafter, Samantha's violence first emerges. In many films, female violence is shown as arising in this way, in reaction to sexual harassment. The paradigmatic example of this is, of course, *Thelma and Louise*, in which Louise shoots the man who has tried to rape Thelma. Not all of Charly's violence develops in reaction to sexual harassment, but introducing it in this way alludes to this common way of depicting what provokes women to be violent. Thus, not coincidentally, a deer runs in front of the car right after this moment of sexual harassment. Samantha hits the deer, and then crashes into a tree, after which she is thrown from the car and lands bleeding in the snow. She sees the deer is in pain, and with one quick and violent move, she breaks its neck. Just as in *Natural Born Killers*, the violent woman (Charly appearing for the first time) immediately provokes a sudden change in film form from the traditional narrative course it was taking into a montage of images. The images are blurred and hard to make out—of the deer being hit, an eye opening, and an image of Charly.

Within the next few days, Charly begins to resurface more often. It is the way that she returns that makes this film stand out as the quintessential example of the violent woman film. Some of the first clues that Charly is returning appear only in Samantha's behavior and register as merely stereotypical examples of what society thinks is indicative of a non-motherly, nonfeminine woman. In the scene above, she is able to snap a deer's neck. In another scene, she is mean to her daughter, Caitlin, while they are ice skating. After Caitlin falls and hurts herself, Samantha cruelly says to her, "Stop being a little baby and get up. . . . Life is pain. Get used to it. You will skate all the way to the shore princess and you will not fall again. Am I understood?" This is, of course, not what the usual Rice-Krispee-treat-making suburban mother is depicted as saying to her daughter. As it turns out later, Caitlin's wrist is broken, and when Samantha is Samantha again, she feels much remorse and can't even remember what she said to Caitlin on the ice. Even in these two examples, it seems that there is a split becoming evident between Samantha and whoever she was in her past. The way splitting functions with the violent woman in other films (such as *Tomorrow Never Dies, Courage Under Fire,* and *G.I. Jane*) is manifested literally in this film. *The Long Kiss Goodnight* offers us an example of a woman who actually has two distinct identities—an actual, rather than a theoretical, split between her violent half and her feminine half.

Many of the scenes depicting this literal split are shot within a dream-like or fantastical mise-en-scène. Rather than, for example, recovering her memories independently or with the aid of a therapist or just thinking about her past, Samantha seems to have real encounters with her past, that is, with Charly. While in the hospital recovering from the car crash, Samantha closes her eyes and the scene changes to Samantha standing on a cliff in her hospital gown starring at a full-length mirror. The image in the mirror all of a sudden changes from her own image to Charly's. The background is filled with lightening, thunder, and other loud noises. The characteristics that mark Charly as different than Samantha (both played by Geena Davis) are her appearance and her attitude—to say nothing of her violence itself. Charly smokes, and in fact this is one of the first things that Charly tells Samantha, that she wants a cigarette. The mise-en-scène emphasizes their differences: Charly's hair is short, straight, blond, and slicked back. She wears heavy eye makeup and tight fitting clothing. The splitting of the woman in this film, therefore, also runs along the lines of the two traditional opposite images of women: in other words, the whore and the faithful wife.

Charly shocks and scares Samantha, and at one point Charly literally attacks her. In this scene, Samantha is watching herself in a mirror in a hotel, and Charly appears in the place of her image in the mirror and then tries to swipe at Samantha with a knife. This scares Samantha, and as if she is fighting some stranger (rather than another side of herself), she fires a gun she has found at the mirror. In this scene, then, the violent woman provokes the feminine woman into using violence. The two women, however, remain separate until near the end of the film. Once Charly has fully reemerged, she takes over, and the split is remedied by the erasure of one of the women. Charly cuts Samantha's long hair, throws out her clothes, and so forth. She also begins swearing, which other characters note throughout the film. She even startles her private investigator, Mitch, and he reacts by saying "back when we first met, you were like: ah fooey I burned the darn muffins. Now you go into a bar, and sailors come running out. What's up with that?" Mitch also suggests that Charly has taken up her old behavior with such gusto (without at all being affected by the woman that she has been for eight years) because she wants to erase the real feelings she has towards Hal, Caitlin, and the life she had with them.[12] In other words, the violent woman needs to erase all reminders of the feminine woman in order to survive.

In this way, *The Long Kiss Goodnight* seems to depict only stereotypical women. Charly represents the stereotypical male fantasy of a bad girl or whore—promiscuous and violent—while Samantha represents the stereotypical male fantasy of a good girl or faithful wife—feminine and in need of protection. Stereotypes most often work toward ideological purposes, but they are not wholly reliable. There is always the chance that the woman can embody the stereotype too fully or challenge the stereotype, which then disrupts the very social order it was meant to uphold.[13] The battle between these two stereotypes in *The Long Kiss Goodnight* offers us an example of the role of fantasy in sexual relations and the role of violence in male fantasies of women. The film itself even addresses this connection between the identities of Samantha and Charly and fantasy. This occurs in a scene in which Samantha has a chance to discover the truth of her identity but rejects it.

This opportunity arises when a man whom Mitch and Samantha find tells them that he knows her whole story. The man is Nathan Waldman (Brian Cox), who was at one point a father figure to Charly and actually trained her to be an assassin. Upon finding her alive, he tries to tell Samantha about her real identity. Waldman says to her, "It was a fantasy for Christ's sake. Samantha Cain never existed. You wrote the whole bloody thing." Essentially, Waldman, the father figure, is explaining to the traditional feminine woman that she is only a fantasy and that her "real" identity is the violent woman. Samantha can't believe him, and Mitch finds it impossible to believe as well. Samantha replies, "No, it's not a fantasy. I'm in the goddamn PTA." Samantha and Mitch decide that Waldman is setting them up, and they escape from him. As the spectators of the film, we know from previous scenes and clues that actually Waldman is telling the truth. At this juncture in the film, however, Samantha and Mitch decide to leave and to ignore this man, who is the one person who could disclose Samantha's identity. That is to say, Waldman could have anchored Samantha's identity, symbolized it, but instead, she ignores him and leaves the question of her identity unanswered.[14]

This also offers us an example of the contingent nature of identity. Here, even when faced with her real identity, Samantha can't recognize it. In fact, neither identity is presented as more real than the other one is. When faced with the question—who is the fantasy, Samantha or Charly?—the film nicely formulates the idea that both these identities are based in fantasy. The film accomplishes this by attempting to combine the two identities rather than choose one over the other. In the last scene, Sam (the new combination of Samantha and Charly) has long blond hair, a little bit of makeup, and wears a loose but sexy (it is slit up the front) dress. In this way, the film combines not only her attributes but also her appearances. In one sense, it is, of course, a combination that lessens the threat of the violent woman, as Sam has given up her CIA work and gone back to being a caring mother, loving girlfriend, and a schoolteacher. But the combination also shows that we can't separate the violent woman from the schoolteacher—or the whore from the mother. This imperils the fantasies surrounding Samantha and Charly because those fantasies depend on their separation. Our fantasies of femininity unravel, as Slavoj Žižek puts it, when we recognize, "Woman is not Mother and Whore, but *the same woman* is Mother in the private sphere and Whore in the public sphere."[15]

The fact that the melding of Samantha and Charly form an uneasy combination is emphasized by the mise-en-scène surrounding Sam, Hal, and Caitlin in front of their new home, which is perched on top of a mountain. Instead of moving back to suburbia, they have chosen to live isolated on this mountaintop, not embedded in any community. Sam and Hal are eating dinner outside and watching Caitlin play with a goat. All of a sudden, Sam throws her dinner knife, as if into a bull's eye, into a nearby stump. After this, she looks at Hal and shrugs her shoulders, as if there is nothing she can do about that silly little violent impulse of hers. The camera then pulls back to reveal their house, which is surrounded not by people but by nature, indicating that Sam's identity, which combines both violence and femininity, is even less socially acceptable than her other two identities.

Samantha was a part of the suburban American fantasy, and Charly was a part of the urban American fantasy, but Sam cannot fit into either of these spaces. Since the mystery of her identity has been solved, and even the president of the United States himself thanked her for her help in uncovering the criminal operations of Mr. Perkins, it would seem only normal that she could then go back to the white picket fence house and friendly community that her violence originally forced her to leave. She is unable, however, to go back to either of her previous habitats and must instead live out in the wilderness. Connecting these three identities (Samantha, Charly, and Sam) with three different spaces (the suburb, the city, the wilderness) actually makes explicit the very nature of fantasy. Elizabeth Cowie, in her *Representing the Woman*, suggests that fantasies are not the object of desire but instead the setting for desire. She explains:

> Fantasy as a mise-en-scène of desire is more a setting out of lack, of what is absent, than a presentation of a having, a being present. Desire itself coming into existence in the representation of lack, in the production of a fantasy of its becoming present. It can be seen, then, that fantasy is not the object of desire, but its setting.[16]

The key point regarding prevailing fantasies about women is that they exist in two separate "settings." What is most important about these two settings (the whore and the faithful wife) is that fantasy keeps them separate. In other words, the duality itself is the key to this fantasy. This is why it is much easier for a good girl to become a bad girl or vice versa during the course of a film rather than for the two to be combined.

In some ways, *The Long Kiss Goodnight* also attempts to show the dependence of society on this duality. Indeed, the film seems to suggest that underneath every housewife is a violent woman. Samantha has repressed Charly, the violent woman, through her amnesia. The return of the repressed is, if not inevitable, then always a possibility. The film also suggests, however, that inside every violent woman is a suburban housewife. This is illustrated when at one point Mitch tries to convince Charly that Samantha's personality had to come from somewhere. He thinks that Samantha is what Charly would be if she stopped hating herself.[17] All it would take for Charly to be less violent is for her to begin to like herself more. In these depictions, *The Long Kiss Goodnight* reveals the never ending cycle that informs traditional fantasies of femininity, as each one continually tries to undermine the other. This is precisely, however, the relationship that these positions always have and need in order to continue as dueling fantasies. Moreover, characters do often pass from one position to the other without causing any kind of disruption or trauma to society. This kind of movement does not disrupt ideology but actually reinforces it by accentuating the duality of women rather than collapsing it. The reason such a smooth transition doesn't work in *The Long Kiss Goodnight*, however, is that both these fantasies structure the same woman at the same time. Although this cycle is similar to that of other films featuring violent women, it is played out much more literally due to the actual split that occurs on screen. I would suggest that the woman's violence prevents both fantasies from working as they normally do. The violence of the woman doesn't fit into either fantasy and this prevents the kind of ideological security that fantasy usually encourages.

In this way, then, the violent woman often reveals the contingent nature of the fantasy of femininity. Public outcry over real female murderers, films that depict violent women as innately complex and political, and films that depict the violent woman disrupting all relationships she encounters all indicate the ambiguous nature of her relationship with the social order as such. *The Long Kiss Goodnight* depicts this ambiguity through its attempt to integrate the violent woman into society by combining her with traditional femininity. Its almost comical and sometimes awkward depiction of these two stereotypes (the violent woman and the passive woman), existing uncomfortably in one woman, depicts most honestly, I would say, the excessive images society scrambles to produce when it finds itself face-to-face with the trauma of a violent woman. More often than not, we are unable to comprehend the complexities of femininity as an identity that includes violence (or the complexities of maleness as an identity that excludes violence). *The Long Kiss Goodnight*, through its surreality and inability to fully integrate the violent woman, understands the unending cycle of trauma and conflict that the violent woman causes. That is to say, even in the realm of fantasy, we are not truly safe from the violent woman and the underlying social antagonism that she brings to light.

Notes

Introduction

    1. J. David Slocum, "Violence and American Cinema: Notes for an Investigation," in *Violence and American Cinema*, ed. J. David Slocum (New York: Routledge and Kegan Paul 2001), 1–2.

    2. One notable exception is Frank Tomasulo's detailed investigation into the relationship between film form and violence in Martin Scorsese's *Raging Bull*. See Frank Tomasulo, "Raging Bully: Postmodern Violence and Masculinity in *Raging Bull*," in *Mythologies of Violence in Postmodern Media*, ed. Christopher Sharrett (Detroit: Wayne State University Press, 1999), 175–197.

    3. Slocum sums up the content of past theory on film violence by saying: "Briefly put, the guiding forces of most of the centuries social and institutional attention to film violence has been on censorship itself or effects on viewers, or institutional modes of regulation, specific social concerns, or marginalized groups—all worthwhile projects, but rarely allowing for a more synthetic understanding of film violence" (J. David Slocum, "Violence and American Cinema: Notes for an Investigation," in *Violence and American Cinema*, ed. J. David Slocum, [New York: Routledge and Kegan Paul, 2001], 9).

    4. Slocum, "Violence and American Cinema," p. 5.

    5. All contemporary work specifically on the violent woman (including my own) is also indebted to more general work on the image of the working or action-oriented woman in Hollywood, such as Yvonne Tasker's *Working Girls*, for mapping out the kinds of roles that contemporary working or nontraditional women tend to play in Hollywood films.

    6. One notable exception is Jeffrey Brown's "If Looks Could Kill," a fascinating psychoanalytic discussion of stripper films that cross into the

rape revenge genre. See Jeffrey Brown, "If Looks Could Kill: Power, Revenge, and Stripper Movies," in *Reel Knockouts: Violent Women in the Movies*, eds. Martha McCaughey and Neal King (Austin: University of Texas Press, 2001), 52–77.

7. Several film theorists refer to this pattern in filmic violence, which was originally inspired by Linda Williams's reading of pornography and was based on genre critics' discussion of musicals. See Linda Williams, *Hard Core: Power, Pleasure, and the "Frenzy of the Visible"* (Berkeley: University of California Press, 1999); and Marsha Kinder, "Violence American Style: The Narrative Orchestration of Violent Attractions," in *Violence and American Cinema*, ed., J. David Slocum (New York: Routledge and Kegan Paul, 2001), 63–102.

8. Certainly, there were theorists who discussed violence within larger projects on other topics. Within his book on the contemporary auteur, for example, Robert Kolker says, "Violence is an easy way to command emotional response under the pretence of 'realism.'" (Robert Phillip Kolker, *A Cinema of Loneliness: Penn, Kubrick, Scorsese, Spielberg, Altman*, 2d ed. [New York: Oxford University Press, 1988], 52). This kind of descriptive statement does not, however, theorize violence as a structuring principle.

9. Christian Metz, *Film Language: A Semiotics of the Cinema*, trans. Michael Taylor (Chicago: University of Chicago Press, 1974), 95.

10. Echoing Gunning, Peter Kramer's "Clean Dependable Slapstick" also suggests that the narrative in silent cinema is simply a smoke screen for the real reason that the audience is attending, namely, to see the spectacle of movement, comedy, and violence. He explains that, "Right from the beginnings of extended filmic storytelling, the film industry's discourse about stylistic norms served not merely as a prescription for filmmakers, but also as a rhetorical smoke screen for audiences, obfuscating the very attractions that were at the heart of their entertainment experience." (Peter Kramer, "'Clean, Dependable Slapstick': Comic Violence and the Emergence of Classical Hollywood Cinema," in *Violence and American Cinema*, ed. J. David Slocum [New York: Routledge and Kegan Paul, 2001], 105). Thus, Kramer details the way that critics and studios at the time contributed to this smoke screen for purposes of respectability, but everyone was aware of the real reasons audiences went: the violent spectacle.

11. Tom Gunning, "'Now You See It, Now You Don't': The Temporality of the Cinema of Attractions," in *Silent Film*, ed. Richard Abel (New Jersey: Rutgers University Press, 1996), 73.

12. Slocum, "Violence and American Cinema," p. 4.

13. In "Violence American Style," Marsha Kinder provides an analysis of the patterns that emerge in the relationship between violence and narrative in American film—which she calls the "American NOVA: The Narrative Or-

chestration of Violent Attractions"—and investigates its cultural implications. (Marsha Kinder, "Violence American Style: The Narrative Orchestration of Violent Attractions," in *Violence and American Cinema*, ed., J. David Slocum [New York: Routledge and Kegan Paul, 2001], 68). She reveals that by combining the rhythmic expectations of violent spectacle and comic elements most dramatic narrative intentions are completely elided.

14. Leo Charney argues, "Violence, like sex, becomes a way to feel present; or, more accurately, to mime presence, to manufacture a sensation of presence, in the face of the impossibility of presence." (Leo Charney, "The Violence of a Perfect Moment," in *Violence and American Cinema*, ed. J. David Slocum [New York: Routledge and Kegan Paul, 2001], 46). I would, however, challenge Charney's claim that violence indicates our need for a sense of presence. Charney likens our desire to watch violence to drug addiction in which you need more and more to accomplish less each time. But I would argue that when filmmakers lessen the narrative, and thus remove the suspense or the cultural poignancy, violence is no longer as traumatic. Instead, it merely hints at the idea of trauma. Charney suggests that we crave violence because we crave presence in a world that seems replete with absence. In contrast, I would propose that we live in a world of over-presence, and that our delight in violent spectacle overtaking narrative is a desire to avoid any sign of absence, any engagement with trauma.

15. For more extensive discussions of narrative and the history of narrative theory see David Bordwell, *Narration in the Fiction Film* (Madison: University of Wisconsin Press, 1985); Peter Brooks, *Reading for the Plot: Design and Intention in Narrative* (Cambridge, MA: Harvard University Press, 1984); Christian Metz, *Imaginary Signifier: Psychoanalysis and the Cinema*, trans. Celia Britton (Bloomington, IN: Indiana University Press, 1982).

16. In fact, David Bordwell explicitly contends that the distinction between *szuyhet* and *fabula* has no relationship to ideology and ideological analysis whatsoever. Nonetheless, Bordwell's conception remains so close to Metz's that its helpfulness in the project of ideological analysis is apparent.

17. For Metz, the fundamental ideological dimension of film narrative lies in the way that *discours* is hidden by *histoire*. Jean-Louis Baudry explains this same idea when he says, "the spectator identifies less with what is represented, the spectacle itself, than with what stages the spectacle, makes it seen, obliging him to see what is sees; this is exactly the function taken over by the camera as a sort of relay. Just as the mirror assembles the fragmented body in a sort of imaginary integration of the self, the transcendental self unites the discontinuous fragments of phenomena, of lived experience, into unifying meaning. Through it each fragment assumes meaning by being integrated into an 'organic' unity" (Jean-Louis Baudry, "Basic Effects of the Cinematographic Apparatus," in *Movies and Methods*,

vol. 2, ed. Bill Nichols [Berkeley: University of California Press, 1985], 540).

18. Louis Althusser, "Ideology and Ideological State Apparatus, " in *Lenin and Philosophy and Other Essays*, trans. Ben Brewster (New York: Monthly Review Press, 1971), 162, Althusser's emphasis.

19. Ernesto Laclau, and Chantal Mouffe, *Hegemony and Socialist Strategy: Towards a Radical Democratic Politics* (New York: Verso, 1985), 125, Laclau and Mouffe's emphasis.

20. Karl Marx, *Grundrisse*, trans. Martin Nicolaus (New York: Penguin, 1993), 286.

21. Jacques Lacan, *The Seminar of Jacques Lacan, Book XX: Encore: On Feminine Sexuality, The Limits of Love and Knowledge, 1972–1973*, trans. Bruce Fink (New York: W. W. Norton, 1998), 79, Fink's emphasis.

22. Slavoj Žižek, *The Sublime Object of Ideology* (London: Verso, 1989), 173.

23. Jacques Lacan, *Television: A Challenge to the Psychoanalytic Establishment*, trans. Jeffrey Mehlman (New York: W. W. Norton and Company, 1990), 3.

24. This psychoanalytic approach of seeing an originary trauma manifesting itself in myriad ways in the psyche and throughout culture/ideology has affected other disciplines, as well. For example, Laclau and Mouffe extend their Marxist discussion of antagonism beyond class conflict to the markers of identity (race, gender, sexuality, and so on). That is to say, they see the failure of wholeness, of ideology, as reflected in multiple antagonisms in society, such as the antagonism of race or gender.

25. The trauma of this meaningless origin also moves ideology to constantly create narratives that explain origin as such. For example, the intense struggle between creationism and evolutionism represents the trauma of not being sure of one's origin. While it might seem that the staging of this struggle could represent a gap in ideology, it could also act as a further ideological ruse to assume that underneath this struggle there must lie the real answer to the origin rather than assuming that underneath this struggle there lies no good answer.

26. Not surprisingly, cultural texts also mimic this structure of desire. For example, film narratives often hide the truth from the viewer until the final resolution. The viewer is only given enough information to rouse her/his curiosity but not enough to feel mastery over the scenario. In his discussion of film narrative, Tom Gunning says, "Narrative invokes the spectator's interest (and even desire, in a psychoanalytical model) by posing an enigma. The enigma demands a solution and [. . .] the art of narrative consists in delaying the resolution of that enigma, so that its final unfolding can be delivered as a pleasure long anticipated and well earned."

(Tom Gunning, "'Now You See It, Now You Don't': The Temporality of the Cinema of Attractions," in *Silent Film*, ed. Richard Abel [New Jersey: Rutgers University Press, 1996], 73). Just as with the symbolic's concern with the Real and an individual's search for the object of their desire, the film narrative is structured so that the viewer is concerned with and searching for clues to fill in the gaps in their knowledge.

27. Laura Mulvey, *Visual and Other Pleasures* (Bloomington, IN: Indiana University Press, 1989), 15.

28. Mulvey, *Visual and Other Pleasures*, 16.

29. The project of both Marxism and psychoanalysis is one of bringing antagonism to light to produce social change. Theorists such as Slavoj Žižek, Joan Copjec, Frederic Jameson, and Alain Badiou have worked to illustrate the political implications of psychoanalysis and its link to Marxism.

Chapter 1: *Complementarity and Its Discontents*

1. The popularity of the serials was so great that Paramount even produced a film in technicolor in 1947—George Marshall's *The Perils of Pauline* starring Betty Hutton—that depicted the life and times of Pearl White, the actress who starred as Pauline in the serials.

2. Ben Singer, "Female Power in the Serial-Queen Melodrama: The Etiology of an Anomaly," in *Silent Film*, ed. Richard Abel (New Jersey: Rutgers University Press, 1996), 172–173.

3. By catering to female fantasies of empowerment, serial-queen melodrama helped to attract a wave of new female spectators to the cinema, which was precisely the intent behind them.

4. Ben Singer, "Female Power in the Serial-Queen Melodrama: The Etiology of an Anomaly," p. 173.

5. In order to keep this project to a manageable length, I have had to limit this historical overview of the violent woman in film, not focusing on this figure when she appears in only a few isolated cases (or even when she appears in three or four films within a genre). Needless to say, this does not mean that these films are not important to the history of violent woman in film. But these films, precisely because they are isolated cases, tell us less about the relationship between the filmic violent woman and the social order than those films which are part of a larger trend in filmmaking.

6. These genres sometimes depicted violent women, especially as they progressed into the 1950s and 1960s. For example, George Stevens' *Annie Oakley* (1935), King Vidor's *Duel in the Sun* (1946), and Nicholas Ray's *Johnny Guitar* (1954) are all Westerns that depict a woman resorting to violence or taking up violence in order to better navigate the dangerous environment of

the west (and gender relations that occur within that environment). And Arthur Penn's *Bonnie and Clyde* (1967) and John Cassavetes' *Gloria* (1980) are examples of gangster films whose experimental (or independent) nature included a violent woman in a lead role.

7. James Gilligan, *Violence: Reflections on a National Epidemic* (New York: Vintage Books, 1997), 16.

8. Among other historians, Karen Anderson documents the sociopolitical consequences of the factories subsequently firing these women to make room for the returning soldiers in her *Wartime Women: Sex Roles, Family Relations, and the Status of Women During World War II*. She reports that, "to make matters worse, the heaviest layoffs occurred in those industries in which large numbers of women were employed, especially aircraft and munitions. [. . .] Once they were fired, women workers faced overt discrimination as employers and unions alike ignored the seniority and skills they had developed during the war so that young white males could recover their privileged position in industrial work." (Karen Anderson, *Wartime Women: Sex Roles, Family Relations, and the Status of Women During World War II* [London: Greenwood Press, 1981], 161.)

9. There are many extensive studies on this subject, such as William Chafe, *The American Woman: Her Changing Social, Economic, and Political Roles, 1920–1970*; Maria Diedrich and Dorothea Fischer-Hornung, *Women and War: The Changing Status of American Women From the 1930s to the 1950s*; Susan Hartmann, *The Home Front and Beyond: American Women in the 1940s*; and Leila Rupp, *Mobilizing Women for War: German and American Propaganda, 1939–1945*.

10. In fact, in a review of the film in *Variety* in 1944, the reviewer refers to *Double Indemnity*—the quintessential film noir—as a melodrama, when he says, "*Double Indemnity*, apparently based on a sensational murder of the 20s, has become an absorbing melodrama in its Paramount adaptation" ("Double Indemnity," *Variety*, 1 January 1944).

11. Here I am referring to theorists such as Raymond Borde and Étienne Chaumeton (who coauthored *Panorama du film noir américain*), Nino Frank, Jean Pierre Chartier, Andre Bazin, Francois Truffaut, Jacques Rivette, Claude Chabrol, and so forth.

12. James Naremore, "American Film Noir: The History of an Idea," *Film Quarterly* 49 (1995–1996): 14.

13. Elizabeth Cowie, *Representing the Woman: Cinema and Psychoanalysis* (Minneapolis, MN: University of Minnesota Press, 1997), 125.

14. Of course, there is a long history of feminist theorizations of film noir, which this section draws from and is indebted to. The most important of these from the 1970s and early 1980s are Mary Ann Doane, "*Gilda*: Epistemology as Striptease," *Camera Obscura* 11 (1983): 6–27; Molly Haskell,

From Reverence to Rape: The Treatment of Women in the Movies (Chicago: University of Chicago Press, 1973); Claire Johnston, "Feminist Politics and Film History," *Screen* 16, no. 2 (1975): 115–124; and E. Ann Kaplan, *Women in Film Noir* (London: BFI, 1978).

15. Sylvia Harvey, "Women's Place: The Absent Family of Film Noir," in *Women in Film Noir*, ed. E. Ann Kaplan (London: BFI, 1978), 25. Harvey's essay is representative of the kind of very productive interaction that occurred between film noir and 1970s feminist film theory.

16. This conversion of the femme fatale into the good woman suitable for becoming a wife is precisely what occurs in Robert Montgomery's *Lady in the Lake* (1946).

17. The man who involves himself with the femme fatale is almost always the object of her violence, or he is the one who carries out her violent wishes. Ultramasculinity, toughness, a facility with violence, and cleverness usually characterize this man. His trench coat, cocked hat, suave demeanor, and rough-and-ready good looks physically represent the underlying masculine attitude of the male detective figure. But he is also vulnerable in some way and seems to lack control over his world. His worst flaw—but one that film noir always depicts as understandable—is his "fatal attraction" to the femme fatale. Walter Neff in *Double Indemnity* even says that he knows what he is getting into with Phyllis but that he can't help himself. This, of course, is the flaw that drags him away from a lawful existence and the possibility of a normal family life while pulling him into the obscene underbelly of society that the femme fatale inhabits. Humphrey Bogart, Glenn Ford, Edward G. Robinson, Robert Mitchum, and Fred MacMurray were some of the famous actors that played these male characters. Their reputations as screen icons added to the characters' masculine images. Ultimately, however, all this masculinity put together doesn't seem to be able to nullify or change the threatening dimension of the femme fatale.

18. Frank Mott, *The Employment Revolution: Young American Women in the 1970s* (Cambridge: The MIT Press, 1982), 1.

19. At this time, a few explicitly feminist films appeared, depicting alternate visions of what might happen with the elision of gender difference. Specifically, Lizzie Borden's *Born in Flames* (1983) depicts women using violence to further feminist causes. This independent film, which did not reach a large audience, brings together concerns of gender, race, and class, as Borden imagines what a multicultural female revolution would look like in a futuristic socialist society.

20. For an in-depth discussion of the cultural/political context surrounding the Blaxploitation film, see Ed Guerrero's *Framing Blackness: The African American Image in Film* (Philadelphia: Temple University Press,

1993), 69–111; and Mark A. Reid's *Redefining Black Film* (Los Angeles: The University of California Press, 1993), 69–83.

21. Guerrero, *Framing Blackness*, p. 98.

22. Donald Bogle recounts the box office history of Gordan Parks, Jr.'s *Shaft* (1971): "This little picture, which its studio, MGM, thought might make a little money, instead made a mint—some $12 million within a year in North America alone—and single-handedly saved MGM from financial ruin" (Donald Bogle, *Toms, Coons, Mulattoes, Mammies, & Bucks: An Interpretive History of Blacks in American Films* [New York: Coninuum, 1994], 238).

23. While critics often read Blaxploitation films as generic, I think it is also appropriate to make the comparison to New Wave European movements (such as Italian neorealism or the French New Wave): Blaxploitation films concentrated on gritty realism, lasted only a short while, and yet had a significant impact on film form and content (affecting racial representations, the role of music in cinema, and the representation of violent women, to name a few examples).

24. Ed Guerrero, "Black Violence as Cinema: From Cheap Thrills to Historical Agonies," in *Violence and American Cinema*, ed. J. David Slocum (New York: Routledge and Kegan Paul, 2001), 216.

25. Exploitation films also influenced these female centered Blaxploitation films. In Eric Schaefer's extensive investigation of Exploitation films made during the classical Hollywood period, he explains that these films can be understood in part by the categories under which they fall, such as sex hygiene films, drug films, and burlesque films. And he suggests that "exploitation films relied on forbidden spectacle to differentiate themselves from classical Hollywood narrative films and conventional documentaries. As such, they were related to the cinematic tradition Tom Gunning has called 'the cinema of attractions.'" (Eric Schaefer, *"Bold! Daring! Shocking! True!": A History of Exploitation Films, 1919–1959* [London: Duke University Press, 1999], 95). Schaefer's definition of Classical Exploitation aptly describe the exploitation films of the 1960s and 1970s as well. And though he doesn't mention any exploitation films featuring violent women, it is no surprise that eventually some later forms of exploitation films did feature violent women. Randall Clark provides the key link, however, in his look at contemporary Exploitation films when he points out their relationship to Blaxploitation films. He says: "It is, in fact, typical of the differences between mainstream and exploitation films that even when the Hollywood studios were producing Blaxploitation films, they avoided films about powerful African American women. That was left to the exploitation film producers." (Randall Clark, *At a Theater Or Drive-In Near You: The History, Culture, and Politics of the American Exploitation Film*

[London: Garland Publishing, 1995], 158). Indeed, Pam Grier started her career in "women in prison" Exploitation films and subsequently American International Pictures (a production studio well known for it's exploitation films) also produced *Sheba, Baby* (1975), *Foxy Brown* (1974), *Friday Foster* (1975), *Cleopatra Jones* (1973), *Cleopatra Jones and the Casino of Gold* (1975), and *TNT Jackson* (1974). Obviously, this indicates that the topic of violent women could only be handled by those already used to working with marginalized topics, but it also means that the violent woman was then conceived of as titillation for American audiences.

26. The criminal mastermind who the Blaxploitation heroine fights against is quite often a maniacal white woman. In this way, the film pits woman against woman (with the added tension of racial difference) and sidesteps the possible trauma of seeing a woman fight and win against a male adversary.

27. Nonetheless, it is important to come back to Ed Guerrero's point about Blaxploitation as a whole, which is that, regardless of its limitations, the violence in Blaxploitation films remains connected to political struggle, he suggests, "while the genre is full of fantasmatic moments of popcorn violence, like Foxy Brown (Pam Grier) triumphantly displaying the genitals of her archenemy in a jar, or vampire Blacula (William Marshall) energetically dispatching several white L.A. cops in *Blacula* (1972), blaxploitation violence, in most cases, referenced black social reality, or transcoded, however fancifully, black political struggles and aspirations of the times." (Ed Guerrero, "Black Violence as Cinema: From Cheap Thrills to Historical Agonies," in *Violence and American Cinema*, ed. J. David Slocum [New York: Routledge and Kegan Paul, 2001], 214). Following Guerrero's point, I would add that the violent women in Blaxploitation films also, "however fancifully," represent the struggle that black women were going through as they worked for racial and gender equality.

28. Carol Clover, *Men, Women and Chain Saws: Gender in the Modern Horror Film*, (Princeton, NJ: Princeton University Press, 1994), 6.

29. Clover, *Men, Women, and Chainsaws*, p. 35.

30. But not all horror film heroines are young girls. In fact, in rape revenge films, such as Lamont Johnson's *Lipstick* (1976), Abel Ferrara's *Ms. 45* (a.k.a. *Angel of Vengeance*) (1981), and Meir Zarhi's *I Spit on Your Grave* (a.k.a *Day of the Woman*) (1977), the story often involves a mature white woman from the city (who has her own career and money) who is raped by men from the country.

31. This does not mean, of course, that these films were feminist projects. More often they are male fantasies of women being beaten and tortured, followed by the sadomasochistic fantasy of the torturers being tortured in return. Clover even suggests that the primary audience for these

films—adolescent boys—switches identification when the woman starts fighting back. Thus, they have the pleasure of being the aggressor in the beginning and the end.

32. Considering the long history of Hollywood racism, it is not surprising that this more mainstream trend begins with violent white women. Black actresses do not appear in these mainstream action roles until the mid-1990s.

33. Interestingly, Lyne's *Unfaithful* (2002) is about a stay-at-home mom whose spontaneous affair with a beautiful young man drives her husband to violence and almost ruins her family. One might wonder in what scenario Lyne imagines women *not* driving men crazy and ruining the family. Certainly in 2002, the working woman is no longer the new burden to contemporary society that she was in the late 1980s, and the stay-at-home mom has become more acceptable to feminist women as well. *Unfaithful* suggests that for Lyne the sexual woman is a destructive force whether she is a working woman without a family or a stay-at-home mother with a family.

34. Quoted in Susan Faludi, *Backlash: The Undeclared War Against American Women* (New York: Doubleday, 1991), 121.

35. He wasn't the only one on the film crew that felt this way. Michael Douglas also said: "If you want to know, I'm really tired of feminists, sick of them. They've really dug themselves into their own grave. Any man would be a fool who didn't agree with equal rights and pay but some women, now, juggling with career, lover, children, wifehood, have spread themselves too thin and are very unhappy. It's time they looked at *themselves* and stopped attacking men. Guys are going through a terrible crisis right now because of women's unreasonable demands." (Quoted in Faludi, *Backlash*, p. 121).

36. Gabriele Griffin, "Introduction," in *Feminist Activism in the 1990s*, ed., Gabriele Griffin, (London: Taylor and Francis, 1995), 3.

37. This backlash could even be seen in the now seemingly outdated 1980s films such as *Parenthood, Baby Boom, Kramer vs Kramer,* and so on, that attempted to investigate the effect of the working woman on the American family.

38. It is important to mention here a group of films that I do not concentrate on: television movies of the week. These films often investigate the theme of the abused woman who fights back with violence. Exploring the hardships of real women (or of the average woman), these films clearly carry on the tradition of melodrama, which also addressed the actual hardships of female existence. Susan Smith, Tonya Harding, and Elaine Bobbit are only the more sensational and well-known real women that have found their stories represented in a television movie of the week. More often, the frustrations and abuses of ordinary women that eventually lead to an erup-

tion of violence are the subject. The quintessential example of this is the 1980s television movie, Robert Greenwald's *The Burning Bed* (1984), which depicted a woman who reacted violently to being battered by her husband.

39. In fact, the issues that graced the covers of *Time* and *Newsweek* were of real-life career women and the way women's careers were affecting the family, instead of on violent women in film or women in general in film.

40. See chapter 3 for an in-depth discussion of the public's reaction to *Thelma and Louise*.

41. The only other depiction of violent women—which I will not address at length but which are important relative to this trend—is the violent heroine of several popular television series, such as *Buffy the Vampire Slayer*, *La Femme Nikita*, *Zena: Warrior Princess*, and *Dark Angel*. In these series, the violent heroine is presented week after week with problems she must use her brains and her strength to solve.

42. Ernesto Laclau, and Chantal Mouffe, *Hegemony and Socialist Strategy: Towards a Radical Democratic Politics* (New York: Verso, 1985), 124, Laclau and Mouffe's emphasis.

Chapter 2: *Expressions of Masculinity*

1. Graeme Newman, *Understanding Violence* (New York: J. B. Lippincott Company, 1979), 38.

2. Lee Clark Mitchell, "Violence in the Film Western," in *Violence and American Cinema*, ed. J. David Slocum (New York: Routledge and Kegan Paul, 2001), 176.

3. This is obviously the case in the United States military, where even today women are technically not allowed in combat positions because the military—and the society at large—relies on an image of violence as an exclusively male domain. But within the hierarchy of the military itself, some organizations exude more masculinity than others. The Marines and the Navy SEALs—who see more intense action in battle—have an image of being tougher and manlier because of the intensity of the violent circumstances in which they find themselves. In *The Morning After*, her extensive study on sexual politics at the end of the cold war, Cynthia Enloe points out that combat, "the risking of death, in the name of a larger cause," is the most masculine activity that one can engage in, as well as the only way to enter first-class citizenship. (Cynthia Enloe, *The Morning After: Sexual Politics at the End of the Cold War* [Berkeley: University of California Press, 1993], 57). Violence and first-class citizenship, for Enloe, are intimately connected. Prison psychoanalyst James Gilligan echoes this point when he observes that "a man is often thought to be more 'manly' if he has been to war and seen

violent action." (James Gilligan, *Violence: Reflections on a National Epidemic* [New York: Vintage Books, 1996], 30). To become a "real man," one must affirm one's ability to endure and commit acts of violence. And the more violent these acts are, the more manly the subject who perpetuates them.

4. *One False Move* not only reveals this connection between masculinity and violence, but also critiques it. Franklin relies on traditional ideas and images of masculinity, but he also uses this to critique hypermasculinity (in the character of the rampaging Pluto) and nostalgic masculinity (in the character of the narcissistic Dixon) by showing their destructive effects on women and the community (as their violence leaves families torn apart and one woman's life in particular destroyed). Throughout this study of masculine violence, Franklin also investigates the racism in small town America in a way that illustrates the connections between racism, violence, and concepts of masculinity.

5. Steven Neal, "Prologue: Masculinity as Spectacle," in *Screening the Male: Exploring Masculinities in Hollywood Cinema*, eds. Steven Cohan and Ina Rae Hark (New York: Routledge and Kegan Paul, 1993), 11.

6. For further details see my discussion in the introduction and/or Marsha Kinder, "Violence American Style: The Narrative Orchestration of Violent Attractions," in *Violence and American Cinema*, ed. J. David Slocum (New York: Routledge and Kegan Paul, 2001), 63–100.

7. Masculinity certainly seemed to change from the overt spectacle of masculinity in the 1980s to a more feminized man in the early 1990s. Susan Jeffords explains: "By seeming to step back from their own spectacle, these men [in the early 1990s] are presumably leaving space for Hollywood's version of 'difference,' or what it prefers to characterize as 'justice' and 'equality.' What Hollywood culture is offering in place of the bold spectacle of male muscularity and/as violence, is a self-effacing man, one who now, instead of learning to fight, learns to love." (Susan Jeffords, "Can Masculinity Be Terminated?" in *Screening the Male: Exploring Masculinities in Hollywood Cinema*, eds. Steven Cohan and Ina Rae Hark [New York: Routledge and Kegan Paul, 1993], 245). As the 1990s wore on, however, I would say that the "self-effacing man" that Jeffords initially noticed turned back to violence and more obvious masculinity (although certainly less than the spectacle of Sylvester Stallone or Arnold Schwarzenegger) in films such as David O. Russell's *Three Kings* (1999), John Frankenheimer's *Reindeer Games* (2000), Tony Scott's *Enemy of the State* (1998), and Doug Liman's *The Bourne Identity* (2002).

8. Mark Gallagher suggests that "The elevator sequence in *Speed*, for example, establishes the virility and resourcefulness of an L.A.P.D. officer (Keanu Reeves) and the ruthlessness and vindictiveness of his mad-bomber adversary (Dennis Hopper)." (Mark Gallagher, "I Married Rambo: Specta-

cle and Melodrama in the Hollywood Action Film" *Mythologies of Violence in Postmodern Media,* ed. Christopher Sharrett [Detroit: Wayne State University Press, 1999], 207). Clearly, these two positions (the hero and his adversary) are implicitly degrees of masculinity.

9. William Luhr, "Mutilating Mel: Martyrdom and Masculinity in *Braveheart,"* in *Mythologies of Violence in Postmodern Media,* ed. Christopher Sharrett (Detroit: Wayne State University Press, 1999), 230.

10. Bruce Fink, *The Lacanian Subject: Between Language and Jouissance* (Princeton, NJ: Princeton University Press, 1995), 111.

11. In *Totem and Taboo,* Freud creates a myth of the primal horde in order to try to understand, or posit, where the ideal masculinity originated. He suggests that people originally lived in small hordes that were ruled by an all-powerful father. Freud distills the story—which he points out took many centuries and was repeated time and again—to one primal horde in order to more clearly make his point. The father was jealous of any son who indicated he possessed any strength. He would castrate this son and banish him. Eventually all these brothers banned together and killed the Father so that they could have his enjoyment and power for themselves. They fought viciously among themselves over who would take the Father's place. To end the fighting, all the brothers agreed that no one would take the place of the dead father and all would agree to not possess their mother and sisters. This was the beginning of morality and law. It was also the beginning of the ideal masculinity that was left behind by the dead father. Freud, therefore, posits ideal masculinity as linked to the very beginning of civilization.

12. Joan Copjec, *Read My Desire: Lacan Against the Historicists* (Cambridge, MA: The MIT Press, 1994), 234.

13. Jacques Lacan, *The Seminar of Jacques Lacan, Book XX: On Feminine Sexuality, the Limits of Love and Knowledge, 1972–1973,* trans. Bruce Fink (New York: W. W. Norton, 1998), 79.

14. Slavoj Žižek, *The Indivisible Remainder: An Essay on Schelling and Related Matters* (New York: Verso, 1996), 161.

15. Quoted in Nancy Gibbs and Timothy Roche, "The Columbine Tapes," *Time* 20 December 1999, 50-51

16. James Gilligan, *Violence: Reflections on a National Epidemic* (New York: Vintage Books, 1996), 111.

17. The whole department congratulates Harry for being heroic, but there is the suggestion that even his injury makes him less manly than Jack, who wasn't injured. In almost every circumstance, the wound contains a double meaning because it is both a sign of masculinity and of its loss.

18. This emasculated image is also coupled with descriptions of Payne's intelligence. He is supposedly highly intelligent, and Payne himself

continually tells Jack not to underestimate him or to assume he is stupid. Although no one doubts his intelligence, everyone does doubt his mental stability. Intelligence is here aligned with craziness. It also connotes lack of masculinity. In *Speed*, the "thinking man" is constantly compared to the hero, Jack. Everyone in the film comments, for example, that Jack never thinks but relies on his gut feelings. Here, gut feelings translates into a kind of bravery that bolsters his masculinity. Harry, in contrast, is the brains of the partnership (as Payne points out), and yet he ends up dead. In this way, the film defines masculinity as non-thinking and physical.

19. Many film theorists writing on violence refer to Girard's theories of violence as well as to Richard Slotkin, *The Fatal Environment: The Myth of the Frontier in the Age of Industrialization, 1800–1890* (New York: Antheneum, 1985) and Georges Bataille, *Visions of Excess: Selected Writings, 1927–1939*, trans. Allan Stoekl (Minneapolis, MN: University of Minnesota Press, 1985), as starting points to understand violence in film and this retributive paradigm.

20. Rene Girard, *Violence and the Sacred*, (Baltimore, MD: Johns Hopkins University Press, 1972), 26.

21. Violence is most often experienced as immediate, as a random act that appears spontaneously (for example, when someone is mugged while they are walking down a city street). In this system, violence becomes a thing with no social ties, a thing we do not understand; we simply experience it. And in this light, attempting to understand it would seem ridiculous because it is something we feel we know, something that we grasp phenomenologically.

22. Georg Lukács, *History and Class Consciousness*, trans. Rodney Livingstone (Cambridge, MA: MIT Press, 1990), 153.

23. I do not think this can be said about all masculine violence. When masculine violence is connected with what Jacques Lacan would call an "act" and Walter Benjamin would call "law creating violence," it can radically change the existing social order. In other words, violence connected with an authentic act disrupts and thus wholly changes the very rules on which society is based.

24. The ideological nature of considering male as active and female as passive is perhaps what prompted Freud to reject this duality as a way of distinguishing masculine/feminine. As Freud puts it in his essay "Femininity," "You soon see how inadequate it is to make masculine behaviour coincide with activity and feminine with passivity." (Sigmund Freud, "Femininity," *New Introductory Lectures on Psycho-Analysis*, trans. James Strachey [New York: W. W. Norton, 1965], 143).

25. Teresa de Lauretis, *Alice Doesn't: Feminism, Semiotics, Cinema* (Bloomington, IN: Indiana University Press, 1984), 140.

Chapter 3: *Female Murderers*

1. Jacques Lacan, *The Seminar of Jacques Lacan, Book I: Freud's Papers on Technique, 1953–1954*, trans. John Forrester (New York: W. W. Norton, 1992), 191.

2. For an excellent detailed history of the American female murderer from the 1600s to 1980s, see Ann Jones, *Women Who Kill* (Boston: Beacon Press, 1996).

3. Collette Soler, "Hysteria and Obsession," in *Reading Seminars I and II: Lacan's Return to Freud*, eds. Richard Feldstein, Bruce Fink, and Maire Jaanus (Albany: State University of New York Press, 1996), 253.

4. Slavoj Žižek, *The Sublime Object of Ideology* (New York: Verso, 1989), 114–115.

5. In other words, all too often the public's reaction to trauma is more like the anti-Semite's turn toward the ideological fantasy than like Freud's attempt to struggle with the hysterical question.

6. Paul Wendkos's *The Legend of Lizzie Borden*, starring Elizabeth Montgomery, is a good example. It aired on television in 1974 and used the Lizzie Borden story to articulate the burgeoning feminist issues of the day. For example, in one scene between the prosecutor and his wife, his wife remarks: "It's just that it seems to me that you men have only yourself to blame if women use their femininity as a last defense. After all you cast us in this role." And the prosecutor responds: "I have never heard you talk like this. Next you'll be asking for the vote." It is not impossible that this conversation might have happened during Lizzie Bordeen's trial. But this topic was certainly not one discussed much in the newspapers in 1892. Feminist politics were, however, an important topic for the 1970s. In this way, the Lizzie Borden story was retold to serve the purposes of 1970s feminism. The story of Lizzie Borden has actually been retold many times, which is a further testimony to the strength of its original impact.

7. "Important Clew," *The Evening Standard* (New Bedford), 6 August 1892, 1.

8. "For Her Life," *The Evening Standard* (New Bedford), 19 June 1893, 1.

9. "Ready for the Ordeal," *The Evening Standard* (New Bedford), 22 August 1892, 3. Author's emphasis.

10. "Lizzie Borden's Arrest," *The Evening Standard* (New Bedford), 15 August 1892, 6.

11. I am indebted to Ann Jones for the idea that Ruth Snyder "had to die."

12. The film community actually paid a lot of attention to the Ruth Snyder case. D. W. Griffith reportedly attended almost the whole trial and scribbled madly in a notebook throughout. And Billy Wilder's *Double*

Indemnity (1944) was based—however loosely—on the Snyder murder case. The reviews of *Double Indemnity* in 1944 all referred to the Snyder trial, which meant that almost twenty years later the case was still fresh in the minds of the public.

13. Ann Jones, *Women Who Kill* (Boston: Beacon Press, 1996), 256.

14. The press did not bring up Ruth's immigrant past often, but when it did bring it up, this past was used against her. For example, one newspaper article noted that the warden demanded that Ruth and her mother stop speaking Swedish to each other, because the jail was afraid they were somehow smuggling secrets. ("Gray Ready For Trial For Snyder's Murder," *New York Times*, 7 April 1927, 25).

15. "Widow on Stand Swears Gray Alone Killed Snyder: As She Tried To Save Him," *New York Times*, 30 April 1927, 1.

16. Her marriage, from the start, had not been harmonious. Ruth even said: "I began having difficulty with my husband almost immediately after our marriage. I was apparently too giddy and young for his years; while he was only thirty-three at the time, he was like a man of fifty to me. He was not companionable to me at all. He took care of me and my daughter all right from a financial standpoint. We quarreled quite frequently about accounting for the money which he gave me [. . .] He never took me out, and that is why I had to seek the company of others." ("Text of Confession Mrs. Snyder Made," *New York Times* 27 April 1927: 16).

17. Throughout the trial, the press revealed the "immoral" activities of middle-class America: Albert Snyder talked constantly of a previous girlfriend; Gray had had many affairs including several while he was seeing Ruth; and Gray's friends had devised a system in which they helped each other create alibis as they went off to see their mistresses.

18. "Gray Murder Clues Burned in Syracuse," *New York Times*, 1 April 1927, 25.

19. The men during this trial made out amazingly well in the press and public opinion. When the prosecutor cross-examined Ruth, the newspapers reported that her case had been significantly damaged. But when the defense cross-examined Gray, the newspapers reported that Hazelton, the defense lawyer, was a shrewd lawyer who knew all the tricks to stump a witness. The reporters and detectives continually described Gray as thorough, detailed, well-groomed, and gentlemanly. And about Albert Snyder—although he was in actuality a gloomy, temperamental man, who was prone to violence—they wrote that he was the perfect husband who benevolently bought his wife a house in the suburbs.

20. The newspapers gave every detail of Ruth and Gray's affair as it came out in confessions and during the testimony. Every hotel they stopped in, every restaurant they ate in, practically every intimate moment they spent

together became subject to the most painstaking investigations, to the delight of the interested public. Here we have the hysterical response in a nutshell.

21. Quoted in Jones, *Women Who Kill*, 257.

22. "Mrs. Snyder Fights Back As The State Assails Her Especially on Insurance," *New York Times*, 3 May 1927, 1.

23. "Gray Denies Wish To Kill, Insists Woman Dominated," *New York Times*, 6 May 1927, 1.

24. This accusation was most likely false. No one could prove that Ruth had an affair other than the one with Gray. She herself often proclaimed that he was the only man—outside of her husband—that she had ever been involved with.

25. "Snyder Was Tricked Into Big Insurance, State Witness Says," *New York Times*, 26 April 1927, 1.

26. In a description of her testimony, the newspapers reported: "She was very precise, very decisive. In denying some of the worst charges her voice had an aggressive and angry ring. She spoke in low tones. She was never shrill, even when in a frightening mood. Her enunciation was clear." ("Text of Mrs. Snyder's Story of Husband's Murder Told on the Witness Stand Yesterday," *New York Times*, 30 April 1927, 10). Obviously her failure here was in not being the traditional or stereotypical female and instead conducting herself calmly and determinedly.

27. "Snyder Jury Hears Gray's Confession Accusing Woman," *New York Times*, 28 April 1927, 1.

28. "Mrs. Snyder Fights Back As The State Assails Her Especially on Insurance," *New York Times*, 3 May 1927, 1.

29. "Text of Mrs. Snyder's Story," p. 10.

30. "Widow on Stand," *New York Times*, 30 April 1927, 1.

31. "Text of Mrs. Snyder's Story," p. 10.

32. Murphy, Clay. "Union Newsstand thrives with Smith as cover story," *Herald-Journal*, 6 August 1995, <http://www.teleplex.net/SHJ/Smith/trial/newsstan.html> (22 August 1997).

33. "Susan Smith: Despite a speedy conviction, she remains a frightening enigma," *People Weekly*, 25 December 1995, 67.

34. Of course, this type of murder is not unheard of; instead, it is a story that has been told—albeit in hushed tones—since *Medea*. And recent news stories about young mothers who have dumped their newborns in order to continue on with their lives—and the reaction that these stories received—emphasizes the constancy of this type of murder and the female anguish that it ultimately represents.

35. "Life of a Mother Accused of Killing Offers No Clues," *New York Times*, 6 November 1994, A1.

36. "Life of a Mother," *New York Times*, 6 November 1994, A1.

37. Bill Hewitt, "Does She Deserve To Die?," *People*, 13 March 1995, 79.

38. "David Smith: His Own Story," *People*, 7 August 1995, 73.

39. "Sex, Betrayal and Murder," *Time*, 17 July 1995, 33.

40. The media's general conflation with female promiscuity and female criminality, for example, allowed the public to pass a quick verdict on Aileen Wuornos. Wuornos, discussed by the press as the first female serial killer, worked as a prostitute before she was arrested (her victims were some of the men who hired her). While her story provoked press coverage, Patty Jenkins's *Monster* (2003), and several made-for-TV movies, her prostitution and her lesbianism provided the media with "the reason" for her violence. These aspects of her life were easily co-opted into traditionally stereotypical and homophobic fantasies that served to cover over the trauma of her violence.

41. "Sex, Betrayal and Murder," p. 33.

42. The letter that Tom Findlay wrote to Susan in which the prosecutors found motive for Susan's murder—the fact that he didn't want to continue their relationship because of her children—also reveals the class issues in this case. Findlay continually refers to their backgrounds as too different to reconcile and tells her not to pay attention to the Union boys she grew up with as she attempts to better herself.

43. As in the two previous cases discussed, the men in this case made out very well in the press. Tom Findlay continually earned such descriptions as "the good-looking, twenty-seven-year-old son of the boss" ("Sex, Betrayal," p. 35). David Smith, of course, had the sympathy of the nation as he wept through his testimony about his two boys. And even though Bev Russell sexually abused Susan most of her life, the press often recounted the fact that he was paying for Susan's defense and that he was the one who kept the family together.

44. Steve Wolf, "Elegy for Lost Boys: A Swift, Dramatic Trial Finds Susan Smith Guilty of Murdering Her Sons," *Time*, 31 July 1995, 32.

45. Hewitt, "Does She Deserve To Die?," *People*, 13 March 1995, 79.

46. I am not suggesting that Susan was giving a rehearsed performance—although this was a charge during the trial. I am only concerned with the way she acted and the way it was interpreted by the media.

47. Hewitt, "Does She Deserve To Die?," *People*, 13 March 1995, 78.

48. The only female violence that seems acceptable is violence which is justifiable. Presumably, Susan Sarandon's response to questions about the violence in *Thelma and Louise* only further provoked the media. She commented: "The violence I liked, in a way, because it is not premeditated. It is primal, and it doesn't solve anything." (Quoted in Richard Schickel, "Why Thelma and Louise Strikes A Nerve," *Time*, 24 1991, 56.) Sarandon's comment stands out because the words "primal" and "violence" are not normally associated with women. And when people use "violent" to describe

a woman's actions, they usually pair it with the word "justifiable" in order to render it more acceptable. "Justifiable" usually applies to violence in which the woman protects herself, her home, or her children (under the right circumstances). A good example of this type of violence is the violence committed by Beth Gallagher (Anne Archer) in Adrian Lyne's *Fatal Attraction* (1987). Gallagher shoots Alex Forrest (Glenn Close) as Forrest is trying to kill her and ruin her family. This violent act works to protect the family and its patriarchal order by counteracting the traumatic violence of her nontraditional rival. Thus, this kind of female violence is not as traumatic and instead seems justified because it has a more defined symbolic space.

49. Rod Lurie, "On the Road with Susan Sarandon," *Los Angeles Magazine*, May 1991, 30.

50. In many ways, the femmes fatales of the 1930s and 1940s also fit into this description. The reviews about Barbara Stanwyk at the time that *Double Indemnity* came out are full of praise for her extreme sexiness and sexual villainy. One review even made a point to recount how the enlisted service men reacted with such excitement when they first saw her that Billy Wilder thought that the rest of his film would be ignored.

51. Jim Jerome, "Riding Shotgun: In the battle of the sexes, Thelma and Louise's Geena Davis is armed and dangerous," *People*, 24 June 1991, 90.

52. Larry Rohter, "The Third Woman of Thelma and Louise," *New York Times*, 5 1991, 55.

53. For a more detailed discussion of this idea and a detailed analysis of the film itself, see Lynda Hart, *Fatal Women: Lesbian Sexuality and the Mark of Aggression* (Princeton, NJ: Princeton University Press, 1994), 68–80.

54. Fred Bruning, "A lousy deal for women—and men," *Maclean's*, 12 April 1991, 9.

55. Margaret Carlson, "Is This What Feminism Is All About?," *Time*, 24 June 1991, 57.

56. Carlson, "Is This What Feminism Is All About?," p. 57.

57. Hart, *Fatal Women*, p. 73, Hart's emphasis.

58. Sheila Benson, "Thelma & Louise is a betrayal of feminism," *Los Angeles Times*, 24 May 1991, F2.

59. See John Leo, "Toxic Feminism on the Big Screen," *U.S. News and World Report*, 10 June 1991; Fred Bruning, "A Lousy Deal for Women—and Men," *Maclean's*, 12 April 1991; Asa Baber, "Guerrilla Feminism," *Playboy*, October 1991 (to name just a few).

60. Many of the articles help to create a corresponding ideological fantasy to the trauma of the violent woman in *Thelma and Louise* by changing focus and discussing how unfairly the male characters are portrayed in this film. This speaks directly to men's fear that their own positions in society might be disrupted. Although written in a tongue and cheek manner, which

might be expected from an article in *Playboy* on *Thelma and Louise*, the essence of critics' fears is best summed up in Asa Baber's reaction: "Davis and Sarandon play tough, gritty, beautiful women. As a man watching them, I was attracted to them at first, and I did like them—until I realized that if I met them on the street, they would probably blow me away if I violated their standards of protocol and etiquette. [. . .] The most primitive message behind *Thelma and Louise* is that a lot of men need killing these days. This is an acceptable, even amusing proposition in our contemporary society. And I suggest that, as men, we had better be alert to it. (Asa Baber, "Guerrilla Feminism," p. 45). This fear is clearly the same as that voiced during trials of female murderers when the lawyers and police said that if the courts don't punish these violent women it will be open season on every husband.

61. The real female murderers were not left completely undefended by feminists of the time. For example, Ann Jones points out that feminists took up the cause of the despoiled maiden in the mid-1800s when poor young women were seduced and left by more prosperous men. During this time, there were several publicized court cases involving these young women killing—or trying to kill—the men who abandoned them. Feminists came to these trials to help the young lady in question and publicly further their causes. Jones recounts the end of one of these trials: "Amelia Norman went home with 'a highly respectable lady' and then to 'the bosom of the family' of Mrs. Lydia Maria Child, one of America's most famous 'lady authors' and an outspoken abolitionist who had campaigned for Norman's release and sat by her side during the trial. Up in Concord, feminist theoretician Margaret Fuller—who did not altogether approve of fallen women or of the sentimental Mrs. Child—nevertheless praised her for taking up this worthy cause." (Jones, *Women Who Kill*, p. 148).

62. Quoted in Richard Schickel, "Why *Thelma and Louise* Strikes a Nerve," *Time*, 24 June 1991, p. 54.

Chapter 4: *Romancing Trauma*

1. J. David Slocum, "Violence and American Cinema: Notes for an Investigation," in *Violence and American Cinema*, ed. J. David Slocum, (New York: Routledge and Kegan Paul, 2001), 17–18.

2. *Buffy the Vampire Slayer*—in a parody that emphasizes the contradictions between femininity, violence, and the history of the male action film—also makes reference to this tradition when Buffy says, in the middle of a struggle with a vampire: "Oh good, the feeble banter portion of the fight!"

3. There are exceptions to this rule of nonromantic endings; these exceptions, however, tend to exist in extreme situations or environments. Particular genres—such as comedy (as in *Lethal Weapon 3*), fantasy, or science fiction—can provide unrealistic environments that distance the viewer and thus provide an unthreatening context within which to explore the violent woman. But the majority of mainstream Hollywood films that feature a violent woman do not end with a romance. For a discussion of the exceptions to this rule, see chapter 5.

4. In this sense, one might say here that the future destruction of the Earth functions as a fetish, allowing us to disavow the far more traumatic constitutive failure of the sexual relationship.

5. Though we can—and do—think about homosexual relationships in terms of complementarity, male/female complementarity is nonetheless one of the chief rationales for homophobia.

6. Joan Copjec, *Read My Desire: Lacan Against the Historicists* (Cambridge, MA: The MIT Press, 1994), 235.

7. Aristophanes' speech is most often thought of in terms of male/female complementarity. But in the actual speech, Aristophanes focuses more on complementarity between men and boy lovers than male and female lovers. He even suggests male and female exist primarily for procreation rather than for love.

8. Plato, *Symposium*, trans. Robin Waterfield (Oxford: Oxford University Press, 1994), 29.

9. Plato, *Symposium*, p. 27.

10. Jacques Lacan, *The Seminar of Jacques Lacan, Book XX: Encore: On Feminine Sexuality, The Limits of Love and Knowledge, 1972–1973*, trans. Bruce Fink (New York: W. W. Norton, 1998), 32.

11. Sigmund Freud, *Three Essays on the Theory of Sexuality*, trans. James Strachey (San Francisco, CA: HarperCollins, 1962), 2.

12. Slavoj Žižek, *The Metastases of Enjoyment: Six Essays on Woman and Causality* (New York: Verso, 1994), 155.

13. Slavoj Žižek, *The Sublime Object of Ideology* (New York: Verso, 1989), 116.

14. Jacques Lacan, *Seminar XX*, p. 47.

15. As Lacan says: "What makes up for the sexual relationship is, quite precisely, love." (Jacques Lacan, *The Seminar of Jacques Lacan, Book XX, Encore: On Feminine Sexuality, the Limits of Love and Knowledge, 1972–1973*, trans. Bruce Fink [New York: W. W. Norton, 1998], 45).

16. Bruce Fink, *The Lacanian Subject: Between Language and Jouissance* (Princeton, NJ: Princeton University Press), 1995, 105, Fink's emphasis.

17. Jacques Lacan, *The Four Fundamental Concepts of Psychoanalysis*, trans. Alan Sheridan (New York: W. W. Norton, 1978), 276.

18. Lacan also notes the primary status of this insight for psychoanalysis: "analytic discourse is premised solely on the statement that there is no such thing, that it is impossible to found (*poser*) a sexual relationship. Therein lies analytic discourse's step forward and it is thereby that it determines the real status of all other discourses." (Lacan, *Seminar XX*, p. 9).

19. Jacques Lacan, *Le Séminaire de Jacques Lacan, livre XIV: La Logique du fantasme, 1966–1967*, 1 March 1967, author's translation.

20. Sigmund Freud, *An Outline of Psychoanalysis*, trans. James Strachey (New York: W. W. Norton, 1949), 70.

21. Lacan, *Séminaire XIV: La logique du fantasme*, 7 June 1967, author's translation.

22. Lacan, *Séminaire XIV: La logique du fantasme*, 7 June 1967, author's translation.

23. Joan Copjec, *Read My Desire: Lacan Against the Historicists* (Cambridge, MA: The MIT Press, 1994), 212, Copjec's emphasis.

24. Of course, many of our famous male icons in films are associated with ultramasculine violence. But even men who play mostly romantic parts in comedies and dramas can easily (and convincingly) take up violence. Tom Hanks even dressed as a woman in *Bosom Buddies* before taking on romantic parts, but no one found it unbelievable when he took on a very violent and masculine role in Steven Spielberg's *Saving Private Ryan* (1998). In fact, *Saving Private Ryan* is a film that concentrates on violence and masculinity, and yet it stars mostly actors known for their romantic roles (Matt Damon, Tom Hanks, and Edward Burns). But this does not present a problem because part of a male actor's masculinity rests on his ability (however long it may be hidden) to be violent if he has to be. If he's successful with women, the public expects him to be equally successful with violence. In other words, male actors move easily—indeed are expected to move—between these two roles.

25. This film is also important to look at because it is indebted to and is attempting to update the classical film noir (especially *Double Indemnity*).

26. Mary Ann Doane, *Femmes Fatales: Feminism, Film Theory, Psychoanalysis* (New York: Routledge and Kegan Paul, 1991), 25.

27. Slavoj Žižek, *The Indivisible Remainder: An Essay on Schelling and Related Matters* (New York: Verso, 1996), 161.

28. Žižek *Indivisible Remainder*, pp. 160–161.

29. Teresa de Lauretis, *Alice Doesn't: Feminism, Semiotics, Cinema* (Bloomington, IN: Indiana University Press, 1984), 121.

30. As is often the case (and as I discuss in more detail in the conclusion), action films starring violent women often rely on racist stereotypes of African-American men in order to define the strength of the violent woman. While this does not really apply to Jack's partner Buddy Braggs

(Ving Rhames), it does apply to the African American male character whom Karen overpowers while trying to find out where Jack has escaped to. In this scene, Karen visits Kenny (Isaiah Washington) looking for information. In a typically racist characterization, Kenny (depicted as an ill-mannered gangsta figure) tries to manhandle Karen with the suggestion of rape. Proving her calm approach to dangerous situations, Karen forcefully overpowers Kenny. Using racist stereotypes of black men for both comedy and to define the strength of the white hero is a common tool in mainstream American cinema and is similarly appropriated here to prove the strength of the violent woman. Although typical in American cinema, such racist depictions in the service of defining the hero become, I would argue, awkward and stand out in films with violent women. The stereotypes of strong women and the ways in which the image of the weak woman has for so long reinforced traditional gender definitions contrasts with the use of racism in defining the violent woman, which leads to scenes (like this one in *Out of Sight*) that seem campy and over the top. In these cases, the multiple layers of cultural tension make it difficult for Hollywood to deploy racism in the traditionally seamless way.

31. Martha McCaughey, *Real Knockouts: The Physical Feminism of Women's Self-defense* (New York: New York University Press, 1997), 200.

32. A good example of this is John Woo's *Broken Arrow* (1996), in which the woman is tough and violent but is not allowed to have full control over a situation in which violence takes place. The film starts out surprisingly. In the first scene, Terry Carmichael (Samantha Mathis) seems to be violently unrelenting as she fights with Captain Riley Hale (Christian Slater) and does not let up just because he tells her to. After this first scene, Hale and Carmichael team up together against the "bad guys," and though Carmichael is very capable of violently overpowering her attackers, Hale is the one who finishes every fight. Not surprisingly, however, while a romance is hinted at, they do not end up in a romantic union at the end.

33. McG's *Charlie's Angels* (2000) operates in a similar way to de-emphasize the violent female. Combining humor and an over-the-top film style, *Charlie's Angels* lessens the traumatic impact of its spectacular female violence. Even still, the conclusion of the film completely de-emphasizes the romantic relationships of the three female detectives, despite the numerous men who have pursued them throughout the film.

34. Linda Williams, *Hard Core: Power, Pleasure and the "Frenzy of the Visible,"* (Los Angeles: University of California Press, 1989), 77.

35. McCaughey, *Real Knockouts*, p. 22.

36. Fink, *Lacanian Subject*, p. 109.

37. Copjec, *Read My Desire*, pp. 226–227.

38. As a result, one can never represent femininity directly. As Paul Verhaeghe points out, "femininity can only be represented through another idea that takes its place" (Paul Verhaeghe, *Does the Woman Exist?: From Freud's Hysteric to Lacan's Feminine*, trans. Mark du Ry [New York: The Other Press, 1999], 39).

39. Serge André, *What Does a Woman Want?*, trans. Susan Fairfield (New York: The Other Press, 1999), 61.

40. Lacan, *Seminar XX*, p. 73.

41. The violence in *Thelma and Louise* is done out of anger, and this is what most critics reacted against. In subsequent action films with violent women, the woman's violence has been given more justification—whether it be that she is saving her kids, doing her job, or that she is just plain crazy. These films provide explorations that are varied but are anything but an average woman expressing her anger.

42. Renata Salecl, *(Per)versions of Love and Hate* (New York: Verso, 1998), 72.

43. The violent woman unsettles all cultural definitions that seem fixed, and thus in America there are always racial issues implicitly involved in all films about violent women. For a detailed analysis of this, see chapter 7.

44. Kimberly Springer, "Waiting to Set It Off: African American Women and the Sapphire Fixation," in *Reel Knockouts: Violent Women in the Movies*, eds. Martha McCaughey and Neal King, (Austin: University of Texas Press, 2001), 173.

45. Springer, "Waiting to Set It Off," p. 194.

46. Ibid., p. 180.

47. Lynda Hart, *Fatal Women: Lesbian Sexuality and the Mark of Aggression* (Princeton, NJ: Princeton University Press, 1994), 17.

Chapter 5: *Violent Women in Love*

1. John Cawelti, "Bonnie and Clyde: Tradition and Transformation," in *Focus on Bonnie and Clyde*, ed. John Cawelti (Englewood Cliffs, NJ: Prentice-Hall, 1973), 1–2.

2. Robert Phillip Kolker, *A Cinema of Loneliness: Penn, Kubrick, Coppola, Scorsese, Altman*, (New York: Oxford University Press, 1980), 52. Kolker's enthusiastic description aside, Penn's *Bonnie and Clyde* (although extremely influential) was not the only influence on this new era of violence on film and television. The coverage of the Vietnam War also heavily influenced depictions of violence. News agencies reported this war in far more gory detail than previous wars. Television played a crucial role in this: uncen-

sored images of dead and wounded bodies appeared nightly on the news. This kind of exposure to the details of violence produced a jaded public, which also led the way to more blood and violence in film. Less mainstream genres, such as the 1950s exploitation films and horror films, had been experimenting with gruesome violence as well, which eventually also exerted some influence on mainstream cinema.

3. Another important factor in the film's emphasis of the noncomplementary nature of the sexes is the fact that in Penn's *Bonnie and Clyde*, Clyde is impotent. This emphasizes the impossibility of any man adequately filling the masculine role with a violent woman. And Bonnie's potency—her ability to use both gun and pen more effectively than Clyde—also works to explore the effect of the violent woman on the dynamics between men and women.

4. Many theorists feel that Stone's attempt to critique the overpresence of the image in contemporary society failed. For example, Philip Simpson argues that "the hyperkinetic, fetishized visuals seem a too-literal expression of Stone's surface protest against a violence-begetting media" (Philip L. Simpson, "The Politics of Apocalypse in the Cinema of Serial Murder," in *Mythologies of Violence in Postmodern Media*, ed. Christopher Sharrett, [Detroit: Wayne State University Press], 125). Or as Jane Capulti suggests, "Stone purports to mock fan adulation of Mickey and Mallory, yet the film itself is similarly star struck" (Jane Capulti, "Small Ceremonies: Ritual in *Forrest Gump*, *Natural Born Killers*, *Seven* and *Follow Me Home*," in *Mythologies of Violence in Postmodern Media*, ed. Christopher Sharrett, [Detroit: Wayne State University Press], 153).

5. Jacques Lacan, *The Seminar of Jacques Lacan, Book III: The Psychoses, 1955–1956*, trans. Russell Grigg (New York: W. W. Norton, 1993), 322.

6. The purpose of ideology, of course, is to simulate a sense of immediacy where none exists. That is to say, ideology covers over the lack of immediacy and makes our mediated interactions with each other seem immediate. For a thorough critique of ideology's role in fostering a sense of immediacy, see Georg Lukács, *History and Class Consciousness*, trans. Rodney Livingstone (Cambridge, MA: The MIT Press, 1968).

7. As Žižek explains in *The Sublime Object of Ideology*, "the *point de capiton* [the quilting point] is the point through which the subject is 'sewn' to the signifier, and at the same time the point which interpellates individual into subject by addressing it with the call of a certain master-signifier [. . .] in a word, it is the point of the subjectivation of the signifier's chain" (Slavoj Žižek, *The Sublime Object of Ideology* [New York: Verso, 1989], 101).

8. Bruce Fink, *A Clinical Introduction to Lacanian Psychoanalysis: Theory and Technique* (Cambridge, MA: Harvard University Press, 1997), 107.

9. *Natural Born Killers* is actually one of the only films that highlight the woman enjoying violence, thus further linking the violent woman's

jouissance with the film's psychotic form. In other words, it is her very *jouissance* that seems to distort the Law and the symbolic order.

10. Slavoj Žižek, *The Indivisible Remainder: An Essay on Schelling and Related Matters* (New York: Verso, 1996), 196.

11. *Natural Born Killers* emphasizes this psychosis in the content of the film as well, when Mickey and Mallory marry themselves. Instead of being married by a religious figure or a justice of the peace (who are all representatives of the law), Mickey and Mallory perform their own ceremony on a bridge over a river in front of only "nature itself." They slit their hands and mingle their blood as a symbol of the marriage bond. Nature, water, and blood are all aligned outside of social Law in this scene. Clearly, this content can be seen as complementing the psychotic nature of the film form.

12. Actually, the film itself explains the murderous nature of both Mickey and Mallory in terms emblematic of the 1990s. The film attributes their violence to a history of sexual and physical abuse they endured as children and to a surfeit of television watching. Thus, even though the form of the film seems a radical break from Hollywood, the ultimate reasons for their actions are quite conventional. In this sense, *Natural Born Killers* is just a typical Hollywood film. Compared to this, Penn's *Bonnie and Clyde* is much more radical, precisely because it avoids any suggestion of the character's motivations and past experiences.

13. At the end of the film itself, Mickey and Mallory walk off into the distance together. What is left behind is the notion of an actual violent couple existing within the social order. The violent couple disrupts the social bond because their violence begets an ever-increasing amount of further violence. For example, the news anchor is so affected by this couple he adopts their rampaging destructiveness—as if they are contagious. Thus, the film serves to remind us why we stick to our masculine and feminine roles in the first place.

14. Lewis's Faith is not a violent woman in this film, but coming so soon after her much-discussed performance as Mallory in *Natural Born Killers*, Lewis' presence in the film cannot be ignored. Her "violent past" lingers in the background of Faith's nonviolent characterization. In some ways, this encourages the audience to expect Faith to fight back when necessary and thus inevitably provides suspense or at least surprise when Faith is incapable of such actions.

15. Christina Lane, "The Strange Days of Kathryn Bigelow and James Cameron," in *The Cinema of Kathryn Bigelow: Hollywood Transgressor*, eds. Deborah Jermyn and Sean Redmond (New York: Wallflower Press, 2003), 194.

16. *Strange Days* can be considered a science fiction film partly because it deals with how advanced technology might affect our lives in the future.

Although this film is set in the—at the time—not too distant future (the last days of 1999), the mise-en-scène is chaotic and out of control. Almost every shot that takes place outside reveals hundreds of wandering, rioting, and chaotic groups of people—most of whom are clashing with the police. Unlike *Natural Born Killers*, the camera movements themselves are not chaotic; instead, the chaos appears within the mise-en-scène. This does, however, work similarly to *Natural Born Killers* in that the violent woman seems to provoke a chaotic environment. The contradictions and trauma that surround the violent woman manifest themselves, in these two films, metaphorically, through film form and a chaotic mise-en-scène.

17. Carol M. Dole, "The Gun and the Badge: Hollywood and the Female Lawman," in *Reel Knockouts: Violent Women in the Movies*, eds. Martha McCaughey and Neal King, (Austin: University of Texas Press, 2001), 92.

18. Shot in a gritty and realistic style, *Girlfight* has more in common with John Avildsen's *Rocky* (1976) than with other violent women films modeled on high-budget male action films.

19. That Kusama is an independent female filmmaker and that *Girlfight* was never slated for a huge mainstream release has, I believe, everything to do with this. The film's relative popularity, however, also suggests that audiences are interested in this more complicated depiction of the violent woman.

20. This is different from a hero like Mel Gibson in the *Lethal Weapon* series, who seems to fall in love in each film and, subsequently, experience the devastation of the death—or near-death—of his lover.

21. The one exception to this well-known Bond film rule is that Eunice Gayson, who plays one of Bond's lovers in Terence Young's *Dr. No* (1962), reappears briefly at the beginning of Terence Young's *From Russia with Love* (1963).

22. See, for example, Tania Modleski, *Feminism Without Women: Culture and Criticism in a "Postfeminist" Age* (New York: Routledge and Kegan Paul, 1991), 140–164; Alexander Doty, *Making Things Perfectly Queer: Interpreting Mass Culture* (Minneapolis, MN: University of Minnesota Press, 1993), 103, 127–128; and Jacquie Jones, "The Construction of Black Sexuality: Towards Normalizing the Black Cinematic Experience," in *Black American Cinema*, ed. Manthia Diawara (New York: Routledge and Kegan Paul, 1993), 247–256.

23. In "The Gun and the Badge," Carol Dole also analyzes this splitting in several films involving violent women. Her essay revolves around the films that feature what she calls "split personalities," films that separate a female character's "feminine and masculine attributes." She sees this split personality as a new mode in films that represents female law enforcers. She analyzes Sidney Lumet's *Stranger Among Us* (1992) and Renny Harlin's

Long Kiss Goodnight (1996) as presenting the woman trapped in two com-
peting personalities, while she sees Steven Soderbergh's *Out of Sight* (1998)
as putting the female cop in two different genres throughout the film. Ultimately, she suggests that "these Hollywood containment devices familiar
from first-wave films [. . .] didn't have much more success in satisfying the
audience than they had had in the past." (Carol M. Dole, "The Gun and the
Badge: Hollywood and the Female Lawman," in *Reel Knockouts: Violent
Women in the Movies*, eds. Martha McCaughey and Neal King, [Austin: University of Texas Press, 2001], 97).

Chapter 6: *Feminity on the Front Line*

1. Soviet, Chinese, and Israeli war films include depictions of women
warriors, and they deserve their own investigation concerning the relation-
ship between women, violence, and the military. See Denise Youngblood,
"A War Remembered: Soviet Films of the Great Patriotic War," *American
Historical Review*, June 2001, 839–56. Here, however, I will concentrate on
Hollywood military films.

2. In *Ground Zero: The Gender Wars in the Military*, Linda Bird Francke
explains that women during World War II flew for the Army Air Forces as
civilian volunteers. They logged sixty million miles between 1942 and 1944,
flying every kind of new fighter plane from the factories on the West Coast
to the embarkation centers on the East Coast. They were given no insurance
or benefits, and the thirty-eight women who died on these test runs were
not entitled to money for burials. It wasn't until 1977 that Congress officially recognized them as "military." This is just one of hundreds of stories
about how women were involved in wars, but because they weren't supposed to be, they weren't recognized by the military. The military relied on
these women, but the military also relied far more on traditional gender definitions and thus were simply unable to recognize these women's achievements officially (i.e., symbolically).

3. Quoted in Linda Bird Francke, *Ground Zero: The Gender Wars in the
Military* (New York: Simon and Schuster, 1997), 23.

4. Cynthia Enloe, *Sexual Politics At the End of the Cold War* (Berkeley:
University of California Press, 1993), 174.

5. Servicewoman Melissa Rathbun-Nealy (an Army truck driver) and
Army flight surgeon Major Rhonda Cornum were both POWs during the
Gulf War. Although the country was hysterical about possible sexual harassment, both women reported that they were not raped, and the harassment they experienced did not go beyond the physical torture that the male
prisoners experienced. Both women suggested that while it may have been

hard for their male compatriots to watch their harassment, it was equally as hard for them to watch their captors beating and torturing the men. The media and Congress continued, however, to only focus on the sexual harassment issue. In other words, America stared at the reality of the female POW and chose not to believe what it saw.

6. Leela Jacinto, "Girl Power: Women Join the Boys in Combat, But Not without a Fight," January 14, 2003. http://abcnews.go.com/sections/world/DailyNews/women030114_military.html (May 26, 2003), ABCNEWS.com.

7. It is revealing, however, that *Courage Under Fire* also depicts the violent white woman and a violent Latino male as not only adversaries but also as totally incompatible. Thus, while the main racial relationship between a white woman and an African American man is resolved as harmonious, there still exists within the film a racial relationship which is not only not harmonious, but also actually fatal (it is Monfriez's anger at Walden which gets Walden killed, and Walden's death eventually leads to Monfriez's suicide). Obviously, this subplot makes what seems like a conclusive ending more ambiguous.

8. Serling's investigation of Walden also becomes a way for Serling to reassert his floundering masculinity. At one point in the film, he is kicked off the case because he will not okay the medal without further investigation. Even though he is kicked off the case, he continues investigating for personal reasons, personal reasons that revolve around the fact that he has had a questionable experience in combat for which he was awarded a medal. Serling, however, feels that he didn't deserve it and feels his symbols of masculinity slipping away from him. He in unable to be with his wife and be a good father to his kids until he works out this crisis in his masculinity. He continues his investigations of Walden because he feels that finding the truth of her identity will also solve his own identity crisis. After figuring out the mystery of the violent white woman and okaying the medal ceremony, he is able to properly accept his own medal and return to his family. It is no coincidence that what allows him to reclaim his masculinity is proving that the violent white woman is no threat to America.

9. It is much more effective ideologically to have those who occupy sites of would-be trauma themselves demonstrate that they pose no threat, than to have someone else do it for them. This is an ideological operation oft-performed in American film, but perhaps nowhere more emphatically than in John McTiernan's *The Hunt For Red October* (1990). This film deals with two sites of possible trauma in a single character—Soviet submarine commander Ramius (Sean Connery). Ramius is at once a potentially insane Russian and a submarine commander with numerous nuclear missiles under his thumb. On both of these counts, however, Ramius himself,

throughout the course of the film, assures us that our fears are for naught. He is not really insane, but only wants to defect to the United States. And though he controls nuclear weapons, he would sooner give them to the Americans than fire the missiles at the United States.

10. Recent United States military scandals have highlighted these fears and ideological definitions. During testimony surrounding the Talehook scandal, for example, accused officers claimed that they didn't think they were doing anything wrong because they were just acting like the characters in *Top Gun*, a film that clearly relies on traditional gender definitions.

11. Francke, *Ground Zero*, p. 156.

12. Georg Lukács, *History and Class Consciousness*, (trans. Rodney Livingston, Cambridge, MA: The MIT Press, 1968), 87.

13. Lukács, *History and Class Consciousness*, p. 99.

14. Slavoj Žižek, *For The Know Not What They Do: Enjoyment as a Political Factor* (New York: Verso, 1991), 241.

15. Žižek, *For The Know Not What They Do*, p. 242.

16. Senator De Haven brings the issue up by presenting an internal Naval report that she has acquired concerning a downed female aviator. She says that she is "struck by the ill-spirited tenor" of the report. There are innuendoes about the aviator's performance and even mention of her sexual activities the weekend before. DeHaven concludes that she has never seen an aviator treated like this before in all her seven years on the committee. It is no coincidence that the content of this initial report is remarkably similar to the story of *Courage Under Fire*. In this sense, *G.I. Jane* is almost literally attempting to answer, or present the sequel to, the crisis of the violent woman in *Courage Under Fire*.

17. Jordan has this opportunity to begin with, of course, because of a very political, feminist move by Senator DeHaven. Jordan's individual nonpolitical motives are only possible due to the highly political move that gave her the opportunity.

18. The scene also has additional importance because Demi Moore did actually shave her head during the shoot. This allows us to see more clearly the effect of the elision of gender difference. When I saw this film at a theater, a young man called out just before Moore began to clip, "Don't do it"—an exclamation clearly provoked by the fear that cutting off her hair would cut off her femininity. This undoubtedly is many people's reaction as they watch Moore's long hair tumble to the ground. Reassuringly, however, Moore's good looks are not erased with this gender erasure, which is presumably one of the reasons the filmmakers chose Moore to play the role. That so much is at stake in this scene indicates the ways in which femininity is so heavily defined by symbolic markers of difference, such as long hair.

19. Not coincidentally, when Geena Davis becomes most violent in *The Long Kiss Goodnight*, she bursts forth with precisely the same exclamation. This line has become something like the calling card of the violent woman—it occurs also in *Thelma and Louise*—indicating the way in which films often masculinize the violent woman at the height of her violence.

20. Royce, in fact, is assigned, by chance, to track Jordan's progress for the Secretary of the Navy. This is an ironic twist in the film, which emphasizes further the constant investigation—even from her own mate—that the violent woman most endure. It also gives Royce—as the mate of the violent woman—a chance to conclude that her violence is truly just attached to her job and not her femininity. After his investigation of her, he is able to fully embrace her when she comes home, because he verifies that she is doing this just for career advancement (not to be around a bunch of "hard core" guys, as he originally accuses her of desiring).

Chapter 7: *Conclusion*

1. That Geena Davis plays this role of the conflicted violent woman cannot be completely separated from her role in *Thelma and Louise*. In *Thelma and Louise*, Davis's character rejects domesticity and eventually embraces violence and ultimately death. If *Thelma and Louise* is completely unable to imagine the violent woman integrated back into society, then *Long Kiss Good Night* wrestles with this precise question as it desperately tries to find a way to combine the domestic and violent woman. Davis' past performance as Thelma informs this characterization both in that Davis is an actor willing to embrace the action heroine and to metaphorically attempt to resurrect Thelma from what seemed like an inevitable end.

2. The contingency of her choice is emphasized by the fact that the few memory shreds that she thought she still held onto from her past were actually lies that she was using during an undercover mission.

3. It is not insignificant that this man from Samantha's past learns that she is still alive when he sees a news report that shows her dressed up as Mrs. Claus in the town Christmas parade. Even when she most fully occupies the traditionally feminine role (as Mrs. Claus), Samantha is nonetheless visible as Charly to those who know what to look for.

4. At the beginning of the film, we see Mitch try to masquerade as these roles that he has failed in (police officer and father). In fact, in the first scene that he appears he masquerades as a police officer in order to hustle some money out of a man caught with a prostitute (who is herself working with Mitch). And in another scene, Mitch masquerades as a father: he presents his son with a Christmas gift that he knows his ex-wife won't allow

his son to keep, but nonetheless he and his son go through the motions of the exchange to at least pretend that they have somewhat of a normal father/son relationship. This type of masquerade further aligns Mitch with the feminine. As Mary Ann Doane points out, masquerade involves a woman using her femininity—something that she does but that men do not do. Doane says: "The very fact that we can speak of a woman 'using' her sex or 'using' her body for particular gains is highly significant—it is not that a man cannot use his body in this way but that he doesn't have to. The masquerade [. . .] is constituted by a hyperbolization of the accoutrements of femininity." (Mary Ann Doane, *Femmes Fatales* [New York: Routledge and Kegan Paul, 1991], 26). Masquerade here is clearly associated with femininity; men, because they feel their masculinity as something *not* put on, do not resort to it. The fact that Mitch does shows the distance separating his identity from ideal masculinity.

5. As is typical in many films, Mitch is aligned with the city while Samantha is aligned with the suburbs. When Charly emerges, it is not surprising to find that her apartment is also in the city. That is to say, as is stereotypical in American imagery, the violent woman—along with the African-American male—does not belong in the suburbs.

6. Two examples of this would be the films of Frank Capra and the films of Steven Spielberg. It is difficult to imagine a more ideological film than *It's A Wonderful Life* (1946), and yet that film also depicts, perhaps more powerfully than any film of its time, the antagonism between big capital and small town American life. Though the film concludes by smoothing over this antagonism, it does at least depict it—and depict it in an extreme form, so that the ideological work it is able to do can be all the greater. The same thing is clearly evident is a film like *Jurasic Park* (1993).

7. Ed Guerrero, *Framing Blackness: The African American Image in Film* (Philadelphia, PA: Temple University Press, 1993), 240.

8. It is somewhat significant that Ridley Scott directed both of these films. He himself obviously sees black masculinity and violent white femininity as occupying similar positions within society but is unwilling to really investigate this relationship in any kind of depth.

9. In neither film, however, does this alignment lead to a possible love (or complementary) relationship. One could argue that this might be a case in which complementarity—if it could be achieved between these two positions—actually disrupts the social order.

10. *The Long Kiss Goodnight* has one particularly egregious scene in which we see Samuel Jackson depicted naked, chained, shivering, and scared in the basement of one of the criminal's barns. Samantha finds him this way after she frees herself and attempts to save him. Why would the film show Mitch in this way? On the level that I have been discussing, it

seems to fit the attempt by the film to show the male in a more feminine light, in the light of someone who needs protection. After this rescue, Mitch jokes with Charly that in dangerous situations he will be waiting for her to rescue him (and, in fact, each time she does rescue him). But the image of Samuel Jackson naked and chained seems too strikingly similar to slave imagery. The scene would have played just the same if Charly had found Mitch dressed and sitting handcuffed to a chair—but the film instead resorts to an image loaded with racist symbolism. This reveals the extreme lengths to which the film goes to racialize the black man who is paired with the violent white woman.

11. As we saw in chapter 4, this is a fear that society often has about women and violence. There is the sense that a woman's violence will always end up out of control. Whereas a limit always constrains masculine violence, no matter how criminal, no such limit stands in the way of the woman's violence—hence the threat that it might spiral out of control.

12. In fact, Mitch makes this observation after rejecting her suggestion that they have sex. He implies that she's trying to sleep with an African American man to get as far away as she can from her white bourgeois life. But Mitch prevents her from doing this by rejecting her and eventually helps lead her back toward that life. This intervention on his part further solidifies his role as the one that investigates, tames, and sets straight the violent white woman.

13. This is why Slavoj Žižek claims in the *Plague of Fantasies* that "an ideological edifice can be undermined by a too-literal identification" (Slavoj Žižek, *The Plague of Fantasies* [New York: Verso, 1998], 22). If we identify with an ideological injunction completely or if we live out a stereotype as fully as possible, we effectively subvert the stereotype.

14. The rejection of Waldman is an exemplary instance of the radicality of *The Long Kiss Goodnight*: in rejecting him, Samantha refuses the entreaties of the good father, the father who could provide an assurance of identity and security. It isn't that Samantha doesn't want this assurance, but that she can't be sure that it is actually reliable. In the paranoid universe of the film, there is no way to tell the good father from the bad father—and no way to tell which identity is "real."

15. Slavoj Žižek, *The Metastases of Enjoyment: Six Essays on Woman and Causality* (New York: Verso, 1994), 148.

16. Elizabeth Cowie, *Representing the Woman: Cinema and Psychoanalysis* (Minneapolis, MN: University of Minnesota Press, 1997), 133.

17. Mitch echoes here another traditional way of understanding the violent woman. That is to say, it is common to see the violent woman as a female masochist who has just inverted her masochism. Instead of hating and hurting herself, she directs it onto others.

Index